STEAK AND CAKE

MORE THAN 100 RECIPES
— TO MAKE —
ANY MEAL A SMASH HIT

ELIZABETH KARMEL

PHOTOGRAPHS BY STEPHEN HAMILTON

WORKMAN PUBLISHING · NEW YORK

Library of Congress Cataloging-in-Publication Data
Names: Karmel, Elizabeth, author.
Title: Steak and cake : more than 100 recipes to make any meal a smash hit / Elizabeth Karmel ; photographs by Stephen Hamilton.
Description: New York : Workman Publishing, [2019]
Identifiers: LCCN 2018054776 | ISBN 9780761185741 (alk. paper)
Subjects: LCSH: Cooking (Beef) | Beef steaks. | Cake. | LCGFT: Cookbooks.
Classification: LCC TX749.5.B43 K37 2019 | DDC 641.6/62--dc23
LC record available at https://lccn.loc.gov/2018054776
ISBN 978-0-7611-8574-1

Food photography copyright © Stephen Hamilton
Photograph on page 240 from the collection of Elizabeth Karmel
Steak layer cake illustration by Bob Blumer

Workman books are available at special discounts when purchased in bulk for premiums and sales promotions as well as for fund-raising or educational use. Special editions or book excerpts can also be created to specification. For details, contact the Special Sales Director at the address below or send an email to specialmarkets@workman.com.

Workman Publishing Co., Inc.
225 Varick Street
New York, NY 10014-4381
workman.com

WORKMAN is a registered trademark of Workman Publishing Co., Inc.

Printed in the United States of America
First printing April 2019

10 9 8 7 6 5 4 3

STEAK AND CAKE

DEDICATION

*This book is dedicated to the bakers
I grew up with and their cakes
that have stood the test of time:
my Grandmother Odom,
my mother, Marylin, and
my sister Mary Pat—
all of whom firmly believe that
you should eat dessert first!*

*And to all the steak lovers who
believe that cake is an after-dinner treat—
most notably my father, Big Lou.
This book has something for all of us!*

CONTENTS

LET THEM EAT CAKE—AND STEAK!

Who doesn't love steak and cake?! After all, it's everyone's favorite Saturday night menu choice. And it has a certain ring to it. I'd be willing to bet that it is *the* universal favorite meal for friends, family, the boss—and, of course, a birthday. It really doesn't matter what day of the week it is. Steak and cake turn any day, and any occasion, into a special one.

That's what I thought when I created the title and menu for my Saturday night class more than a decade ago at the Institute of Culinary Education (ICE). I filled the menu with a variety of steaks and a selection of my favorite cakes, and because it was a festive Saturday night, I paired the dishes with a few of my favorite wines.

Students flocked to my Steak and Cake classes, resulting in a very long waiting list. When I stopped teaching the class a few years ago, I decided that the subject matter would make a fun cookbook. A main-course steak and a slice of cake—as my editor, Suzanne Rafer, says, "What's not to love?"

WHY I WROTE THIS BOOK

People who know me know that there are two things that I almost never order in a restaurant—one is steak and the other is cake. This is because I can always make a better steak at home and I can always bake a better cake. Every time I break my rule and order either one out, I am sorely disappointed. Often the steak is flavorless and tastes like warm water, and inevitably the cake is dry.

So, the two reasons that I wrote this book:

1. To give people the basic tools needed to choose and cook steak and to bake luscious cakes. (It always surprised me how many of my students had never purchased, much less cooked, a steak, mostly because they didn't know what kind of steak to buy at the store. Nor had they baked a cake, because they thought that it was so much harder than it really is.)

2. To empower people to create their favorite restaurant-style meals in their own home.

DINNER PARTY SOLVED!

Once you've mastered how to buy and cook steak at home, and how to make a simple cake for dessert, you've got the restaurant versions beat and a dinner party at the ready. And the secret is that it is much easier than most people think.

Though I offer pairings of steak, sides, and cake, I urge you to use them loosely and put together your own favorite combinations. I want *Steak and Cake* to be fun for everyone. This is a book made for celebrations, and it should be more about the occasion than the meal—so don't be rigid, and make your own rules. Including drinking what you want with what you make! If you like white wine, drink it with your steaks—don't feel pressured to drink red. I often drink Champagne from appetizers to steak to cake.

Years of teaching my class at ICE showed me the cakes that people loved to bake and eat. Further "anecdotal" testing was at my restaurants in New York City and Washington, DC, where I created both the savory (meats and sides) and sweet (dessert) menu. I used that flavor "research" when I chose the steak and cake recipes that I wanted to include in the book because I wanted the book to be full of crowd-pleasers, not esoteric or trendy recipes.

This book ended up being a delicious collection of my favorite flavors and an homage to both my Southern heritage and the recipes of my family. In that way, this is the most personal book that I have ever written. It is akin to publishing my personal recipe box. You now have all the steak and cake, sauce, and side recipes that I make for my friends and family when they come to my house for dinner. I hope that your friends and family enjoy them as much as mine do!

Warm wishes,

Elizabeth

ABOUT THIS BOOK

For me, it was recipes first things first. Once I had the essential steaks and cakes, I paired them as I would if I were having you over to my house for dinner. The pairings, highlighted by beautiful color photography taken by my friend Steve Hamilton and his team, make up the heart of the book. In fact, what you see on the pages was our lunch, snacks, dinner, and even breakfast for the ten days of the photo shoot. Very little went to waste as we happily devoured it all.

Page through the pairings, but remember there are no hard and fast rules. In fact, every steak recipe and every cake recipe has two other "match up" suggestions in case you want to veer slightly from the script. And you can also go full-on rogue and match up any steak and any cake from the whole book.

Because the best steaks are cooked simply and by two basic methods (grill and cast-iron or carbon-steel pan), most of my recipes are differentiated and complemented by the compound butters, sauces, and sides that go with the steaks. So, following The Steaks and Their Cakes is a chapter of those sauces and sides that accompany the main event.

Finally, the back of the book is where the technical information lives—in a Steak Primer and a Cake Primer.

THE STEAK PRIMER

Think of it as Steak 101. The most important part of the Steak Primer is the explanation of all the different cuts of steak—where they come from, their flavor profile, and what the grades of beef mean. I've created a Steak Grid with the help of meat industry giants whom I am lucky enough to call friends, Pat LaFrieda and the folks at Certified Angus Beef. My Steak Grid includes price references and flavor and texture notes, and which major muscle the steak comes from. It is not exhaustive but includes the cuts of steak that are cooked most often and that I focus on in the book. I've also included recipes for the basic methods for cooking steak. If you are like many of my former ICE students and don't even know how to buy a steak, this section will help you figure it out.

THE CAKE PRIMER

Think of it as Cake 101. The Cake Primer is not a complicated baking "encyclopedia." Although there are cakes in the book for serious bakers, like My Mother's Freshly Grated Coconut Cake, the book is geared toward the home cook who wants to make a great-tasting dessert to serve after a great steak. In the primer, I have provided all the information you need to become a good cake baker, but not so much information that you become overwhelmed. I've included tips for preparing the pan so the cake won't stick (Baker's Joy is your best bet), a glossary of pans—shapes and materials—and basic recipes.

I drilled the basics down to three classic cakes—white, yellow, and chocolate—and a selection of icings, glazes, and frostings, including buttercreams and stabilized whipped creams that you can use to create layer cakes, sheet cakes, cupcakes, and the like for those occasions that call for a traditional cake instead of one of the more specialized cakes that are paired with the steaks.

A LITTLE SOMETHING EXTRA

As lagniappe, or a little something extra, I have included three additional recipes for the more advanced baker, including my mother's signature Wild Persimmon Christmas Fruit and Nut Cake. This is a very personal Karmel family holiday dessert tradition that my mother created. Because she passed away before this book was published, I wanted to share her legacy of this unique and special recipe that up until now has only been given to friends and family. I promise you that if you can get your hands on wild persimmon pulp and you make this cake, you will be a lifelong fruitcake lover. It's the real deal, not the much maligned commercial Christmas fruitcake.

This small but powerful book is a collection of time-tested and well-loved recipes that I hope will provide you with inspiration for a lifetime of great dinners!

"Bone" appétit!

STEAK AND CAKE

THE STEAKS
AND
THEIR CAKES

COWBOY STEAK

WITH WHISKEY BUTTER

WHISKEY BUTTERMILK BUNDT CAKE

THE STEAK

The cowboy steak is a bone-in ribeye that is as dramatic as it is delicious. It makes a show-stopping entrance at any dinner table. I am not sure when restaurants began to refer to the bone-in ribeye as a cowboy steak, but I always imagined it was because it is the steak that matches the personality of the handsome, macho, boot-wearing, horse-riding wildcat cowboys—and cowgirls—who cook steaks al fresco and eat outdoors on the range. If you can't find a cowboy steak, my whiskey butter will pair well with any of your favorite steaks.

Serves 4

4 bone-in ribeye steaks (about 1 pound each and 1 to 2 inches thick)

Extra-virgin olive oil

Kosher salt and freshly ground black pepper

Whiskey Butter (recipe follows)

Chopped fresh parsley, for garnish (optional)

Grilling Method: Direct/Medium-High Heat

❶ Preheat the grill with all burners on high. Once preheated, adjust the temperature to medium-high heat for direct grilling.

❷ Wrap the steaks in paper towels to rid them of excess moisture. Replace the paper towels as needed.

❸ Just before grilling, brush both sides of the steaks with olive oil and season with salt and pepper.

❹ Place the steaks on the cooking grate, cover, and cook for 5 to 6 minutes per side for a perfect medium-rare (135°F on an instant-read thermometer). When you turn the steaks onto their second sides, you may only need to cook them for 3 to 4 minutes more, depending on the thickness and how rare you like the steak. Note that all meat with a bone takes longer than boneless meat, and bone-in ribeyes can cook longer than a New York strip and still be rare inside.

❺ Remove the steaks from the grill and place a pat of Whiskey Butter on each as it rests for at least 5 minutes before serving.

❻ Serve the steaks warm with an additional pat of Whiskey Butter and garnish with chopped parsley, if desired.

THE MATCHUPS

WHISKEY BUTTERMILK BUNDT CAKE, *recipe follows*

GINGERBREAD WITH ORANGE MARMALADE AND GRAND MARNIER GLAZE, *page 11*

CHOCOLATE-COCONUT CANDY BAR CAKE, *page 89*

WHISKEY BUTTER

This is my favorite compound butter! The butter mellows the uncut bourbon as it melts on the hot steak, adding a depth of flavor and whiskey sharpness to the savory steak. You can make the Whiskey Butter up to a week in advance.

Makes 1 log; generous ½ cup

1 shallot, minced

1 tablespoon bourbon whiskey

1 cup (2 sticks) unsalted butter, at room temperature

1 tablespoon minced fresh parsley

½ teaspoon Worcestershire sauce

½ teaspoon Dijon mustard

½ teaspoon fine sea salt

Freshly ground white pepper to taste

❶ Place the shallot in a small bowl and add the bourbon. Let soak for about 10 minutes. No need to drain.

❷ Add the butter, parsley, Worcestershire sauce, mustard, salt, and white pepper to the whiskey-soaked shallot. Mix well, mashing with the back of a fork to make sure all the ingredients are incorporated.

❸ Drop the butter in spoonfuls in a row on a piece of plastic wrap or parchment paper. Roll the butter up in the wrap and smooth it out to form a round log about 5 inches long.

❹ Twist the ends to seal and refrigerate the wrapped butter until it's hard and easy to slice, at least 2 hours. This recipe will make more than you need, but if it is well wrapped, it will keep in the refrigerator for up to 1 week and in the freezer for 1 month.

WHISKEY BUTTERMILK BUNDT CAKE

THE CAKE

Mark Twain would have loved this cake, as he is known for saying, "Too much of anything is bad, but too much good whiskey is barely enough." This cake is spiked with whiskey in the batter, in the syrup, and in the glaze, which creates complex layers of flavor that he might agree is just enough! The cake is both light and tangy (from the buttermilk and the nutmeg) and sharp and sweet (from the vanilla and the bourbon), which gives it a quiet sophistication. However, rest assured it doesn't taste like a whiskey bomb. It is good the day you make it but even better the next day, once all of the flavors meld together.

Serves 12

Baking spray, for preparing the pan

1 cup (2 sticks) unsalted butter, at room temperature

2½ cups granulated white sugar

4 large eggs, at room temperature

3 cups all-purpose flour

¼ teaspoon baking soda

⅛ teaspoon fine sea salt

Scant ⅛ teaspoon freshly grated nutmeg

¾ cup buttermilk

¼ cup bourbon, such as Maker's Mark

1 generous teaspoon pure vanilla extract

Whiskey Syrup (recipe follows)

Whiskey Glaze (recipe follows)

Pan: 12-cup Bundt pan

❶ Position a rack in the center of the oven and preheat the oven to 325°F. Spray the Bundt pan with baking spray.

❷ Cream the butter and sugar together with an electric mixer on medium-high speed until light and very fluffy, 3 to 5 minutes. Add the eggs one at a time, beating well after each addition.

❸ Whisk the flour, baking soda, salt, and nutmeg together in a small bowl. Pour the buttermilk into a glass measuring cup to the ¾-cup mark. Add ¼ cup bourbon. Add the vanilla and stir to combine.

❹ Add the flour mixture and the buttermilk mixture to the butter mixture alternately in batches, beating well after each addition. Stop the mixer and scrape down the side of the bowl as necessary.

❺ Pour the batter into the prepared pan, leveling the top with a spatula. Lightly tap the cake pan down on the counter to make sure the batter is evenly distributed and to remove excess air bubbles.

❻ Bake until the cake pulls away from the side of the pan and a toothpick inserted in the center comes out clean, 55 to 60 minutes.

❼ Cool in the pan for 10 minutes before turning out onto a wire cooling rack to glaze. Place a sheet of waxed paper under the rack to catch any drips. Brush the cake with the warm Whiskey Syrup. Drizzle the glaze over the cake immediately following the layer of syrup. Let cool for 2 to 3 hours before slicing.

WHISKEY SYRUP

A sugar syrup spiked with bourbon flavors that moistens the cake. You can use a flavored sugar syrup on any cake when you want to add another layer of flavor or to add moistness.

¼ cup filtered or bottled water

¼ cup granulated white sugar

2 tablespoons bourbon, such as Maker's Mark

Pour the water into a glass measuring cup. Add the granulated sugar. Microwave on high for 1 minute. Remove and stir to combine—all of the sugar should be melted and mixed into the water. If it isn't, microwave for 30 seconds more. Add the bourbon and stir well. Set aside 3 tablespoons for the glaze and reserve the rest for brushing the cake before glazing it.

WHISKEY GLAZE

The white whiskey glaze delivers a bourbon note in the first bite. The cake batter is made with bourbon and pairs with the buttermilk to create a delicate vanilla cake with a deeper flavor, but the Whiskey Syrup and the Whiskey Glaze remind you that the spirit is alive!

1½ cups confectioners' sugar, or more if needed

⅛ teaspoon fine sea salt

⅛ teaspoon freshly grated nutmeg

1 tablespoon heavy (whipping) cream, or more if needed

3 tablespoons Whiskey Syrup (see above), or more if needed

Mix the confectioners' sugar, salt, and nutmeg together in a small bowl. Add the cream and 2½ tablespoons of the Whiskey Syrup. Stir together. Taste and add more syrup if you want the flavor to be stronger. If the glaze is too stiff, add a little more of the syrup or cream; if it is too loose, add a little more sugar. Taste and make sure the salt, nutmeg, and Whiskey Syrup are balanced.

THE MATCHUPS

COWBOY STEAK WITH WHISKEY BUTTER,
page 5

COFFEE-RUBBED TENDERLOIN WITH GARLIC CHEESE GRITS AND REDEYE GRAVY GLAZE,
page 107

SIZZLIN' STEAK KEBABS WITH SALSA VERDE,
page 143

RED-HOT CAST-IRON STEAK

WITH PERFECT CRUST

GINGERBREAD

WITH ORANGE MARMALADE AND GRAND MARNIER GLAZE

THE STEAK

If you make this steak according to my directions, I can guarantee you two things: Your kitchen will get very smoky, and your steak will be very crusty—in all the right ways! This stovetop method is like an extreme culinary sport since the pan is preheated over high heat for about 5 minutes before the steak is cooked. When the smoke clears, you are left with a gorgeous caramelized crust that covers the steak from end to end. For that reason, I prefer a flat-bottomed cast-iron or carbon steel skillet instead of one with raised "grill" ridges. Note: This technique is best suited to a boneless steak served rare.

Serves 1 or 2

1 boneless New York strip or ribeye steak (16 to 20 ounces and 1 to 2 inches thick)

Coarse kosher salt or Maldon sea salt

Freshly ground black pepper (optional)

Pan: 10½-inch cast-iron or carbon steel skillet

Method: Stovetop

❶ Preheat the oven to 325°F (optional; see Note).

❷ Wrap the steak in paper towels to rid it of excess moisture. Replace the paper towels as needed.

❸ Meanwhile, place a dry cast-iron skillet on the stove and preheat over high heat until a drop of water sprinkled on the surface "dances" and evaporates instantly.

❹ Just before cooking, scatter the salt lightly but evenly over the pan. Place the steak at the top edge of the pan. Let the steak cook and sizzle for 1 minute, then, using tongs, flip it so the raw side of the steak is at the bottom edge of the pan. This placement is important because the cooking process cools down the temperature of the cast iron and you want each side of the meat to be exposed to the same hot surface.

❺ Press down gently to ensure even contact between the steak and the pan. Let the steak cook and sizzle until there is a nice even crust, 1 minute more. Using tongs, hold the steak vertically and brown the fat on the edges. This also allows the pan to heat up again.

❻ Repeat cooking the first side of the steak at the top edge of the pan for another minute. Flip the steak and place the second side at the bottom edge of the pan for 1 minute more. Repeat browning the edges if necessary, about 30 seconds on each edge.

❼ At this point, the steak should look done and have a deep-brown caramelized crust on each side. Check for doneness: The meat should feel tight and slightly springy, not raw and mushy, to the touch. If using an instant-read thermometer, insert it horizontally (through the thickness) into the center. Rare is 125°F, and that is the temperature that I prefer. Medium-rare is 135°F. If you want your steak cooked more in the center, once it has the crust on it slip the cast-iron pan into the preheated oven (see Note on page 10).

❽ Remove the steak to a wire cooling rack set on a sheet pan and let rest for 10 minutes. You can tent it lightly with aluminum foil but not so tightly that the steak will begin to steam. Slice and serve with freshly

THE MATCHUPS

GINGERBREAD WITH ORANGE
MARMALADE AND GRAND
MARNIER GLAZE,
recipe follows

GRANDMOTHER ODOM'S
APPLE CAKE, *page 108*

DOUBLE-DUTCH CHOCOLATE
GUINNESS BUNDT CAKE WITH
CHOCOLATE GUINNESS GLAZE,
page 133

ground pepper if desired—you shouldn't need to add any salt.

Note: I have found that if you put the steak in the preheated oven when it reaches 100°F on an instant-read thermometer, it will reach about 130°F after 15 minutes. Once you take the steak out and let it rest, it will continue cooking, ending at 135°F. This is not a rule, but rather a guideline based on my experience.

Steak and the Grill Pan

You may read this recipe and wonder, like my friend Rebecca Freedman, why anyone would cook a steak indoors any other way. In my Steak 101 (page 213), I recommend a ridged grill pan for indoor cooking. It is the classic sear on the stovetop and finish in the oven method that restaurants the world over use. I recommend this method because it is simple, effective, and not very smoky, and you get great grill marks.

The red-hot cast-iron skillet method used in this recipe is more advanced, and although the crust results are superior, it is much more hands-on, and it is more easily mastered by someone who already feels confident with the stovetop-to-oven Steak 101 method.

GINGERBREAD

WITH ORANGE MARMALADE AND GRAND MARNIER GLAZE

THE CAKE

This cake is perfect for the fall, when the crisp, cool air conjures up cravings for cinnamon, cloves, ginger, and molasses. I can't think of a nicer way to satisfy those desires than with a big hunk of sweet and spicy gingerbread. I've created a bittersweet orange marmalade glaze spiked with Grand Marnier to add a refined layer of flavor to the dark gingerbread. Don't worry if the cake sinks a little in the middle. It won't affect the flavor at all.

Makes 16 squares

Baking spray, for preparing the pan

2½ cups all-purpose flour

2 teaspoons baking soda

½ teaspoon baking powder

6 teaspoons ground ginger

2 teaspoons ground cinnamon

½ teaspoon ground cloves

½ teaspoon fine sea salt

1 cup (2 sticks) unsalted butter, at room temperature

1¼ cups (packed) light brown sugar

2 large eggs, at room temperature

1 cup unsulfured molasses, preferably Grandma's

¾ cup cream stout or Guinness, flat and at room temperature

Orange Marmalade and Grand Marnier Glaze (optional; recipe follows)

Confectioners' sugar, for garnish (optional)

Lemon Cream, for serving (optional; recipe follows)

Sweetened Whipped Cream, for serving (recipe follows)

Pan: 9 x 13-inch cake pan

❶ Position a rack in the center of the oven and preheat the oven to 350°F. Spray the pan with baking spray.

❷ Whisk the flour, baking soda, baking powder, ginger, cinnamon, cloves, and salt together in a large bowl.

❸ Cream the butter and sugar with an electric mixer on medium-high speed until light and very fluffy, 3 to 5 minutes. Add the eggs one at a time, beating well after each addition. Beat in the molasses. Lower the mixer speed to medium. Beat in the flour mixture and cream stout alternately, one-third at a time. (The batter may curdle at this point or when you add the beer, but don't worry; it will get creamy again as you continue beating.) Beat until completely combined—do not overbeat. Stop the mixer and scrape down the side of the bowl as necessary.

❹ Spoon the batter into the prepared pan and lightly tap the pan down on the counter to make sure the batter is evenly distributed and to remove excess air bubbles.

❺ Bake until the cake pulls away from the sides of the pan and a toothpick inserted in the center comes out clean, 50 to 60 minutes.

❻ Cool the cake in the pan for 10 minutes before glazing. Brush with the glaze while still warm. If not using the glaze, let cool completely and dust with confectioners' sugar instead before serving. Eat warm or at room temperature with Lemon Cream or Sweetened Whipped Cream, if desired, on the side.

ORANGE MARMALADE AND GRAND MARNIER GLAZE

Mix marmalade with Grand Marnier for a sweet glaze that is perfect for gingerbread as well as fall fruit, squash, and sweet potatoes.

Makes about 1 cup

> 1 cup favorite orange or clementine marmalade
>
> 2 tablespoons Grand Marnier, or more if needed
>
> Pinch of fine sea salt, or more if needed

1 Place the marmalade in a small heavy-bottomed saucepan and melt over low heat, stirring occasionally so it doesn't burn.

2 When the marmalade is melted, add the Grand Marnier and stir to combine. Add the salt and stir again.

3 If the glaze is too thick, add more Grand Marnier, 1 teaspoon at a time. Mix and taste. Adjust seasoning if necessary.

THE MATCHUPS

RED-HOT CAST-IRON STEAK WITH PERFECT CRUST, *page 9*

T-BONE WITH NDUJA BUTTER AND EASY MUSHROOM TARTS, *page 70*

LONDON BROIL WITH ROASTED CHERRY TOMATOES ON THE VINE AND BURRATA CHEESE, *page 134*

LEMON CREAM

Gingerbread and lemon are a classic flavor combination—and if you really want to gild the lily, you can not only glaze the gingerbread but also serve it with this Lemon Cream.

Makes about 2½ cups

> 3 tablespoons EAK's Lemon Curd (page 70), or best-quality store-bought lemon curd
>
> 1 cup heavy (whipping) cream, whipped to soft peaks

Gently fold the lemon curd into the whipped cream. Refrigerate until ready to use.

SWEETENED WHIPPED CREAM

Perfect on its own or used in other recipes like the Lemon Cream above.

> 1 cup heavy (whipping) cream
>
> 2 tablespoons confectioners' sugar
>
> 1 generous teaspoon pure vanilla extract
>
> Small pinch of fine sea salt (less than ⅛ teaspoon)

1 Place a mixing bowl and (preferably whisk) beater in the freezer for at least 15 minutes, but preferably 30 minutes.

2 Place the cream in the chilled bowl and whisk just until soft peaks are formed. Add the sugar, vanilla, and salt, and continue beating until stiff peaks form. Refrigerate any leftover whipped cream in a nonreactive container with a tight lid. It will keep for up to 1 day.

KNIFE & FORK COUNTRY CLUB STEAK SANDWICH

WITH BLOODY MARY SALAD WITH HORSERADISH VINAIGRETTE

AND

CLASSIC SOUR CREAM COFFEE CAKE

THE STEAK

When I was growing up in North Carolina, the local country club was our second home, and the grill was open all day for lunch or snacks. My favorite menu item was a steak sandwich. The steak was a very thin ribeye that was pan-fried and placed on toasted white bread. It wasn't a sandwich in the classic sense, but I loved the way the toast soaked up all of the grilled beef juices and provided a base for the steak. To make it equally satisfying in my adult life, I pair it with a grown-up salad made from my favorite Bloody Mary garnishes and dressed with a spicy horseradish vinaigrette.

Serves 4

4 boneless ribeye steaks (about 8 ounces each and ½ inch thick)

Extra-virgin olive oil

1 teaspoon kosher salt

1 teaspoon whole black peppercorns, coarsely ground

2 tablespoons unsalted butter

Chopped fresh parsley, for garnish (optional)

4 to 8 slices favorite white bread, toasted

Bloody Mary Salad with Horseradish Vinaigrette (page 175)

Grilling Method: Direct/Medium Heat

❶ Preheat the grill with all burners on high. Once preheated, adjust the temperature to medium heat for direct grilling.

❷ Wrap the steaks in paper towels to rid them of excess moisture. Replace the paper towels as needed.

❸ Just before grilling, brush both sides of the steaks with olive oil and season with the salt and pepper. Place 4 slices of toast on a large serving platter.

❹ Place the steaks on the cooking grate directly over the heat, cover, and cook for 2 to 3 minutes on each side for medium-rare (135°F on an instant-read thermometer). Remove the steaks from the grill and place each on a piece of toast. Let rest for 4 to 5 minutes. This allows the toast to absorb any juices from the steaks.

❺ Top each steak with ½ tablespoon of the butter and sprinkle with parsley, if desired. Serve with the Bloody Mary Salad on the side and extra toast, if desired.

THE MATCHUPS

CLASSIC SOUR CREAM COFFEE CAKE,
recipe follows

CLASSIC KEY LIME CHEESECAKE
WITH PECAN CRUST, *page 113*

ROSE WHITE'S FAMOUS CARAMEL CAKE, *page 243*

CLASSIC SOUR CREAM COFFEE CAKE

THE CAKE

This will be a favorite of anyone who likes a delicate sour cream cake and a hefty dose of cinnamon-pecan streusel—which is just about everyone! I've served it at brunch, afternoon coffee, and dinner. I even made it at one of my restaurants in mini Bundt shapes, and it soon became a signature dessert. If you use a Bundt-shaped cupcake-style tin, this recipe will make 12 minis and take less time to bake.

Serves 6 to 12

FOR THE CAKE

Baking spray, for preparing the pan

1 cup (2 sticks) unsalted butter, at room temperature

1½ cups granulated white sugar

1¼ cups full-fat sour cream (not light or nonfat)

2 large eggs

1 teaspoon pure vanilla extract

2 cups all-purpose flour

1 teaspoon baking powder

½ teaspoon baking soda

½ teaspoon fine sea salt

FOR THE CINNAMON-PECAN FILLING

1 cup chopped pecans

¾ cup (packed) dark brown sugar

¼ cup granulated white sugar

1 tablespoon ground cinnamon

Pinch of fine sea salt

Pan: 12-cup Bundt tin or 10-inch tube pan

❶ Position a rack in the center of the oven and preheat the oven to 325°F. Spray the cake pan with baking spray.

❷ Make the cake: Cream the butter and 1½ cups granulated sugar together with an electric mixer on medium-high speed until light and very fluffy, 3 to 5 minutes. Add the sour cream, eggs, and vanilla and mix again until well incorporated.

❸ Mix the flour, baking powder, baking soda, and ½ teaspoon salt together in a medium-size bowl. Add the flour mixture to the butter mixture a little at a time until well mixed. Stop the mixer and scrape down the side of the bowl as necessary.

❹ Make the filling: Combine the pecans, brown sugar, ¼ cup granulated sugar, cinnamon, and a pinch of salt in a large bowl. Mix well.

❺ Spoon one-third of the batter into the pan. Sprinkle a third of the filling evenly over the top to cover the batter. Cover the filling with another third of the batter, and top with three-quarters of the remaining filling. Cover with the final third of the batter. Smooth the top with a spatula and sprinkle with the remaining filling. Lightly tap the pan down on the counter to make sure the batter is evenly distributed and to remove excess air bubbles.

❻ Bake until the cake pulls away from the side of the pan and a toothpick inserted in the center comes out clean, 50 to 60 minutes. Start testing for doneness after the cake has baked for 40 minutes, since ovens and pans vary in the way they bake. Remove the cake from the oven and let cool in the pan on a wire cooling rack for 10 minutes. Remove the cake from the pan; if you've baked the cake in a tube pan, invert it so it's top side up. Cool completely before slicing.

CARNE ASADA

WITH AVOCADO AND TOMATO SALAD

MY SISTER'S FAVORITE LEMON-BLUEBERRY BUNDT CAKE

THE STEAK

This international mash-up of a meal is courtesy of an amazing clover, avocado, and tomato salad that I had in Paris. One bite of the fresh, slightly grassy salad made me yearn for a big, bold Mexican carne asada. The avocado and tomato are universal partners, but it was the clover, a microgreen, that begged for roasted garlic, lime, and oregano—all hallmarks of the classic carne asada. If you can't find clover, use baby arugula as I did in the photo on the facing page.

Serves 4 with leftovers

2 to 4 prime ribeye steaks (about 16 ounces each and 1½ inches thick)

1 tablespoon New Mexico (or any other) chile powder

1 tablespoon chipotle chile powder, if available, or 1 additional tablespoon New Mexico chile powder

1 tablespoon granulated white sugar

1½ teaspoons smoked paprika

1½ teaspoons freshly ground white pepper

1 teaspoon dried oregano, preferably Mexican

1 teaspoon granulated garlic

1 teaspoon freshly ground black pepper

Extra-virgin olive oil

Kosher salt

Lime wedges, for serving

Avocado and Tomato Salad (page 176)

Grilling Method: Combo/Medium Heat

❶ Wrap the steaks in paper towels to rid them of excess moisture. Replace the paper towels as needed.

❷ Combine the chile powders, sugar, paprika, white pepper, oregano, granulated garlic, and black pepper in a medium-size bowl.

❸ Brush the steaks all over with a thin coat of olive oil. Generously coat the meat with the chile powder rub mixture. Cover the steaks with waxed paper or plastic wrap and refrigerate for 30 minutes.

❹ Preheat the grill with all burners on high. Once preheated, adjust the temperature to medium heat for direct grilling.

❺ Season the steaks all over with salt just before cooking. Place the steaks on the cooking grate over direct heat. Cover and cook for 3 to 4 minutes, then turn them and reset the grill for indirect heat. Make sure all 4 steaks are placed over indirect heat.

❻ Cover and cook for 10 to 15 minutes more for medium-rare (135°F on an instant-read thermometer).

❼ Remove the steaks from the grill and let rest for 5 to 10 minutes before serving. Slice and serve with lime wedges and the Avocado and Tomato Salad.

THE MATCHUPS

MY SISTER'S FAVORITE
LEMON-BLUEBERRY BUNDT
CAKE, *recipe follows*

RETRO CHOCOLATE
CUPCAKES WITH A SWEET
MASCARPONE CENTER,
page 53

MARGARITA TRES LECHES
CAKE WITH STRAWBERRY
PAVÉ, *page 150*

Choosing Your Tongs

After the grill, I think the right tongs are the most important piece of equipment you need for great grilling. Traditionally, the tongs that are sold for "grilling" are too large, too long, awkward, and not at all precise. They might look impressive, but they give even master grillers two left hands. It is very difficult to turn the food on the grill with these tongs. That is why I strongly recommend investing in 12-inch, long-handled, locking chef tongs. They cost under $10 and are a perfect length for keeping your hands away from the heat (OXO makes a great pair).

TONG TIP:
I like having two pairs of tongs, one to handle raw food (marked with red tape: *Stop! Raw food touched these.*) and the other to handle cooked food (marked with green tape: *Go! Cooked food touched these.*). Only use the "red" tongs for raw food and the "green" tongs for cooked food. This will keep your outdoor cooking safe by helping to prevent cross-contamination.

MY SISTER'S FAVORITE LEMON-BLUEBERRY BUNDT CAKE

THE CAKE

My sister goes bananas for blueberries. So it's no surprise that she does backflips for this rich lemon cake, which is baked in layers with blueberries that have been tossed in flour, brown sugar, and cinnamon. The simple technique prevents the blueberries from falling to the bottom of the cake and creates a "blueberry streusel" that flavors the entire cake as it bakes. The result is so tasty that you might find yourself hiding it—as my sister does—from the rest of the family!

Serves 12

FOR THE CAKE

Baking spray, for preparing the pan

1 cup (2 sticks) unsalted butter, at room temperature

2 cups granulated white sugar

4 large eggs

1½ teaspoons pure lemon extract

1½ teaspoons pure vanilla extract

3 cups all-purpose flour

Zest of 1 lemon

2 teaspoons baking powder

½ teaspoon fine sea salt

1 cup whole milk

FOR THE BLUEBERRIES

⅛ cup all-purpose flour

2 tablespoons (packed) dark brown sugar

½ teaspoon ground cinnamon

1 pint blueberries, rinsed and dried

FOR THE GLAZE

½ cup fresh lemon juice

1 tablespoon heavy (whipping) cream

Pinch of fine sea salt

1 box (1 pound) confectioners' sugar, sifted

Pan: 12-cup Bundt pan

❶ Position a rack in the center of the oven and preheat the oven to 350°F. Spray the cake pan with baking spray.

❷ Make the cake: Cream the butter and granulated sugar with an electric mixer on medium-high speed until light and very fluffy, 3 to 5 minutes. Add the eggs, one at a time, beating well after each addition. Beat in the extracts.

❸ Whisk the flour, lemon zest, baking powder, and salt together in a medium-size bowl. Add the flour mixture and the milk alternately to the butter mixture in batches, beating well after each addition. Stop the mixer and scrape down the side of the bowl as necessary.

❹ Mix the flour, brown sugar, and cinnamon together in a medium-size bowl. Add the blueberries and toss to coat. Pour one-third of the batter into the prepared pan. Layer with half the blueberries. Pour half the remaining batter over the blueberries. Top that layer with the remaining blueberries, then top the blueberries with the remaining batter. Lightly tap the cake pan down on the counter to make sure the batter is evenly distributed and to remove excess air bubbles.

❺ Bake until the cake pulls away from the side of the pan and a toothpick inserted in the center of the cake comes out clean, 60 to 70 minutes.

❻ Cool for 10 minutes in the pan, then remove the cake from the pan onto a wire cooling rack and cool for 10 minutes longer before glazing.

❼ Meanwhile, make the glaze: Place the lemon juice, cream, and salt in a medium-size bowl. Add the confectioners' sugar and stir to combine.

❽ To glaze, place a sheet of waxed paper under the rack to catch any drips. Drizzle the glaze over the warm cake—it will go on white but become transparent as it dries. Cool completely before serving.

THE MATCHUPS

CARNE ASADA WITH AVOCADO AND TOMATO SALAD, *page 18*

FIRST-PLACE SMOKED AND CHARRED TENDERLOIN WITH GRILLED MEXICAN STREET CORN SALAD, *page 103*

STEAK TACOS WITH 1-2-3 GUACAMOLE, CARROT-JALAPEÑO RELISH, AND CHIPOTLE CREMA, *page 147*

AN INDOOR/OUTDOOR

TOMAHAWK STEAK

AND

BAKED CINNAMON-SUGAR DOUGHNUT PUFFS

WITH DARK CHOCOLATE BOURBON
DIPPING SAUCE

THE STEAK

A few years ago, I had the pleasure of eating at NoMI—the restaurant at the top of the Park Hyatt in Chicago. The chef served us an Imperial aged Japanese Wagyu tomahawk steak for two. The steak was first roasted in the oven, set aside to rest, and then seared on a plancha. It was presented with the bone and then sliced and served. I loved the steak, the technique, and the presentation, so I decided to make this idea the centerpiece of a dinner party that my friend Bob Blumer and I were throwing in Los Angeles. I ordered a Certified Angus Beef tomahawk that weighed about 3 pounds, and it came beautifully Cryovac-ed. It was begging to be my sous vide experiment. I didn't open the wrapping to season the steak—which ended up being a happy decision. I don't think seasoning on the steak adds anything except visual appeal. It was almost embarrassingly easy. If you want to fancy it

up a bit, you could serve the steak with the Caviar Butter on page 24 or the Whiskey Butter on page 5 instead of brushing it with melted butter.

Serves 2 hungry souls

> 1 tomahawk steak (about 3 pounds and 3 to 4 inches thick), vacuum-sealed
>
> Extra-virgin olive oil
>
> Kosher salt
>
> 8 tablespoons (1 stick) unsalted butter, melted
>
> 2 large sprigs rosemary (optional)
>
> Fleur de sel, for serving

Special Equipment: Vacuum sealer (such as Cuisinart vacuum sealer); ChefSteps Joule sous vide circulator

Grilling Method: Direct/Medium-High Heat

❶ Make sure that your tomahawk steak is sealed in an airtight Cryovac package either from your butcher or by using a vacuum sealer.

❷ Fill a large rectangular pot such as a turkey roaster or a Cambro container (a large heavy-duty plastic rectangular tub) with water. Secure the sous vide circulator to the pot. Set the temperature to 140°F. Once the temperature reaches 140°F, place the wrapped steak in the water. Let cook at 140°F, uncovered, for 4 hours for medium-rare.

❸ Remove the steak from the water. Pat the wrapper dry, and place the steak in its wrapper in the refrigerator overnight.

❹ The next day, just before you serve the steak, preheat the grill with all burners on high. Once preheated, adjust the temperature to medium-high heat for direct grilling. Or preheat a large stovetop grill pan to hot.

❺ Remove the steak from its wrapper and blot dry with a paper towel. Brush all over with olive oil and season with sea salt.

THE MATCHUPS

BAKED CINNAMON-SUGAR
DOUGHNUT PUFFS
WITH DARK CHOCOLATE
BOURBON DIPPING SAUCE,
recipe follows

RED VELVET FOUR-LAYER
CAKE, *page 72*

CLASSIC KEY LIME
CHEESECAKE WITH
PECAN CRUST, *page 113*

6 Place the steak on the grill, cover, and sear for 2 to 3 minutes on each side to char the outside and warm the center.

7 Let the steak rest for 5 to 7 minutes, then slice off the bone. Place the slices on a platter and brush with melted butter. (I like to use a couple of large sprigs of rosemary as the butter brush.) Sprinkle with fleur de sel and serve.

CAVIAR BUTTER

No need to break the bank on the caviar used to make this lush butter. Moderately priced California sturgeon will do just fine (I like Tsar Nicoulai).

Makes 1 log; generous ½ cup

> 8 tablespoons (1 stick) unsalted butter, at room temperature
>
> ⅛ teaspoon freshly ground white pepper
>
> 1 ounce caviar

1 Place the butter and white pepper in a small bowl. Mix well, mashing with the back of a fork to make sure the pepper is incorporated. Fold in almost all of the caviar, being as gentle as possible to make sure that you don't pop the caviar. Reserve the remainder for garnish.

2 Drop the butter in spoonfuls in a row on a piece of plastic wrap or parchment paper. Roll the butter up in the wrap and smooth it out to form a round log about 5 inches long.

3 Twist the ends to seal and refrigerate the wrapped butter until it hardens and is easy to slice, at least 2 hours.

4 Cover the top of the steak with thick slices of the butter and garnish with the remaining caviar. This recipe will make more than you need, but if it is well wrapped, it will keep in the refrigerator for up to 1 week and in the freezer for 1 month.

Does a Steak Knife Matter?

I think that it does! I had the distinct pleasure of testing out this notion at the legendary Chicago steakhouse Gene & Georgetti when I went to lunch with Alex Delecroix, the French-born US representative from Opinel. When Alex arrived, he brought with him two very sharp Opinel knives and placed them on the table. The waiters gathered around the table to look at the beautiful knives with rare Finnish wood handles and the traditional slight S shape of a French table knife. The smooth, shiny metal blade glistened, and you could see the edge with your naked eye. As the waiters admired the knives, we ordered, and I commented to Alex that you know you're in the correct steakhouse when the waiters, who have been serving steak for 40 years, are still so passionate about steak that the appearance of shiny new (to them) steak knives draws a crowd. Nothing jaded about Gene & Georgetti!

We both ordered the "petite strip"—a 10-ounce New York strip that was cooked perfectly to medium-rare. As I used my knife, I noticed that it cut through the steak smoothly with little effort. I commented that it was a pleasure to eat the steak with such a small but mighty and sharp knife. I was cutting each piece of steak into small bites because I was enjoying both cutting and savoring the flavor. I then decided to do a side-by-side taste and asked the waiter for the traditional steak knife that is serrated and much larger. The not-sharp serrated blade literally "sawed" through the steak, leaving a ragged edge, while the smooth, sharp blade of the Opinel knife made a simple cut with very little effort and left an almost shiny and very smooth texture on the cut piece of steak.

At that moment, I realized that I needed to urge everyone to use a sharp, non-serrated knife for the best results and a much more enjoyable steak experience.

BAKED CINNAMON-SUGAR DOUGHNUT PUFFS

WITH DARK CHOCOLATE BOURBON DIPPING SAUCE

THE CAKE

When I lived on the Upper East Side of New York, I frequented a fantastic bakery called Yura. As a cook myself, I loved the setup as much as the pastries. It was an open commissary kitchen for several restaurants with a walk-up counter for ordering. As you waited in line, you could watch the bakers make cakes and pies and all manner of homespun baked goods. Among the array of deliciousness displayed on the counter, there was one very small item that looked like a mini muffin coated in cinnamon and sugar. The texture of the crumb inside was less dense and more like a cake than a muffin, and it had the telltale cinnamon flavor and a pop of nutmeg as well. It was called a "puff," or at least that is what my friends and I called it. A puff with a double-shot cappuccino was morning heaven! Once you try these baked doughnut puffs, I guarantee that they will replace your fried doughnut craving with a new one! They are so good that I often make them for dessert with a dark chocolate dipping sauce, because even doughnuts are better with a little chocolate!

Makes about 33 minis

FOR THE PUFFS

Baking spray, for preparing the pan

2 cups all-purpose flour

1½ cups granulated white sugar

2 teaspoons baking powder

1 generous teaspoon ground cinnamon

1 scant teaspoon freshly grated or ground nutmeg

Pinch of ground cardamom

½ teaspoon fine sea salt

2 large eggs, lightly beaten

1 cup whole milk

3 tablespoons unsalted butter, melted

2 teaspoons pure vanilla extract

FOR THE TOPPING

½ cup granulated white sugar

1 teaspoon ground cinnamon

⅛ teaspoon fine sea salt

8 tablespoons (1 stick) unsalted butter, melted

Dark Chocolate Bourbon Dipping Sauce
(optional; recipe follows)

(If you use a standard mini cupcake tin, the yield will be about 33 puffs. If you use an extra-mini cupcake tin, as we did at the photo shoot, the yield will be about twice as many and the baking time will be reduced to about 12 minutes.)

❶ Position a rack in the center of the oven and preheat the oven to 350°F. Spray the pan with baking spray.

❷ Make the puffs: Whisk the flour, 1½ cups sugar, baking powder, 1 teaspoon cinnamon, nutmeg, pinch of cardamom, and ½ teaspoon salt together in a large bowl. In a second bowl, whisk together the eggs, milk, 3 tablespoons butter, and vanilla. Add the egg mixture to the flour mixture a little at a time, stirring well after each addition.

❸ Transfer the batter (which is fairly thin) to a liquid measuring cup and pour it into the cupcake cups, filling them about three-quarters full.

❹ Bake until the tops of the puffs look dry and a little nubby and a toothpick inserted in the center of a puff comes out clean, 16 to 18 minutes.

❺ Meanwhile, make the topping: Mix the ½ cup sugar, 1 teaspoon cinnamon, and ⅛ teaspoon salt together in a shallow bowl.

❻ Let the puffs cool on a wire cooling rack for 2 to 3 minutes, then remove them from the tin and let cool on the rack for 1 minute more.

❼ While the puffs are still warm, dip the tops in the 8 tablespoons melted butter and swirl them all over in the cinnamon-sugar mixture. Place the puffs back on the wire rack to cool completely. Eat when cool, with or without the chocolate dipping sauce, and place any leftovers in an airtight container. They will keep for 3 days.

DARK CHOCOLATE BOURBON DIPPING SAUCE

The bourbon is optional, but I think it makes a big difference. It doesn't taste boozy; it just deepens the flavor and marries the doughnuts and the chocolate. You can make the chocolate sauce up to 2 days in advance. Gently warm just before serving.

Makes about ⅔ cup dipping sauce

⅓ cup heavy (whipping) cream

6 ounces bittersweet or semisweet chocolate (chips or block chocolate, chopped)

1 tablespoon bourbon (optional)

½ teaspoon pure vanilla extract

1 to 2 tablespoons granulated white sugar (optional)

Place the cream in a small saucepan and heat over medium-low heat to almost boiling. Remove the pan from the heat and add the chocolate. Stir until it's melted and well combined. Add the bourbon, if using, and vanilla, while stirring continuously. Taste, and if you like it a little sweeter, add the sugar; otherwise leave it as is. The puffs are covered in cinnamon sugar, so I like the chocolate sauce without any added sweetening.

THE MATCHUPS

AN INDOOR/OUTDOOR TOMAHAWK STEAK,
page 22

STEAK AND TRUFFLED EGGS, *page 32*

BEEF TENDERLOIN KEBABS
WITH BACON, SHALLOTS, AND MUSHROOMS,
page 80

CECE'S CAST-IRON LEMON STEAK

AND

HOUSTON BANANA LOAF CAKE

THE STEAK

This unusual steak preparation was inspired by the classic Tuscan steak, and it includes a white wine and capers pan sauce that you would normally think to serve with veal or chicken. It was created by Cece Campise, a pastry chef by training who worked for many years for chef Art Smith and at Chicago's upscale Italian restaurant Spiaggia. Cece is an excellent cook and a wonderful entertainer, and she says that her signature sauce makes the steak dish lighter than a traditional red wine and cream sauce. I have to agree. It's a wonderful summertime steak—or anytime you want a little sunshine on your dinner table.

Serves 4 to 6

2 boneless New York strip steaks (about 16 ounces each and about 1½ inches thick)

1 tablespoon extra-virgin olive oil

Kosher salt

4 tablespoons (½ stick) unsalted butter

3 small shallots, peeled and sliced in rings

2 cloves garlic, peeled and chopped

½ cup crisp white wine, such as chardonnay or pinot grigio

1 generous tablespoon capers in brine

Juice of 1 lemon (4 tablespoons), plus more if needed

Chopped fresh parsley, for garnish

Pan: 12-inch cast-iron skillet

Method: Stovetop

❶ Wrap the steaks in paper towels to rid them of excess moisture. Replace the paper towels as needed.

❷ Heat the olive oil in a cast-iron skillet over medium-high heat for about 1 minute. Season the steaks all over with salt and add them to the pan. Cook for 5 minutes on each side for rare. You will notice that the steaks will get a beautiful crust on them. To test for doneness, insert an instant-read thermometer through the side of the steak into the center. The temperature should be 120°F to 125°F for rare. For medium-rare, cook the steaks for 6 to 7 minutes per side, close to 135°F on the thermometer. (The steaks will continue to cook as they rest, so be sure to take them off the fire when they are 2°F to 5°F less than what you want your final temperature to be.)

❸ Remove the steaks to a wire cooling rack set on a sheet pan and tent with aluminum foil, if desired. Pour off the excess fat from the skillet and allow it to cool down a little.

❹ While the steaks rest, make the sauce: Place the skillet back on the burner over medium-low heat. Melt the butter in the skillet, then add the shallots and garlic. Sweat the shallots until they are translucent, about 3 minutes. Add the wine and increase the heat to medium.

❺ Bring to a boil, stirring constantly. Let the wine reduce slightly, then stir in the capers and lemon juice. Taste for seasoning and add more lemon juice, if necessary.

6 Add the steaks to the bubbling sauce. Baste with the sauce for about 2 minutes. Set the skillet aside for 1 to 2 minutes.

7 Remove the steaks from the sauce and slice them. Fan the slices out on a platter. Top the meat with the sauce and garnish with chopped fresh parsley. Serve immediately.

THE MATCHUPS

HOUSTON BANANA LOAF CAKE, *recipe follows*

POTUS CARROT CAKE, *page 44*

GERMAN CHOCOLATE SHEET CAKE, *page 128*

THE MATCHUPS

CECE'S CAST-IRON
LEMON STEAK, *page 28*

BOB'S STEAK AU POIVRE
WITH FRENCH ONION
CROUTONS, *page 91*

LONDON BROIL WITH
ROASTED CHERRY TOMATOES
ON THE VINE AND BURRATA
CHEESE, *page 134*

HOUSTON BANANA LOAF CAKE

THE CAKE

Banana bread is the universal solution for rescuing overripe bananas—and creating a sweet treat that feels kind of healthy. I was content with the banana bread that I had made all my life until a happy accident led me to the best banana bread ever! I was visiting my sister Catherine in Houston, and her twin girls Nathalie and Olivia wanted to help me bake. We settled on banana bread because there was a bunch of overripe bananas in the house. I wanted each of the girls to have a job, so I divided the recipe into three bowls: bananas and sugar, flour and dry ingredients, and eggs and oil. Each of us mixed our bowl separately, and then we combined the three. The end result is the smoothest, moistest, most flavorful banana bread that I have ever tasted. And it's worth dirtying up three bowls to get it that way! Bake these in disposable pans so you'll have one loaf to give away at the ready.

Makes 2 loaves

- Baking spray, for preparing the pans
- 1½ cups walnut halves
- 3 very ripe bananas
- 1½ cups granulated white sugar
- 1 teaspoon pure vanilla extract
- 1¾ cups all-purpose flour
- 1½ teaspoons baking soda
- ½ teaspoon fine sea salt
- ¼ teaspoon ground cinnamon
- 3 large eggs
- ¾ cup vegetable oil

Pans: 2 disposable aluminum foil loaf pans, about 8 x 3¼ x 3 inches; sheet pan

❶ Position a rack in the center of the oven and preheat the oven to 250°F. Spray the loaf pans with baking spray.

❷ Spread the walnuts out on a sheet pan and toast them until browned and fragrant, about 15 minutes. Stir the nuts after about 10 minutes to ensure even toasting. Remove the nuts from the oven and let cool. Increase the oven temperature to 325°F. When the nuts have cooled, reserve ¼ cup for decorating the tops of the loaves and coarsely chop the rest of them; set the nuts aside.

❸ Meanwhile, mash the bananas with a fork in a small bowl. Add 1 cup of the sugar and the vanilla. Stir until the mixture is completely smooth.

❹ Place the flour in a large bowl and whisk to aerate. Add the remaining ½ cup sugar, baking soda, salt, and cinnamon to the flour and whisk well. Mix the eggs and oil together in a third bowl until emulsified. Add the egg mixture to the flour mixture and mix well. Add the banana mixture and stir with a fork until completely combined. Stir in the chopped walnuts, then divide the batter between the prepared pans. Lightly tap the loaf pans down on the counter to make sure the batter is evenly distributed and to remove excess air bubbles. Scatter the reserved walnut halves on top of the cakes.

❺ Place the loaf pans on a sheet pan to make it easier to pull them out of the hot oven. Bake until the cake pulls away from the sides of the pan and a toothpick inserted in the center comes out clean, about 40 minutes.

❻ Remove the cakes from the oven and let cool in the pans. The banana cakes can be served warm or completely cooled.

STEAK AND TRUFFLED EGGS

AND

LATTE LOAF

WITH HAZELNUT GLAZE

THE STEAK

This is a dish that is perfect for an intimate New Year's Day brunch or a midnight breakfast. To me, it is the ultimate steak and eggs. The soft, custardy eggs are cooked with cream cheese—my secret to soft scrambled eggs—and scented with a generous amount of black truffle pâté before serving. If you like truffles, you will find that truffle pâté beats truffle oil hands down, and the entire room will smell heavenly.

Serves 2

2 New York strip steaks or other favorite "breakfast" steaks (about 8 ounces each and 1 inch thick)

Extra-virgin olive oil

Pinch of kosher salt

¼ teaspoon whole black peppercorns, coarsely ground

1 tablespoon unsalted butter (optional)

Chopped fresh parsley (optional)

Truffled Scrambled Eggs (recipe follows)

Toast, croissants, or biscuits

Grilling Method: Direct/Medium Heat or Stovetop Grill Pan

❶ Wrap the steaks in paper towels to rid them of excess moisture. Replace the paper towels as needed.

❷ **If you are grilling**, preheat the grill with all burners on high. Once preheated, adjust the temperature to medium heat for direct grilling. Just before cooking, brush both sides of the steaks with olive oil and season with salt and pepper. Place the steaks on the cooking grate, cover, and grill for about 4 minutes. Turn the steaks and continue cooking for 3 to 4 minutes more for medium-rare (135°F on an instant-read thermometer).

If you are using a stovetop, preheat a large grill pan over medium-high heat for 1 to 2 minutes. Place the steaks (seasoned as above) in the pan, leaving space between them. Let cook until marked well with grill marks, 2 minutes. Flip the steaks over and let cook on the other side for another 2 to 3 minutes. If serving the steaks immediately, repeat on each side until the steaks have cooked for a total of about 10 minutes for medium-rare (135°F).

If you are not serving them immediately, once the steaks have been seared on both sides—about 5 minutes total—transfer them to a rack set on a sheet pan. This can be done up to 1 hour in advance. Once the steaks have been seared and you are ready to finish cooking them, place them in a preheated 300°F oven to finish cooking. Do not leave the steaks in the oven for longer than 15 minutes, or they will be overcooked.

❸ Remove the steaks from the grill or grill pan or oven and let rest for at least 5 minutes but no longer than 10 minutes before serving.

❹ Top each steak with 1½ teaspoons of the butter and some of the parsley, if desired. Serve with Truffled Scrambled Eggs and your choice of a breakfast bread.

TRUFFLED SCRAMBLED EGGS

If you aren't into truffles, omit the pâté. I promise, these scrambled eggs will still be the best you have ever made. What bread you serve with them is your choice. If steak isn't on the menu, sometimes I grill

thick slabs of multigrain bread. Other times I serve croissants and fruit salad. Most often, it is hot biscuits with butter and molasses.

Serves 2

4 large farm-fresh eggs

2 tablespoons unsalted butter

1½ tablespoons extra-virgin olive oil

Generous pinch of fine sea salt

2 tablespoons cream cheese, cut into 8 cubes

1 tablespoon chopped fresh chives

1 heaping teaspoon black truffle pâté (see Note)

Fleur de sel or other flaky sea salt

Freshly ground black pepper

❶ Crack the eggs into a medium-size bowl and beat them with a fork or a whisk until they are pale yellow in color, about 15 seconds.

❷ Put the butter and olive oil in a cold 8- to 10-inch nonstick skillet and place over medium-low heat. When the butter melts and the oil heats up, add the eggs and salt. Let cook, undisturbed, until a thin layer of cooked egg appears around the edge of the skillet.

Add the cream cheese cubes and chives, sprinkling them over the entire surface of the eggs.

❸ Using a fork or spatula, loosen the eggs all the way around the circumference of the skillet and then across the bottom. Continue to loosen them until they are fluffy and barely set, 2 minutes; the eggs should still look glossy on top and the cream cheese should be completely melted into the eggs. Turn off the heat and let the eggs finish cooking, gently scrambling, if necessary. Add the truffle pâté and gently fold it into the eggs.

❹ Scoop the eggs into a serving bowl, season with fleur de sel and pepper, and serve immediately with the steak.

Note: This pâté is made from chopped truffles and sometimes mushrooms. It is not made from liver.

THE MATCHUPS

LATTE LOAF WITH HAZELNUT GLAZE, *recipe follows*

BAKED CINNAMON-SUGAR DOUGHNUT PUFFS WITH DARK CHOCOLATE BOURBON DIPPING SAUCE, *page 25*

EASY LEMON LOAF, *page 140*

LATTE LOAF

WITH HAZELNUT GLAZE

THE CAKE

If you like hazelnut-flavored coffee, chances are you will love coffee infused with a generous shot of Frangelico. One summer evening while I was on my "cake tour," I made myself an iced Frangelico latte. After one cool, refreshing (and, yes, slightly intoxicating) sip, I was inspired to duplicate the flavors in a cake. I like to think of the result as a "quiet" cake in the sense that the flavors are present, refined, and authentic—just like the Christian monks of northern Italy who created Frangelico. If you are a fan of mocha, add a 1-ounce square of melted unsweetened chocolate to the glaze.

Serves 8

THE MATCHUPS

STEAK AND TRUFFLED EGGS, *page 32*

BOB'S STEAK AU POIVRE
WITH FRENCH ONION CROUTONS, *page 91*

COFFEE-RUBBED TENDERLOIN WITH
GARLIC CHEESE GRITS AND REDEYE GRAVY
GLAZE, *page 107*

FOR THE CAKE

Baking spray, for preparing the pan

3 large eggs

1⅓ cups granulated white sugar

2¼ cups all-purpose flour

3 teaspoons baking powder

1 teaspoon fine sea salt

2 teaspoons espresso powder

1⅓ cups heavy (whipping) cream

1½ teaspoons pure vanilla extract

FOR THE HAZELNUT GLAZE

2 tablespoons Frangelico liqueur

2 tablespoons heavy (whipping) cream

1¼ cups confectioners' sugar, sifted

Pinch of fine sea salt

Pans: 9 x 5 x 3-inch loaf pan; sheet pan

❶ Position a rack in the center of the oven and preheat the oven to 325°F. Spray the cake pan with baking spray.

❷ Make the cake: Beat the eggs and granulated sugar together with an electric mixer on medium-low speed until light and smooth, about 3 minutes. Whisk the flour, baking powder, and 1 teaspoon salt together in a medium-size bowl. In a small bowl, dissolve the espresso powder in the 1⅓ cups cream and add the vanilla.

③ Add the flour mixture and the cream mixture to the egg mixture alternately in batches, beating well after each addition. Stop the mixer and scrape down the side of the bowl as necessary.

④ Pour the batter into the prepared pan and lightly tap the pan down on the counter to make sure the batter is evenly distributed and to remove excess air bubbles.

⑤ Place the loaf pan on a sheet pan to make it easier to pull it out of the hot oven. Bake until the cake pulls away from the sides of the pan and a toothpick inserted in the center comes out clean, 55 to 60 minutes.

⑥ Meanwhile, make the glaze: Combine the liqueur, cream, confectioners' sugar, and a pinch of salt in a small bowl. Beat with a fork until smooth.

⑦ Remove the cake from the oven and let cool in the pan for 15 minutes. Place a sheet of waxed paper underneath a wire cooling rack to catch any drips, then invert the cake onto the rack and remove the pan. Flip the cake over and let cool before icing with glaze. The cake should sit uncovered until the glaze is set, about 2 hours, before serving.

PRIME NEW YORK STRIP STEAK ROAST

WITH BARBUTO-INSPIRED ROASTED POTATOES

CHOCOLATE LAYER CAKE

WITH COCOA-FRANGELICO FROSTING

THE STEAK

My friend Pete Savely knows how to throw a dinner party for his Chicago crew: one part prime beef, one part good Champagne (rosé for me), and one part potato (for another friend, Healy). Recently, he has gotten into roasting whole prime strip roasts and cutting them into ¾-inch steaks once they're cooked and rested. It's a very relaxing way to host a steak cookout for a large gathering. The potato preparation frequently changes—my favorite is a potato dish that is baked, broken into pieces, and fried. Here I am adapting Jonathan Waxman's "patate" from his iconic New York restaurant, Barbuto. They are my favorite version of these potatoes. I hope it does Pete proud.

Serves 8 to 10

6 to 7 pounds prime New York strip roast (about 11 inches long)

Extra-virgin olive oil

About 1 tablespoon kosher salt

About 1 teaspoon freshly ground black pepper

Barbuto-Inspired Roasted Potatoes (page 181)

Grilling Method: Indirect/Medium-High Heat or Oven Method

❶ Preheat the grill with all burners on high. Once preheated, adjust the temperature to medium-high heat for indirect grilling. Or preheat the oven to 450°F.

❷ Wrap the meat in paper towels to rid it of excess moisture. Replace the paper towels as needed.

❸ Brush the roast all over with olive oil and season with salt and pepper.

❹ **If using a grill,** place the meat, fat side up, in the middle of the cooking grate (make sure that no burners are on under the roast). Close the lid.

   If using the oven, place the meat in a roasting pan fitted with a rack; place the pan in the oven.

❺ Roast the meat for 45 minutes and then check the internal temperature with an instant-read thermometer inserted in the center of the roast. Depending on what the temperature is, generally it should take another 15 to 20 minutes to come to 120°F for rare (see Note). If you like your meat cooked more, you can leave it in the oven for another 5 to 10 minutes, but be aware that it will continue to cook a little as it rests.

❻ Tent the roast loosely with aluminum foil and let stand 10 minutes before slicing into ¾-inch-thick steaks. Serve with the Barbuto-Inspired Roasted Potatoes.

Note: If you want to eat the steak rare, watch it carefully while you are cooking. It takes under an hour for a 6½-pound roast to reach a rare center. A good meat thermometer is key to your success, because the meat will go from rare (120°F to 125°F) to medium-rare (130°F to 135°F) in a New York minute! Always remove a large piece of meat when it reaches 5°F below your desired degree of doneness, as it will continue to cook 5°F more as it rests.

THE MATCHUPS

CHOCOLATE LAYER CAKE
WITH COCOA-FRANGELICO FROSTING,
recipe follows

POTUS CARROT CAKE, *page 44*

GRANDMOTHER ODOM'S APPLE CAKE, *page 108*

CHOCOLATE LAYER CAKE

WITH COCOA-FRANGELICO FROSTING

THE CAKE

This tender and very dark chocolate cake is made with cocoa powder instead of melted unsweetened chocolate. Turn to it whenever you need a rich chocolate cake. Here the layers are frosted with a light, sweet chocolate frosting that complements their chocolate flavor. Frangelico is a sweet liqueur made from hazelnuts. The addition of Frangelico gives the frosting a slightly nutty flavor that enhances the light cocoa notes. If you like a lot of frosting, you will need to increase the recipe. This recipe will fill and frost a 9-inch round two-layer cake with a thin layer of frosting. I think it is the perfect frosting-to-cake ratio, but it may not be enough in our "more is more" Instagram society.

Serves 12

2 layers Chocolate Cake (page 230)

COCOA-FRANGELICO FROSTING

2 boxes (2 pounds) confectioners' sugar, or more if needed, sifted

4 generous tablespoons unsweetened cocoa powder

2 pinches fine sea salt

1 cup (2 sticks) unsalted butter, at room temperature

2 teaspoons pure vanilla extract or other extract

2 tablespoons heavy (whipping) cream, or more if needed

2 tablespoons Frangelico, or more if needed

❶ Bake the cake layers and set aside to cool.

❷ Make the frosting: Sift the confectioners' sugar, cocoa powder, and salt together in a medium-size bowl.

❸ Cream the butter until fluffy using an electric mixer on medium speed, about 2 minutes.

❹ Slowly add the sugar mixture to the butter and continue to cream for an additional 1 to 2 minutes. When the sugar is incorporated, add the vanilla, cream, and Frangelico 1 tablespoon at a time until your desired spreading consistency is reached. If it's too stiff, add a little more cream. If it's too loose, add a little more sugar. Taste for balance, and add a touch more salt and vanilla or other flavorings if desired.

❺ Assemble the cake: Carefully trim a thin slice off the rounded top of one of the layers to even it out. Place the trimmed layer, bottom side up, on a serving plate. Place about ¼ cup of frosting in the center of the cake layer and spread it out toward the side, making a smooth, even layer. If you want a thicker frosting layer, add more frosting and spread it out to make it even. (As a general rule, I allow ½ cup of frosting to fill between layers.) Place the second cake layer, top side up, over the frosting and press lightly to adhere. Place 1 tablespoon of frosting on the side of the bottom layer and, using a butter knife or offset spatula, spread it up to frost a portion of both layers. Continue frosting the side of the layers 1 tablespoon at a time. Once the side is done, place ¼ cup of frosting on the top and spread it evenly out toward the side, adding more frosting as necessary to frost the entire cake.

THE MATCHUPS

PRIME NEW YORK STRIP STEAK ROAST
WITH BARBUTO-INSPIRED ROASTED POTATOES,
page 36

COWBOY STEAK WITH WHISKEY BUTTER,
page 5

GRILLED TENDERLOIN WITH DECADENT
HORSERADISH CREAM AND YORKSHIRE PUDDING,
page 111

Regular

Dutch Processed

CLASSIC NEW YORK STEAKHOUSE STRIP

WITH BEEFSTEAK TOMATOES AND SIZZLING THICK BACON AND ONIONS

POTUS CARROT CAKE

THE STEAK

This is a classic restaurant steak preparation. I call for New York strips because that is my favorite cut of steak, but this recipe will work well with any cut. This rub-enhanced steak is the "kicked up" version of a basic grilled steak. When you make the rub, consider doubling or tripling it. It is a great flavor addition for any cut of beef and keeps for months in an airtight container. That way, this recipe is reduced to: oil, sprinkle, and grill! A big bonus when you're short on time!

Serves 4

4 New York strip steaks (12 to 16 ounces each and about 1½ inches thick)

1 tablespoon whole black peppercorns, toasted in a skillet (see Note)

¼ teaspoon dried rosemary

1 tablespoon kosher salt or coarse sea salt

1 teaspoon dry mustard

½ teaspoon granulated garlic

Extra-virgin olive oil

Beefsteak Tomato and Vidalia Onion Salad with Steak Sauce Dressing (page 177)

Sizzling Thick Bacon and Onions (recipe follows)

Grilling Method: Direct/Medium-High Heat

Special Equipment: Spice grinder

❶ Preheat the grill with all burners on high. Once preheated, adjust the temperature to medium-high heat for direct grilling.

❷ Wrap the steaks in paper towels to rid them of excess moisture. Replace the paper towels as needed.

❸ Coarsely grind the peppercorns in a spice (or coffee) grinder; add the rosemary and grind again. Put the pepper and rosemary mixture in a small bowl and mix in the salt, mustard, and garlic.

❹ Lightly brush the steaks with olive oil. Sprinkle the rub evenly and lightly on both sides of the steaks. (Too much rub will overseason the meat.)

❺ Place the meat on the cooking grate directly over the fire. Cover, cook about 3 minutes for good grill marks, then turn the steaks. Grill for 6 minutes on the second side, then turn the steaks again and grill for 3 minutes more on the first side for medium-rare (135°F on an instant-read thermometer).

❻ Remove the meat from the grill and place on a clean platter. Let the steaks rest for 5 minutes before serving with the tomato and onion salad and the bacon and onions.

Note: Place the peppercorns in a small cold skillet. Turn the heat to low and let toast, shaking occasionally, until you can smell the aroma of the pepper, about 5 minutes. Don't place over high heat, or the pepper will burn.

SIZZLING THICK BACON AND ONIONS

This dish can also be served as an appetizer—but you might be tempted to make it for breakfast. It is oven-baked bacon and the best that I have ever eaten!

Serves 4 to 6

> 1 pound best-quality slab bacon
>
> ¼ cup (packed) dark brown sugar
>
> Leaves from 3 sprigs thyme
>
> Kosher salt and freshly ground black pepper
>
> 2 large sweet onions, peeled and cut into thick slices
>
> Extra-virgin olive oil

❶ Preheat the oven to 375°F.

❷ Cut the bacon into ⅛-inch-thick slices. Sprinkle the slices liberally with half the sugar, half the thyme, and salt and pepper on both sides. Place them on a rack set on a sheet pan.

❸ Toss the onion rings in olive oil and season with the remaining sugar, thyme, and salt. Place the onion rings on the rack with the bacon, if there is room. If there isn't room, place on a rack set into a separate sheet pan.

❹ Bake until the bacon is crisp and the onions are golden, about 40 minutes, turning once halfway through the cooking time. Drain on paper towels, then transfer to a serving platter.

THE MATCHUPS

POTUS CARROT CAKE, *recipe follows*

DOUBLE-DUTCH CHOCOLATE GUINNESS BUNDT
CAKE WITH CHOCOLATE GUINNESS GLAZE,
page 133

BANANA PUDDING ICE CREAM CAKE, *page 162*

The Hunt for a Smoky Cocktail

Craft cocktails are all the rage these days, and there isn't a barbecue lover or bartender I know who hasn't pondered how to mash up barbecue and cocktails.

Some people grill fruit to garnish their cocktails, and others use liquid smoke or the fancy Smoking Gun that emits a puff of smoke, but those methods seem a little forced to me. I decided to look in my liquor cabinet and see if there was anything more organic that would make a smoky cocktail.

My brother-in-law, a big fan of single malt Scotch, recommended I start my education with Laphroaig 10-year. That happened to be around the time that I participated in a Scotch tasting taught by Scotch whisky expert and Scotland native Simon Brooking. Laphroaig is made on the Isle of Islay from malted barley. The barley is soaked in water from a nearby stream and dried with the heat of a peat fire. The peat grows on Islay and is hand-cut and dried for three months before it is used as fuel to dry out the wet barley. The smoke from the peat is what gives the barley and the resulting Scotch whisky its distinctive smoky, peaty flavor.

The cocktail needed a neutral spirit to pair with the smoky note. I envisioned an icy vodka martini. You know the kind that I'm talking about—it's so cold that ice crystals of vodka float on the top. What if I took the base of a clean, crisp, cold vodka martini and added a kiss of smoke?

I had the ingredients; how was I going to make the cocktail? I asked a few friends and amateur bartenders what they would do, but none of their ideas panned out. Not wanting to give up, I posed the question to a veteran bartender, and he gave me my answer in a nanosecond! Pour the Scotch into an atomizer and spray the top of the ice-cold vodka martini after it is poured.

That was a game changer! I purchased a stainless-steel atomizer and filled it with single malt Scotch. I chose a very smooth, clean vodka and shook it in a cocktail shaker with a lot of ice. The frosty liquid shimmered in the martini glass, and just before serving it, I sprayed it with a whiff of my smoky Scotch. The atomizer makes all the difference as it distributes the Scotch on the top of the martini and fills the nose with just the right amount of smoky notes. And since smell plays an equal (if not greater) role in helping us determine flavors, it's a powerful way to make a smoky cocktail.

The Smoky Martini

This is a martini that everyone will love. It is still light and crisp from the vodka but has the smoky nose that brown liquor and barbecue lovers crave.

Makes 1 drink

> 2 to 4 ounces favorite vodka
>
> 1 generous cup ice cubes
>
> 2 ounces smoky single malt Scotch, such as Laphroaig 10-year
>
> Cornichon, for garnish (see Note)

Special Equipment: Cocktail shaker, small strainer, martini glass, atomizer (small spray bottle), short bamboo skewer or cocktail pick

Fill the shaker with ice cubes. Add the vodka and shake well. Strain into a martini glass. Fill the atomizer with Scotch and spray the top of the glass twice. Garnish with the cornichon. Serve immediately.

Note: I chose a cornichon (mini pickle) to lend that tangy sharp, briny, salty flavor and complement the vodka, the Scotch, and the smoky world of barbecue. A pickled onion would also work well.

POTUS CARROT CAKE

THE CAKE

This is the recipe that Gerald Ford couldn't get for love or money. My cousin Carol was the chef for America's thirty-eighth president—after he left the White House. When she left his employ to move to the mountains of North Carolina, he missed her carrot cake so much that he begged for the recipe. Since she only passes her recipes down to her family, his request was refused—but luckily for me (and you!), mine wasn't. Carol's secret is the addition of crushed pineapple, which balances the sweetness and adds moisture and just the right amount of tartness. I've adapted the cake for my tastes, adding more carrots, nuts, and cherries to the batter and coconut to the frosting, making it fit for a king—or a president.

Serves 8 to 12

FOR THE CAKE

Baking spray, for preparing the pans

1¾ cups granulated white sugar

1 cup neutral vegetable oil, such as Crisco, or untoasted walnut oil

4 large eggs

2 cups all-purpose flour

1 teaspoon fine sea salt

2 teaspoons baking soda

2 teaspoons ground cinnamon

2/3 cup dried cherries or currants

1½ cups chopped walnuts (English or black walnuts)

4 cups hand-grated carrots

1 can (8 ounces) crushed pineapple, drained

FOR THE FROSTING

8 ounces cream cheese, at room temperature

8 tablespoons (1 stick) unsalted butter, at room temperature

3 cups confectioners' sugar, or more as needed

2 tablespoons heavy (whipping) cream, or more as needed

1 tablespoon pure vanilla extract

2 cups Baker's Sweetened Angel Flake Coconut

½ cup chopped walnuts (English or black walnuts)

Pans: Two 9-inch round cake pans or a 10-inch tube pan

❶ Position a rack in the center of the oven and preheat the oven to 350°F. Spray the cake pans with baking spray.

❷ Make the cake: Beat the granulated sugar, oil, and eggs together with an electric mixer on medium speed until creamy and light in color, 2 to 3 minutes.

❸ Stir the flour, salt, baking soda, and cinnamon together in a large bowl. Add the flour mixture to the sugar mixture and mix well. Stop the machine and scrape down the side of the bowl as necessary.

❹ Fold in the dried cherries, 1½ cups walnuts, carrots, and pineapple, making sure they are well combined.

❺ Pour the batter into the prepared pans. If using layer pans, make sure the batter is evenly divided. Lightly tap each pan down on the counter to make sure the batter is evenly distributed and to remove excess air bubbles.

❻ Bake until the cake pulls away from the sides of the pans and a toothpick inserted in the thickest

THE MATCHUPS

CLASSIC NEW YORK STEAKHOUSE STRIP
WITH BEEFSTEAK TOMATOES AND SIZZLING THICK
BACON AND ONIONS, *page 41*

RED-HOT CAST-IRON STEAK WITH
PERFECT CRUST, *page 9*

PRIME NEW YORK STRIP STEAK ROAST
WITH BARBUTO-INSPIRED ROASTED POTATOES,
page 36

point comes out clean, 25 to 30 minutes for layers and 1 hour for a tube cake.

7 Cool the layers in the pans for 10 minutes before removing them to wire cooling racks to cool completely.

8 Meanwhile, make the frosting: Cream the cream cheese, butter, and 3 cups confectioners' sugar together with an electric mixer on medium speed until fluffy, 2 to 3 minutes. Add 2 tablespoons of cream and the vanilla and mix well. If the frosting is too thin, add more confectioners' sugar, 1 tablespoon at a time. If the frosting is too thick, add more cream, 1 tablespoon at a time. When it is the right consistency for spreading, divide the frosting equally between two bowls. Add about three-quarters of both the coconut and the walnuts to the frosting in one bowl and mix to combine. This will be the filling. Reserve the plain frosting and remaining coconut and walnuts for the top of the cake.

9 Assemble the cake: **If making a layer cake,** carefully trim a thin slice off the rounded tops of the 2 layers to even them out. Place 1 layer, bottom side up, on a serving plate. Spread the top with the filling. Place the second layer over the filling. Frost the top with the plain frosting and leave the sides unfrosted for a rustic look. Sprinkle the top with the remaining coconut and walnuts. (If you prefer to frost the entire cake, you may need to double the cream cheese frosting recipe, omitting the coconut and walnuts in the second batch.)

If making a tube cake, remove the cake from the pan. Invert the cake so it is top side up. For a rustic look, slice the entire cake in half horizontally and spread the cut side of the bottom half with a thick layer of filling before placing the top half back on the cake. Spread the top with the plain frosting and sprinkle with the remaining coconut and walnuts.

Turn a Layer Cake into a Sheet Cake

The beauty of a 9 x 13 x 2-inch pan is that it will hold the same amount of batter as two layer cake pans—pour it in, and you have an instant sheet cake. If you are taking it to a party, you can frost just the top of the cake in the pan and carry and serve from that same pan. If you want to get a little fancier, invert it onto a cooling rack and frost the top and the sides. A cardboard cake board will make this job easier, and Wilton makes cake boards in two sizes, 13 x 19 and 10 x 14. They come in a set of six and are inexpensive on Amazon.

Keep in mind that every pan differs somewhat, so it's best to fill your pan halfway or a little more than halfway with batter to allow for rising. If you have leftover batter—and you often will—make cupcakes or a mini loaf cake. Anything will work, even oven-safe coffee mugs.

NEW YORK STRIP

WITH RED WINE BUTTER AND SPINACH ARTICHOKE CASSEROLE

HOMEMADE CONFETTI BIRTHDAY CAKE

WITH A FLUFFY WHITE CHOCOLATE BUTTERCREAM

THE STEAK

This is a steak dinner tailor-made for celebrating. Legend has it that the famous Chicago-Style Spinach Artichoke Dip from the Hillstone restaurant group was a version of this casserole before customers at Houston's in Chicago started ordering the "vegetable" with a side of corn chips and turned it into an appetizer!

Serves 4

4 New York strip steaks (12 to 16 ounces each and about 1½ inches thick)

Extra-virgin olive oil

1 teaspoon kosher salt

1 teaspoon whole black peppercorns, coarsely ground

4 tablespoons Red Wine Butter
(*Marchand de Vin* Butter; recipe follows)

Chopped fresh parsley, for garnish (optional)

Spinach and Artichoke Casserole (page 190)

Grilling Method: Direct/Medium Heat

❶ Preheat the grill with all burners on high. Once preheated, adjust the temperature to medium heat for direct grilling.

❷ Wrap the steaks in paper towels to rid them of excess moisture. Replace the paper towels as needed.

❸ Just before grilling, brush both sides of the steaks with oil and season with salt and pepper.

❹ Place the steaks on the cooking grate directly over medium heat. Cover and cook for 5 to 7 minutes. Turn the steaks and continue cooking for 5 to 7 minutes more for medium-rare (135°F on an instant-read thermometer).

❺ Remove the steaks from the grill and allow them to rest for 5 minutes before serving. Top each steak with ½ to 1 tablespoon of the Red Wine Butter and a sprinkling of parsley, if desired. Serve with the Spinach and Artichoke Casserole.

THE MATCHUPS

HOMEMADE CONFETTI BIRTHDAY CAKE
WITH A FLUFFY WHITE CHOCOLATE BUTTERCREAM,
recipe follows

ANTHONY'S GRANDMOTHER'S
"EARTHQUAKE CAKE," *page 153*

ROSE WHITE'S FAMOUS CARAMEL CAKE, *page 243*

RED WINE BUTTER (*MARCHAND DE VIN* BUTTER)

The classic *marchand de vin* butter calls for boiling shallots in red wine until the mixture is reduced by half and then adding beef consommé and reducing it again until it is almost dry. If you think that is a lot of work, you are correct! This version is less refined, and the layered flavors come from the addition of Worcestershire sauce and Dijon mustard. Use rough-textured, whole-grain Dijon if you can find it; it makes a big difference in the flavor and texture of this butter. This butter is great with anything that you would normally accompany with a glass of red wine. Make it at least 3 hours in advance of using. This recipe makes enough for 8 to 10 steaks. Wrap any leftover butter tightly in plastic wrap and store for up to 1 week in the refrigerator. The butter is great on all kinds of meat, fish, and vegetables as well. When you take a steak break, try it with sole.

Makes 2 logs; about 1⅓ cups

2 shallots, peeled and minced

2 tablespoons red wine, such as cabernet sauvignon, Shiraz, or zinfandel

1 cup (2 sticks) unsalted butter, at room temperature

3 teaspoons minced fresh parsley

½ teaspoon Worcestershire sauce

½ teaspoon smooth or whole-grain Dijon mustard

Fine sea salt and freshly ground black pepper

❶ Soak the shallots in the wine for 30 minutes. Mash or stir the butter until it is smooth and slightly fluffy. Drain the shallots, reserving 1 tablespoon of the wine; add the shallots to the butter. Mix well, then add the parsley, Worcestershire sauce, Dijon mustard, reserved wine, ½ teaspoon salt, and pepper to taste. Mix well, mashing with the back of a fork to make sure all the ingredients are incorporated. Taste for seasoning. Add more salt if needed.

❷ Drop the butter in spoonfuls on a piece of parchment paper or plastic wrap. Roll up the butter in the wrap and smooth it out to form a round log about 5 inches long. Twist the ends to seal and refrigerate until hard and easy to slice, at least 2 hours. The butter can be made in advance and stored tightly covered in the refrigerator for up to 1 week. Place leftover butter in the freezer for up to 3 months.

HOMEMADE CONFETTI BIRTHDAY CAKE
WITH A FLUFFY WHITE CHOCOLATE BUTTERCREAM

THE CAKE

What could possibly be more *fun* than a homemade confetti-style cake?! In fact, confetti cake is so much fun that it has a cult following—all people who grew up with and love the original Pillsbury Funfetti, which is white cake dotted with colorful sprinkles, frosted, and decorated with more sprinkles! My sisters and I never tasted the cake because my mother didn't use cake mixes, but when I started working on this book, I knew that I had to try it. My first step was to buy the mix and a can of purple frosting. I made the Funfetti "kit" into cupcakes with my twin nieces, who at that time were 12 years old. Despite the fact that they ate up the experience and the cake, I decided that it would be even more fun to make it from scratch. A few weeks later, I was visiting my other sister, who had a houseful of young boys ages 8 to 14. I unveiled my from-scratch confetti cake for them. And, lest anyone think that confetti skews female, the boys devoured the cake—never once commenting on it being girly!

Serves 16

Baking spray, for preparing the pans

1 cup (2 sticks) unsalted butter, at room temperature

2⅔ cups granulated white sugar

4½ cups cake flour or 4 cups all-purpose flour
(I prefer cake flour)

5 teaspoons baking powder

1 teaspoon fine sea salt

2 cups skim milk

1 teaspoon pure vanilla extract

1 teaspoon pure almond extract

6 large egg whites, at room temperature

½ cup multicolor sprinkles, plus 2 tablespoons for decorating the top (see Note on next page)

White Chocolate Buttercream (recipe follows)

Pans: Three 9-inch round cake pans

❶ Position a rack in the center of the oven and preheat the oven to 350°F. Spray the cake pans with baking spray.

❷ Cream the butter and sugar together with an electric mixer on medium speed until smooth and very fluffy, 3 to 5 minutes.

❸ Whisk the flour, baking powder, and salt together in a separate bowl and set aside. Mix the milk, vanilla, and almond extract together in a small bowl.

❹ Add the flour mixture and the milk mixture alternately to the butter mixture in small batches.

Beat well after each addition. Continue beating on medium-low until smooth, 1 to 2 minutes more. Stop the machine and scrape down the side of the bowl as necessary. Set aside.

⑤ Remove the batter blade(s) from the mixer and replace it with the wire whisk. Pour the egg whites into a clean bowl and mix on medium-high speed until they hold soft peaks, about 3 minutes. Gently mix the sprinkles into the batter by hand and then fold the egg whites into the batter using a silicone spatula.

⑥ Divide the batter equally among the 3 prepared pans. Lightly tap each pan down on the counter to make sure the batter is evenly distributed and to remove excess air bubbles.

⑦ Bake until the layers pull away from the sides of the pans and a toothpick inserted in the center comes out clean, 30 to 35 minutes. Cool the layers in the pans for 5 minutes before removing them to wire cooling racks to cool completely.

⑧ Assemble the cake: Carefully trim a thin layer of cake off the rounded tops of the 3 layers to even them out. Place 1 layer, bottom side up, on a cake plate. Place ¼ to ½ cup of frosting in the center of the cake layer and spread it out toward the side until it evenly covers the surface. If you want the layer of frosting to be thicker, add more and spread it out evenly. Place the second layer, bottom side up, over the frosting and press lightly to adhere it. Spread the second layer with frosting, then top with the third layer. Using a butter knife or an offset spatula, place 1 tablespoon of frosting on the side of the bottom layer and spread it up to frost a portion of all 3 layers. Continue frosting the side of the layers 1 tablespoon at a time. Once the side is done, place ¼ cup of frosting on the top and spread it evenly out toward the side, adding more frosting as necessary to frost the entire cake. Decorate the top with the reserved sprinkles.

Note: Be sure to use sprinkles that are all sugar so that they melt into the batter. I prefer the multicolor sprinkles made by Wilton.

WHITE CHOCOLATE BUTTERCREAM

Using Guittard Gourmet White Chocolate Chips in this recipe makes all the difference. They are made for the professional pastry community, but you can buy them on Amazon if you can't find them locally. Alternatively, use any good white chocolate, like Ghirardelli, which is sold in 4-ounce bars.

Makes about 4 cups

> 1 cup (2 sticks) unsalted butter, at room temperature
>
> 4 ounces white chocolate chips, melted
>
> ¼ teaspoon fine sea salt
>
> 2 boxes (1 pound each) confectioners' sugar
>
> 6 tablespoons whole milk
>
> 1 teaspoon pure vanilla extract

Cream the butter and melted white chocolate together with an electric mixer on medium-low speed. Whisk the salt into the sugar in a separate bowl. Mix the milk and vanilla together in a third bowl. Add the sugar and the milk alternately to the butter mixture in small batches. Beat well after each addition. Increase the speed and mix until the buttercream is white and very fluffy, about 2 minutes.

Cover until ready to frost the cake.

THE MATCHUPS

NEW YORK STRIP WITH RED WINE BUTTER AND SPINACH ARTICHOKE CASSEROLE, *page 47*

STEAK DIANE WITH TWICE-BAKED POTATOES, *page 51*

BACON-WRAPPED BEEF TENDERLOIN WITH A GREEN PEPPERCORN AND THYME SAUCE, *page 116*

STEAK DIANE

WITH TWICE-BAKED POTATOES

RETRO CHOCOLATE CUPCAKES

WITH A SWEET MASCARPONE CENTER

THE STEAK

"The only time to eat diet food is while you're waiting for the steak to cook."

—Julia Child

Steak Diane has been loosely linked to the Roman goddess of the hunt, Diana. Her connection may or may not be accurate, but it is a delicious throwback to a simpler time. The essence of it is the rich flavors of beef juices, shallots, brandy, butter, and cream that are reduced to their heart-throbbing essence. When it was my sister Catherine's turn in the kitchen, she would frequently make it for dinner. The traditional recipe she used called for flambéing. I've eliminated the flambé and added both mushrooms and garlic to the rich, boozy sauce. With these additions, I feel the traditional filet mignon is best replaced with a juicy strip steak or a flatiron steak. Powerful Diana, forager of ancient forests, goddess of the moon and domestic animals, would no doubt approve.

Serves 2 to 4

2 flatiron steaks (about 12 ounces each and ¾ inch thick)

⅔ cup beef or veal stock

2 teaspoons Dijon mustard

1½ teaspoons Worcestershire sauce

Extra-virgin olive oil

Kosher salt

2 tablespoons unsalted butter

2 tablespoons finely chopped shallot (1 large shallot)

1 teaspoon minced garlic

8 ounces assorted mushrooms, sliced (about 3 cups)

¼ cup brandy, preferably Cognac

¼ cup heavy (whipping) cream

Snipped fresh chives, for garnish

Cheesy Twice-Baked Potatoes (page 182)

Pan: 12-inch cast-iron or carbon steel skillet

Method: Stovetop

❶ Wrap the steaks in paper towels to rid them of excess moisture. Replace the paper towels as needed.

❷ Whisk the beef stock, mustard, and Worcestershire sauce in a bowl and set aside. Brush the steaks all over with olive oil and season on both sides with salt.

❸ Heat the skillet over medium heat until very hot, 3 to 4 minutes. Place the steaks in the pan and sear until well caramelized and brown, 2 to 3 minutes per side. They should be cooked to medium-rare (135°F on an instant-read thermometer). If you want them more done, continue cooking once you make the sauce below. Remove the skillet from the heat, place the steaks on a plate, and loosely tent with aluminum foil.

❹ Add 1 tablespoon of the butter, all of the shallot, and garlic to the pan juices in the skillet, while stirring continuously. Residual heat from the pan should be hot enough to cook them. Stir until wilted and golden brown, about 2 minutes.

THE MATCHUPS

RETRO CHOCOLATE CUPCAKES
WITH A SWEET MASCARPONE
CENTER, *recipe follows*

DAVID LEBOVITZ'S ORANGE-
GLAZED ALMOND LOAF, *page 104*

PECAN-STUDDED RUM CAKE,
page 144

⑤ Place the skillet over medium-high heat and immediately add the remaining 1 tablespoon butter and mushrooms. Cook, stirring, until the mushrooms are just beginning to brown, about 5 minutes.

⑥ Raise the heat to high and add the brandy. Reduce for 20 seconds, then whisk in the beef stock mixture. Reduce the liquid, stirring continuously, until the sauce is velvety smooth and thickened, 3 to 4 minutes.

⑦ Stir in the cream. If the steaks need additional cooking, reheat in the sauce at this time, or see Note. Serve the steaks whole or cut in slices with the sauce spooned over the meat. Garnish with chives and serve with Cheesy Twice-Baked Potatoes.

Note: If you prefer your steaks medium to well-done, you can also place them in a warm oven (200°F) to continue cooking as you make the sauce.

RETRO CHOCOLATE CUPCAKES

WITH A SWEET MASCARPONE CENTER

THE CAKE

When I feel like eating a classic chocolate cupcake but want to present something with a little more personality, I make these "Hostess"-style cupcakes. The homemade cupcakes are loaded with a sweet mascarpone filling and dipped into a dark chocolate ganache to make the shiny, flat icing. The white squiggles on the top can be easily "penned" with one of the new decorating pens, and just like snowflakes, no two cakes ever turn out the same.

Makes 12 cupcakes

FOR THE CUPCAKES

8 tablespoons (1 stick) unsalted butter, at room temperature

1½ cups granulated white sugar

2 large eggs

1 teaspoon pure vanilla extract

2 cups all-purpose flour

1 cup unsweetened Dutch-process cocoa powder

½ teaspoon fine sea salt

1½ cups buttermilk

1 tablespoon white vinegar

1 teaspoon baking soda

FOR THE MASCARPONE FILLING

8 tablespoons (1 stick) unsalted butter, at room temperature

8 ounces mascarpone cheese

1 box (1 pound) confectioners' sugar

⅛ teaspoon fine sea salt

FOR THE CHOCOLATE ICING

⅓ cup heavy (whipping) cream

6 ounces bittersweet chocolate chips or chopped block chocolate

½ teaspoon pure vanilla extract

Royal Icing (recipe follows)

Pans: Two 6-cup cupcake tins; cupcake liners

Special equipment: Piping bag with large and small tips

① Position a rack in the center of the oven and preheat the oven to 350°F. Line the cupcake tins with cupcake liners.

❷ Make the cupcakes: Cream the 8 tablespoons butter and granulated sugar together with a handheld mixer on medium-high speed until light and fluffy, 3 to 5 minutes. Add the eggs one at a time, beating well after each addition. Beat until smooth and silky. Add the 1 teaspoon vanilla and beat until well combined. Stop the mixer and scrape down the side of the bowl as necessary.

❸ Whisk the flour, cocoa, and ½ teaspoon of salt together in a separate bowl. Add the flour mixture to the butter mixture in thirds, alternating with the buttermilk. Begin and end with the flour. Pour the vinegar into a measuring cup and add the baking soda. (Note: If you do it the other way, it foams a lot.) Whisk this into the batter mixture.

④ Fill each muffin cup three-quarters full with batter. Bake until a toothpick inserted in the center comes out clean, 25 to 28 minutes. Cool on a wire rack for 10 minutes, then remove the cupcakes from the pan to the wire rack.

⑤ Make the mascarpone filling: Cream the 8 tablespoons butter and mascarpone together with a handheld mixer on medium-high speed until fluffy, 2 to 3 minutes. Add the confectioners' sugar and ⅛ teaspoon of salt. Continue beating until fluffy, 1 to 2 minutes. Fill a piping bag fitted with a large tip with the mixture. Poke the pastry tip through the top and into the center of a cupcake. Squeeze about 2 tablespoons of filling into it. Repeat with the remaining cupcakes.

⑥ Make the icing: Place the cream in a small saucepan and heat over medium heat to almost boiling. Remove the pan from the heat and add the chocolate; stir until the chocolate is melted and well combined. Add the ½ teaspoon of vanilla, stirring constantly. If making in advance, cover with plastic wrap and set aside until you are ready to ice the cupcakes (but note that the icing is best made right before you want to ice them).

⑦ Using an offset spatula or the back of a spoon, spread a thin, flat layer of icing over the tops of all of the cupcakes. You can also hold the cupcakes from the bottom and "swirl" the tops in the icing. Let set completely before decorating with the royal icing squiggle.

ROYAL ICING FOR DECORATION

You can make the traditional royal icing with egg whites or meringue powder, but since only a small amount is needed, I like to make this eggless royal icing.

Makes about ½ cup

> 2 teaspoons light corn syrup, such as Karo, or more if needed
>
> 2 teaspoons heavy (whipping) cream or milk, or more if needed
>
> 1 cup confectioners' sugar, or more if needed

Mix the corn syrup and the cream or milk in a small bowl. Mix in the sugar with a fork and stir until creamy and there are no lumps. If it is too thick, add a little more corn syrup and cream. If it is too thin, add a little more sugar. You want to make sure that the icing won't "bleed" and spread when you squiggle it. Place the icing in a decorating bag with a small tip, a decorating pen, or a plastic bag with the tip cut off. If you write a row of fat, cursive, lowercase *e*'s down the center of the cupcake, it will resemble the squiggle decoration on that original filled cupcake.

THE MATCHUPS

STEAK DIANE WITH TWICE-BAKED POTATOES,
page 51

CARNE ASADA WITH AVOCADO AND
TOMATO SALAD, *page 18*

STEAK TACOS WITH 1-2-3 GUACAMOLE,
CARROT-JALAPEÑO RELISH, AND CHIPOTLE CREMA,
page 147

TRI-TIP SANTA MARIA

WITH LOW-AND-SLOW CABBAGE AND OLD-FASHIONED GARLIC BREAD

TURTLE BROWNIE BITES

THE STEAK

When I first started grilling and barbecuing in earnest, everyone I met from the West Coast would reply to the statement that California has no barbecue with "Yes, we do, we have the tri-tip." The first time I had it, it was prepared very simply and had a darkly caramelized crust that was almost black and a glistening fuchsia interior. I thought it was the most beautiful grilled meat that I had ever seen. I've added a touch of brown sugar to the traditional salt, pepper, and dried garlic rub to facilitate an even deeper caramelization of the crust. Because this is California's "barbecue," I've paired it with my favorite barbecued side, a whole cabbage that is barbecued for several hours until the leaves are pluck-able and melt into themselves to make something akin to cabbage confit.

Serves 4 to 6

1 tri-tip steak (1½ to 2 pounds)

1 tablespoon dark brown sugar

1 teaspoon kosher salt

1 teaspoon freshly ground black pepper

½ teaspoon dried Worcestershire powder

1 teaspoon granulated garlic

Pinch of cayenne

Extra-virgin olive oil

Low-and-Slow Cabbage (page 188)

Old-Fashioned Garlic Bread (recipe follows)

Grilling Method: Indirect/Medium-High Heat

❶ Preheat the grill with all burners on high. Once preheated, adjust the temperature to medium-high heat for indirect grilling.

❷ Wrap the tri-tip in paper towels to rid it of excess moisture. Replace the paper towels as needed.

❸ To make the rub, mix the brown sugar, salt, pepper, Worcestershire powder, garlic, and cayenne together in a small bowl (see Note).

❹ Just before grilling, brush both sides of the steaks with the oil and season liberally with the rub.

❺ Place the tri-tip on the cooking grate directly over the fire. Cover, and cook for about 2 minutes for good grill marks. Turn the steak and continue searing over the fire for about 2 minutes more. Move the meat away from the heat, cover, and continue cooking for 15 to 20 minutes more for just under medium-rare or to an internal temperature of 130°F on an instant-read thermometer. Remember, the larger the piece of meat, the longer it will take to cook.

❻ Remove the steak from the grill and allow it to rest for 8 to 10 minutes before slicing against the grain. Serve with Low-and-Slow Cabbage and Old-Fashioned Garlic Bread.

Note: You can double the rub and use half of it for the Low-and-Slow Cabbage on page 188.

THE MATCHUPS

TURTLE BROWNIE BITES,
recipe follows

THE ORIGINAL PB&J CUPCAKES,
page 167

RASPBERRY ROLL-UP WITH
LIMONCELLO WHIPPED CREAM,
page 238

OLD-FASHIONED GARLIC BREAD

This old-school garlic bread rounds out the meal, and if you make an open-faced tri-tip sandwich out of it, you'll be one happy camper!

Serves 4 to 6

6 large garlic cloves, peeled and chopped

½ teaspoon kosher salt

4 tablespoons (½ stick) unsalted butter, at room temperature

¼ cup chopped fresh flat-leaf parsley

Freshly ground black pepper

¼ cup extra-virgin olive oil

1 large loaf ciabatta or Italian bread

2 tablespoons grated Parmigiano-Reggiano cheese

1 Preheat the oven to 350°F.

2 Place the garlic in a food processor and process until minced. If you don't have a food processor, mash the garlic and salt together with a heavy blending fork or the back of a large spoon until a paste forms. Otherwise, add the salt to the food processor, along with the butter, parsley, and pepper, and pulse until combined.

3 Heat the olive oil in a medium-size skillet until warm, about 1 minute. Add the garlic/butter mixture

and stir until well combined. Remove the pan from the heat.

4 Slice the ciabatta bread in half horizontally and spread the garlic butter on both halves. Sprinkle each half with the Parmigiano-Reggiano.

5 Place the bread on a sheet pan and then into the oven, and bake until toasty brown and the butter mixture is absorbed into the bread, 10 minutes. If you want it to be more toasted, turn on the broiler and place the bread underneath for 1 to 2 minutes. Remove from the oven and cut into pieces. Serve immediately.

California's Steak

The tri-tip comes from Santa Maria, California, and is sometimes called Santa Maria steak, in honor of the town that made it popular, or the triangle steak, because of its vaguely triangular shape. It's cut from the bottom sirloin, the muscle group that controls the steer's back legs, and is a lean but juicy cut if grilled to a beautiful hot-pink rare. This cut is sometimes hard to find outside of California, but it is becoming more and more popular. Tri-tips generally weigh between 1½ and 2½ pounds. Be sure to note the weight of your piece and adjust your timing accordingly.

TURTLE BROWNIE BITES

THE CAKE

When we were kids, we would always give our father a box of candy turtles for Father's Day. While I was developing recipes for this book, I decided to update the tradition by creating a turtle cake especially for him. The result was a dark chocolate brownie–like base coated with homemade caramel, chocolate ganache, and toasted pecan halves. It is so rich that it's best served in tiny pieces, and so good that you might not be able to stop at one bite!

Makes 16 average-size pieces, or 48 small bites

Baking spray, for preparing the pan

8 tablespoons (1 stick) unsalted butter

8 ounces Guittard 70% bittersweet chocolate

2 large eggs

1⅔ cups granulated white sugar

2 teaspoons pure vanilla extract

½ teaspoon fine sea salt

1 cup all-purpose flour

⅔ cup coarsely chopped pecans, toasted (see page 85)

Caramel Sauce (recipe follows)

1 pound (about 2½ cups) pecan halves, toasted, for the top

Chocolate Ganache (recipe follows)

Pan: 9-inch square cake pan

❶ Position a rack in the center of the oven and preheat the oven to 350°F. Spray the cake pan with baking spray and line it with a length of heavy-duty aluminum foil or parchment paper, leaving a 2-inch-long overhang on each side of the pan. Smooth the paper evenly on the bottom and up the sides. The overhanging sides will help you remove the cake from the pan once it is done.

❷ Melt the butter and 6 ounces of the chocolate in the top of a double boiler or in a metal bowl set over simmering water. Chop the remaining chocolate into small pieces.

❸ Beat the eggs, sugar, vanilla, and salt together with an electric mixer on medium speed until combined. Add the melted butter mixture to the egg mixture and beat until well incorporated. Add the flour a little at a time, beating until fully incorporated. Stir in the toasted pecans and the reserved chocolate pieces, making sure the batter is evenly mixed. Stop the mixer and scrape down the side of the bowl as necessary. Pour the batter into the prepared pan. Lightly tap it down on the counter to make sure the batter is evenly distributed and to remove excess air bubbles.

4 Bake until the cake pulls away from the sides of the pan, 25 minutes. The center should be moist but not runny—a little chocolate will cling to a toothpick when it is inserted in the cake.

5 Cool the cake in the pan on a wire rack for at least 1 hour or up to 2 hours before assembling. Leave the cake in the pan for assembly.

6 To assemble the cake, set aside 2 tablespoons of the caramel, then pour a layer of it over the top of the brownie cake. Insert the pecan halves evenly into the layer of caramel. Drizzle the caramel and pecan halves with the chocolate ganache, and finish with a light drizzle of the reserved caramel. Allow to cool completely in the refrigerator before removing from the pan and cutting into pieces.

CARAMEL SAUCE

This is the easiest and safest homemade caramel sauce because you add all the ingredients to the pot at the same time. That means no more sputtering and bubbling that happens when you add cream to the molten sugar.

Makes about 2 ½ cups

   1 cup heavy (whipping) cream

   1 cup plus 1 tablespoon granulated white sugar

   ½ cup plus 2 tablespoons light corn syrup, such as Karo

   3 tablespoons unsalted butter, cut into pieces

   ½ teaspoon pure vanilla extract

   ¼ teaspoon fine sea salt

1 Place the cream, sugar, corn syrup, and butter in a large saucepan and bring to a boil over high heat, stirring until the sugar dissolves, about 2 minutes. Reduce the heat to medium-high and cook, stirring occasionally, until the caramel reaches 240°F on a candy thermometer, about 10 minutes. You are cooking it slightly less than you would if you were making candy. If you cook it too long, it will have the texture of toffee and will be too hard.

2 Remove the caramel from the heat and stir in the vanilla and salt. Stir gently to cool a little before pouring over the cake.

CHOCOLATE GANACHE

Because the caramel is sweet, I don't add any sugar to this ganache. If you like your desserts sweeter, feel free to add a couple of tablespoons of granulated sugar.

Makes about ½ cup

   ¼ cup plus 1 tablespoon heavy (whipping) cream

   4 ounces semisweet chocolate, chopped into small pieces

   Pinch of fine sea salt

Heat the cream in a microwave on high to just under boiling, about 1 minute, or in a small saucepan on the stovetop. Add the chocolate to the hot cream and stir vigorously with a fork until all the chocolate is melted. Add the salt and stir until well combined. The ganache will thicken as it cools. If you need to keep it warm, let it sit in the bowl or saucepan in a shallow pan of hot water.

THE MATCHUPS

TRI-TIP SANTA MARIA WITH LOW-AND-SLOW CABBAGE AND OLD-FASHIONED GARLIC BREAD, *page 56*

PRIME NEW YORK STRIP STEAK ROAST WITH BARBUTO-INSPIRED ROASTED POTATOES, *page 36*

STEAK FRITES WITH DIJON BÉARNAISE, *page 155*

TUSCAN STEAK

WITH WHITE ANCHOVY AND TRUFFLE BUTTER AND GRILLED LEMONS

AND

ITALIAN CREAM CAKE

THE STEAK

This preparation of steak is based on the traditional *bistecca alla fiorentina* for which Tuscany is so famous. Since the Chianina beef they use in Italy is unavailable in the United States, I use a porterhouse. But any steak will work as long as it's between 2 and 3 inches thick. A squirt of grilled lemon and a compound butter of white anchovies with a hint of truffle flavor will get you as close to Tuscany as possible without boarding a plane.

Serves 4

1 porterhouse steak (about 3½ pounds and 3 inches thick)

2 tablespoons extra-virgin olive oil, preferably from Tuscany

Kosher or sea salt and freshly ground black pepper

2 lemons, cut in half

White Anchovy and Truffle Butter (recipe follows)

Grilling Method: Combo/Medium-High Heat

❶ Preheat the grill with all burners on high. Once preheated, adjust the temperature to medium-high heat for direct grilling.

❷ Wrap the steak in paper towels to rid it of excess moisture. Replace the paper towels as needed.

❸ Place the steak on a platter and brush it generously on both sides with olive oil. Season with salt and pepper just before grilling.

❹ Place the steak on the grill grate directly over the heat. Cover and cook for about 2 minutes per side to sear in grill marks. Turn off the burner under the steak and finish cooking by indirect heat, 45 to 50 minutes total for rare. Remove from the grill when the temperature reaches 123°F (the Tuscan preference), or higher if you prefer your steak more well-done. If you've purchased a smaller porterhouse that weighs about 2 pounds, grill for 20 to 30 minutes total. Use an instant-read thermometer to check for doneness: A rare steak will read 125°F; medium-rare, 135°F. Let the steak rest for 5 to 10 minutes before slicing.

❺ While the steak is resting, put the lemon halves on the grill, cut side down, over direct heat until the flesh has grill marks and the lemons are warmed through, 5 minutes.

❻ To serve, slice the steak off the bone into individual portions. Serve hot, topped with a shaving of the White Anchovy and Truffle Butter (use a vegetable peeler to shave the butter, cutting across the length of the cold log of butter) and a grilled lemon half on the side for squeezing over the steak.

THE MATCHUPS

ITALIAN CREAM CAKE, *recipe follows*

OLD VIRGINIA'S BEST POUND CAKE,
page 118

OLIVE OIL CAKE WITH ROSEMARY
AND ORANGE AND A CLEMENTINE SALAD,
page 136

Peruvian Steak Salad

Turn leftover steak into a Peruvian-style salad. Mix grilled corn kernels with diced avocado, hearts of palm, mango, and roasted red pepper. Set on a bed of arugula, fresh basil, and sliced celery. Dress with a garlicky vinaigrette and top with sliced steak and a sprinkling of Inka corn or Corn Nuts.

WHITE ANCHOVY AND TRUFFLE BUTTER

This recipe makes more than you'll need for four people, but it keeps for a week in the refrigerator and is terrific in scrambled eggs on Sunday morning.

Makes 1 log; generous ½ cup

8 tablespoons (1 stick) unsalted butter, at room temperature

2 white or regular anchovies in oil, or more if needed (see Note)

1 to 2 teaspoons white truffle oil, or to taste

Coarse sea salt, such as fleur de sel or Maldon, if needed

2 teaspoons minced fresh parsley

❶ Put the butter in a medium-size bowl. In a shallow nonreactive bowl, mash the anchovies with the back of a fork until they resemble a paste. Add the truffle oil to the anchovies and mix with the fork. Work this paste into the softened butter. Taste and adjust the amount of truffle oil, if desired. The butter should be salted enough by the anchovies. If not, add sea salt or another mashed anchovy to the butter until it tastes right.

❷ Mix in the minced parsley, then drop the butter in spoonfuls in a row on a large piece of plastic wrap or parchment paper. Roll the butter mixture up in the wrap and smooth it out to form a log about 4 inches long. Twist the ends to seal and refrigerate until ready to use, at least 2 hours.

❸ Cut the butter into coin-size pieces or shave with a vegetable peeler directly onto hot or warm food to season. This recipe will make more than you need, but if it is well wrapped, it will keep in the refrigerator for up to 1 week and in the freezer for 1 month.

Note: If the anchovies are brined or packed in a vinegar solution, they will be harder to mash with a fork. First, cut them with a knife or snip them with kitchen scissors, and then mash them in a bowl.

ITALIAN CREAM CAKE

THE CAKE

When my sister first started dating her future husband, her future mother-in-law, Sophie, made this cake for her birthday. Mary Pat loved the cake so much that one might think that she married Karl just so she could get the recipe. And I'm glad she did, because now I have the recipe, too. The cake originated with Sophie's sister-in-law, Janice, who grew up with Sophie in Arkansas. No one in the family is Italian, but neither is this cake—it is actually one of the lesser-known great Southern cakes. There are many versions of it, but I am partial to my sister's adaptation, which, in the Italian spirit of using only the finest ingredients, uses all butter and vanilla—no shortening or coconut extract.

Serves 12 to 16

FOR THE CAKE

Baking spray, for preparing the pans

1 cup (2 sticks) unsalted butter, at room temperature

2 cups granulated white sugar

5 large eggs, separated

1 teaspoon baking soda

1 teaspoon pure vanilla extract

1 cup buttermilk

2 cups all-purpose flour

Pinch of fine sea salt

1 cup chopped pecans

1 scant cup Baker's Sweetened Angel Flake Coconut

FOR THE FROSTING

8 ounces cream cheese, at room temperature

8 tablespoons (1 stick) unsalted butter, at room temperature

1 box (1 pound) confectioners' sugar

1 teaspoon pure vanilla extract

2 to 3 tablespoons milk or cream (any type)

Pans: Two 9-inch round cake pans

❶ Position a rack in the center of the oven and preheat the oven to 325°F. Spray the cake pans with baking spray.

❷ Make the cake: Cream the 1 cup of butter and granulated sugar together with an electric mixer on medium speed until very fluffy, 3 to 5 minutes. Add the egg yolks, one at a time, beating well after each addition.

❸ Mix the baking soda and 1 teaspoon of vanilla into the buttermilk in another bowl (this mixture will foam up, so use a big enough bowl). Whisk the flour and salt together in a third bowl. Add the buttermilk mixture and the flour mixture alternately to the butter mixture in small batches. Beat well on medium-low

speed after each addition until well mixed and creamy, 2 to 3 minutes. Add the chopped nuts and coconut to the batter and mix well. Stop the machine and scrape down the side of the bowl as necessary.

❹ Beat the egg whites in a clean, dry bowl until stiff. Fold the egg whites gently into the batter. You do not want to see large pieces of egg whites—none of them should be bigger than a blueberry.

❺ Divide the batter between the prepared cake pans. Lightly tap each pan down on the counter to make sure the batter is evenly distributed and to remove excess air bubbles.

❻ Bake until the layers pull away from the sides of the pans and a toothpick inserted in the center of a layer comes out clean, 30 to 35 minutes. Cool the layers in the pans for 10 minutes before removing them to wire cooling racks to cool completely.

❼ Make the frosting: With an electric mixer on medium speed, beat the cream cheese with the 8 tablespoons of butter until light and fluffy, about 2 minutes. Add the confectioners' sugar and 1 teaspoon of vanilla and continue beating until smooth. Add the milk 1 tablespoon at a time to thin the frosting to a good spreading consistency.

❽ Assemble the cake: Carefully trim a thin slice off the rounded tops of the 2 layers to even them out. Place 1 layer, bottom side up, on a serving plate. Place about ¼ cup of frosting in the center of the cake layer and spread it out toward the side, making a smooth, even layer. If you want a thicker frosting layer, add more frosting and spread it out evenly. (As a general rule, I allow ½ cup of frosting between layers.) Place the second cake layer, top side up, over the frosting and press lightly to adhere. Place 1 tablespoon of frosting on the side of the bottom layer and, using a butter knife or offset spatula, spread it up to frost a portion of both layers. Continue frosting the side of the layers 1 tablespoon at a time. Once the side is done, place ¼ cup of frosting on the top and spread it evenly out toward the side, adding more frosting as necessary to frost the entire cake.

PORTERHOUSE FOR TWO

WITH STEAKHOUSE SPINACH AND
WILD MUSHROOM SAUTÉ

MY MOTHER'S FRESHLY GRATED COCONUT CAKE

THE STEAK

I am wild for wild mushrooms. It is my standard side with steak instead of potatoes. And this sherry-rich wild mushroom ragout is so meaty and flavorful that you could almost forget the steak. I like to serve it with a porterhouse cut that contains the marbled eye of the tenderloin and the more toothsome strip steak. For dinner parties, I like to grill one extra-large porterhouse, which I slice and serve family style with the mushrooms—and a wild time is had by all!

Serves 2

    1 porterhouse steak
(about 2 pounds and 1½ to 2 inches thick)

    Extra-virgin olive oil

    Kosher salt and freshly ground black pepper

    Steakhouse Spinach (page 190)

    Wild Mushroom Sauté (page 186)

Grilling method: Combo/Medium-High Heat

❶ Preheat the grill with all burners on high. Once preheated, adjust the temperature to medium-high heat for direct grilling.

❷ Wrap the steak in paper towels to rid it of excess moisture. Replace the paper towels as needed.

❸ Place the steak on a platter and brush it generously on both sides with the olive oil. Season with salt and pepper just before grilling.

❹ Place the steak in the center of the cooking grate over direct heat. Cover and cook for about 2 minutes per side to sear in grill marks. Turn off the burner under the steak and finish cooking over indirect heat, 20 to 25 minutes total for rare (125°F on an instant-read thermometer) or longer if you prefer your steak more done (135°F for medium-rare). Let the steak rest for 5 to 10 minutes before slicing.

❺ Carve the meat away from the bone into individual portions. Serve hot, with the Steakhouse Spinach and Wild Mushroom Sauté.

THE MATCHUPS

MY MOTHER'S FRESHLY GRATED COCONUT CAKE,
recipe follows

WHISKEY BUTTERMILK BUNDT CAKE,
page 6

CLASSIC KEY LIME CHEESECAKE
WITH PECAN CRUST,
page 113

MY MOTHER'S FRESHLY GRATED COCONUT CAKE

THE CAKE

My mother loves coconut, and she has passed that love on to all of her children and grandchildren! Until I learned how to bake this cake myself, I would request it anytime I went home. The rich white cake and the freshly grated coconut are heavenly. I use sweetened dried coconut in a myriad of cake recipes, but this is one cake for which you must go the extra mile and either buy the freshly grated coconut in the frozen foods aisle of an Asian market or crack a coconut and grate it yourself—you will be richly rewarded with a fabulous cake!

Serves 8 to 12

FOR THE CAKE

Baking spray, for preparing the pans

1 cup (2 sticks) unsalted butter, at room temperature

2 cups granulated white sugar

3 cups cake flour, such as Swans Down

4 teaspoons baking powder

1 teaspoon fine sea salt

1⅓ cups canned light coconut milk (not cream of coconut)

2 overflowing teaspoons pure vanilla extract

6 large egg whites

FOR THE WHITE FROSTING

2½ cups granulated white sugar

1 cup filtered water

1 tablespoon light corn syrup, such as Karo

3 large egg whites, at room temperature

1 overflowing teaspoon pure vanilla extract

2 cups freshly grated coconut (thawed and well drained, if frozen)

EAK's Lemon Curd (optional; recipe follows)

Pans: Two 9-inch round cake pans (see Note)

❶ Position a rack in the center of the oven and preheat the oven to 350°F. Spray the cake pans with baking spray.

❷ Make the cake: Cream the butter and the 2 cups of sugar together with an electric mixer on medium speed until very fluffy, 3 to 5 minutes.

❸ Whisk the flour, baking powder, and salt together in a large bowl. Stir the coconut milk and 2 teaspoons of vanilla together in a separate bowl. Add the flour mixture and the coconut milk to the butter mixture alternately in small batches. Beat well after each addition. Stop the machine and scrape down the side of the bowl as necessary.

❹ With clean beaters, beat the 6 egg whites until they hold stiff peaks. Gently fold the egg whites into the batter and then divide the batter equally between the prepared pans. Lightly tap each pan down on the counter to make sure the batter is evenly distributed and to remove excess air bubbles.

❺ Bake until the layers pull away from the sides of the pans and a toothpick inserted in the centers comes out clean, 30 to 35 minutes. Cool the layers in the pans for 10 minutes before removing them to a wire cooling rack to cool completely.

❻ Make the frosting once the cake is cool and is ready to be frosted. The frosting won't hold and should be used immediately. Mix the 2½ cups of sugar, water, and corn syrup together in a heavy-bottomed saucepan.

Boil, covered, over medium-high heat, without stirring, until an 8-inch thread of syrup spins when poured from a spoon (242°F on a candy thermometer), 6 to 8 minutes. The syrup will be golden in color.

7 While the syrup is cooking, beat the 3 egg whites with an electric mixer until stiff, about 4 minutes. Pour the hot syrup slowly over the egg whites, while continuously beating. Add the teaspoon of vanilla and continue beating until the frosting is fluffy and holds a stiff shape, 2 to 3 minutes. Divide the frosting into 2 batches. Add 1½ cups of the coconut to 1 batch and mix to incorporate.

8 Assemble the cake: Carefully trim a thin slice off the rounded tops of the 2 layers to even them out. Place 1 layer, bottom side up, on a serving plate. Spread the layer with half the coconut frosting or lemon curd, if using. Top that layer with the second one, top side up. Frost the sides and top of the cake with the plain frosting. Spread the remaining coconut frosting on

THE MATCHUPS

PORTERHOUSE FOR TWO WITH STEAKHOUSE SPINACH AND WILD MUSHROOM SAUTÉ, *page 67*

BEEF TENDERLOIN KEBABS WITH BACON, SHALLOTS, AND MUSHROOMS, *page 80*

FIRST-PLACE SMOKED AND CHARRED TENDERLOIN WITH GRILLED MEXICAN STREET CORN SALAD, *page 103*

top of the cake. Sprinkle the top and around the sides of the cake with the remaining coconut.

9 Serve and enjoy your applause! This cake is positively ethereal and actually better made the day before you serve it.

Note: If your cake pans are shallow—less than 2 inches deep—make 3 layers or bake the overflow in a mini loaf pan.

EAK'S LEMON CURD

When I am feeling a little "fancy," I make a batch of lemon curd and use it as a filling between the layers of the coconut cake. The tart lemon cuts through the richness of the fluffy white frosting.

Makes about 1½ cups

- 4 tablespoons (½ stick) unsalted butter, at room temperature
- ¾ cup granulated white sugar
- ¼ teaspoon fine sea salt
- 4 large egg yolks
- ⅔ cup fresh lemon juice, preferably from Meyer lemons
- ¼ cup filtered water
- Zest of 2 Meyer lemons (or zest of 1 regular lemon), grated with a Microplane

1 Cream the butter, sugar, and salt together with an electric mixer on medium speed until light and fluffy, about 2 minutes. Add the egg yolks one at a time, beating well after each addition. Add the lemon juice and water and mix until combined.

2 Pour the mixture into a nonreactive, heavy-bottomed saucepan and cook, stirring frequently, over medium heat until it coats the back of a spoon, 15 to 20 minutes. The curd will go from transparent to opaque to lemon yellow in color. Don't allow the mixture to boil, or it might curdle.

3 Remove the curd from the heat and stir in the zest, mixing well. Pour into a glass bowl and chill before using. Place any extra in a glass jar with a tight-fitting lid. It will keep, refrigerated, for up to 2 weeks.

T-BONE

WITH NDUJA BUTTER AND EASY MUSHROOM TARTS

RED VELVET FOUR-LAYER CAKE

THE STEAK

This is my died-and-gone-to-heaven version of a steak dinner. A grilled T-bone is served with a compound butter made with nduja, which is a spreadable salami from Italy. It rivals my Whiskey Butter (page 5) as my favorite steak topper. The rough and slightly "wildcat" compound butter is tamed by an easy mushroom tart. The tarts are adapted from a recipe Jean-Georges Vongerichten contributed to the *New York Times Magazine* many years ago. They are pure earth wrapped in puff pastry.

Serves 4

- 4 T-bone or porterhouse steaks (about 20 ounces each and 1½ inches thick)
- Extra-virgin olive oil
- 1 teaspoon kosher salt
- 1 teaspoon whole black peppercorns, coarsely ground
- 4 tablespoons Nduja Butter (recipe follows)
- Chopped fresh parsley, for garnish (optional)
- Easy Mushroom Tarts (optional; page 187)

Grilling Method: Combo/Medium-High Heat

1 Preheat the grill with all burners on high. Once preheated, adjust the temperature to medium-high heat for direct grilling.

2 Wrap the steaks in paper towels to rid them of excess moisture. Replace the paper towels as needed.

3 Just before grilling, brush both sides of the steaks with oil and season with the salt and pepper. Place the steaks on the cooking grate directly over the heat. Cover and cook for about 2 minutes. Turn the meat and continue cooking for about 2 minutes more to get good grill marks on both sides.

4 Move the steaks to indirect heat and continue to cook for 10 to 15 minutes more for medium-rare (135°F). Remove the steaks from the grill and allow them to rest 5 to 10 minutes before serving. Top each steak with 1 tablespoon of Nduja Butter and a sprinkling of parsley, if using, while they're resting. Serve with the tarts, if desired.

NDUJA BUTTER

These days, you can find nduja in many supermarkets and specialty food stores. If you can't find it in your town, you can order it from Amazon.

Makes 1 log; generous ½ cup

> 8 tablespoons (1 stick) unsalted butter, at room temperature
>
> ¼ cup nduja (spreadable salami)
>
> Fine sea salt (optional)

THE MATCHUPS

RED VELVET
FOUR-LAYER CAKE,
recipe follows

GINGERBREAD WITH
ORANGE MARMALADE AND
GRAND MARNIER GLAZE,
page 11

FARMERS MARKET
SUMMER FRUIT AND BERRY
CAKE, *page 100*

❶ Mash or stir the butter in a small bowl until it is smooth and slightly fluffy. Add the nduja. Mix together, mashing with the back of a fork to make sure all the nduja is fully incorporated. Taste for seasoning. Add salt only if needed. The nduja should be salty enough. If you do want to add salt, add it slowly, pinch by pinch, because the butter will taste more salty as it sits and the flavors bloom and marry.

❷ Drop the butter in spoonfuls in a row on a piece of plastic wrap or parchment paper. Roll the butter up in the paper or plastic wrap and smooth it out to form a log about 1½ inches in diameter and 4 inches long.

❸ Twist the ends to seal and refrigerate the butter until it's firm and easy to slice. Nduja Butter can be made in advance and stored, tightly covered, in the refrigerator for up to 1 week and in the freezer for up to 1 month.

RED VELVET FOUR-LAYER CAKE

THE CAKE

America is in love with red velvet cake. And that includes me—that is, when the cake is rich and moist and full of chocolate flavor. True red velvet cake is a chocolate cake with a richer, dark red color courtesy of food coloring. Cocoa has a natural red hue once it is baked, but to get that deep red color, you need to add something to the batter—food coloring is the easiest, but there are recipes that call for adding beets.

The origin of the beets, according to Southern tradition, is that after the Civil War, when cocoa was scarce, Southern bakers would stretch it by adding beets to mimic the color. If you have ever had a bright red "red velvet cake," it doesn't include much—if any—cocoa. To me, it is a yellow cake with the food coloring added. In this cake, I have upped the flavor ante by creating a sour cream–cream cheese filling to cut the richness of the cream cheese frosting. This is a four-layer cake, so you will need to split the layers in half once they are completely cool.

Serves 12 to 16

FOR THE CAKE

Baking spray, for preparing the pans

3½ cups cake flour

½ cup unsweetened cocoa powder (not Dutch-process)

1½ teaspoons fine sea salt

2 cups neutral vegetable oil, such as Crisco, or untoasted walnut oil

2¼ cups granulated white sugar

3 large eggs

6 tablespoons (3 ounces) red food coloring or 1 teaspoon red gel food coloring dissolved in 6 tablespoons of water (optional; see Note)

1½ teaspoons pure vanilla extract

1¼ cups buttermilk

2 teaspoons baking soda

2½ teaspoons distilled white vinegar

FOR THE FILLING

8 ounces cream cheese, at room temperature

8 ounces full-fat sour cream, at room temperature

2 cups confectioners' sugar, sifted after measuring, or more as needed

1 teaspoon pure vanilla extract

¼ teaspoon pure lemon extract

1 cup cold heavy (whipping) cream, or more as needed

FOR THE FROSTING

8 ounces cream cheese, at room temperature

8 tablespoons (1 stick) unsalted butter, at room temperature

3 cups confectioners' sugar, sifted after measuring

1 teaspoon pure vanilla extract

Pinch of fine sea salt

Pans: Two 9-inch round, 2-inch deep cake pans

1 Position a rack in the center of the oven and preheat the oven to 350°F. Spray the cake pans with baking spray.

2 Make the cake: Whisk the cake flour, cocoa, and salt together in a large bowl.

3 Beat the oil and granulated sugar together with an electric mixer on medium speed until well blended, 2 to 3 minutes. Add the eggs one at a time, beating well after each addition. With the mixer on low, very slowly add the food coloring, if using, then add the 1½ teaspoons vanilla. Add the flour mixture alternately with the buttermilk to the oil mixture in small batches and beat just long enough to combine. Stop the machine and scrape down the side of the bowl as necessary.

4 Place the baking soda in a small dish, stir in the vinegar, and add it to the batter with the mixer running. Beat for 10 seconds.

5 Divide the batter evenly between the pans. Lightly tap each pan down on the counter to make sure the batter is evenly distributed and to remove excess air bubbles.

6 Bake until the layers pull away from the sides of the pans and a toothpick comes out clean when inserted in the center of a layer, 40 to 45 minutes, but begin testing after the cake bakes for 30 minutes in case your oven runs hot. Cool the layers in the pans for 10 minutes before removing to wire cooling racks to cool completely.

7 Once cool, use a long serrated knife to carefully trim a thin slice of cake off the rounded tops of each layer to even them out. Split each layer in half horizontally. Steady the layer by keeping one hand gently on the top of it as you split it. Level the layers with the serrated knife. Set the crumbles aside for decoration.

8 Make the filling: With an electric mixer, beat the 8 ounces cream cheese and sour cream together on medium speed until smooth, about 2 minutes. Add the 2 cups confectioners' sugar, 1 teaspoon vanilla, and the lemon extract and beat until smooth. Using the whisk attachment, gradually add the cream and whip until the filling is thick enough to spread. Add more sugar or cream as needed to get the right consistency. Then set the filling aside while you make the frosting.

9 Make the frosting: With clean beaters, beat the 8 ounces cream cheese and 8 tablespoons butter together on medium speed until light and fluffy, about 2 minutes. Add the 3 cups confectioners' sugar, 1 teaspoon vanilla, and salt. Beat on low speed to combine. If the frosting is too soft, chill before using until slightly stiff, about 10 minutes.

10 Assemble the cake: Working quickly, place the bottom half of one layer, cut side up, on a serving plate and smooth a generous layer of about one-third of the filling on top. Place the top half of this layer over the filling. Top with another layer of filling. Place the

---

THE MATCHUPS

T-BONE WITH NDUJA BUTTER
AND EASY MUSHROOM TARTS, *page 70*

STEAK AND TRUFFLED EGGS, *page 32*

BACON-WRAPPED BEEF TENDERLOIN WITH A
GREEN PEPPERCORN AND THYME SAUCE, *page 116*

bottom of the remaining cake layer on the filling, cut side up, and top it with the remaining filling. Place the remaining layer over the filling. Frost the sides and top of the cake with a thin layer of frosting—this is the crumb coat. Let set for 1 hour and then frost the sides and the top of the cake with a thicker layer of frosting. Decorate the sides with dried red velvet cake crumbs, if desired.

Note: If you are averse to the red food coloring, don't use it! The cake will taste the same but won't have the same look.

PROSCIUTTO-WRAPPED FILET

WITH BLUE CHEESE AND PECAN BUTTER

APPLE UPSIDE-DOWN CAKE

WITH CRÈME FRAÎCHE

THE STEAK

I f you've ever been to a steakhouse, you've seen the traditional bacon-wrapped filet on the menu. I've updated that offering by wrapping filets mignons with prosciutto and topping them with my favorite Blue Cheese and Pecan Butter. If you have any left over, the butter also makes a delicious spread for crackers and crostini.

Serves 4

4 filets mignons (6½ to 8 ounces each and about 2 inches thick)

1 cup dry red wine, such as cabernet sauvignon

8 slices best-quality prosciutto di Parma

Extra-virgin olive oil

Kosher salt and freshly ground black pepper

Blue Cheese and Pecan Butter (recipe follows)

Special equipment: Wooden toothpicks, soaked in water for at least 15 minutes

Grilling Method: Direct/Medium Heat

❶ Wrap the steaks in paper towels to rid them of excess moisture. Replace the paper towels as needed.

❷ Put the filets in a large, flat, airtight container and pour the wine over them. Cover and place in the refrigerator. Marinate for 1 hour, turning once.

❸ Preheat the grill with all burners on high. Once preheated, adjust the temperature to medium heat for direct grilling.

❹ Remove the filets from the wine and pat them dry with paper towels. Wrap 1 to 2 slices of the prosciutto around the outside edge and bottom of each filet. Secure the ends of the prosciutto with a wet toothpick, if necessary. I usually don't have to do this because the prosciutto adheres to itself. Brush the filets lightly with olive oil and season with salt and pepper.

❺ Place the filets on the grill, top side down to get good grill marks. Cover the grill and cook, turning once halfway through the cooking time, about 10 minutes total. An instant-read thermometer will read 130°F for the rare side of medium-rare.

❻ Remove the steaks from the grill and place them on a clean platter. Immediately top with a slice of the Blue Cheese and Pecan Butter. Let the filets rest for 5 minutes before serving.

THE MATCHUPS

APPLE UPSIDE-DOWN CAKE
WITH CRÈME FRAÎCHE, *recipe follows*

RED VELVET FOUR-LAYER CAKE,
page 72

DAVID LEBOVITZ'S ORANGE-GLAZED
ALMOND LOAF, *page 104*

BLUE CHEESE AND PECAN BUTTER

Think of the best holiday cheese ball, rich with creamy blue cheese and crunchy pecans. When you put this on top of chicken, meaty fish, or steak, you've turned a mealtime staple into a beautiful dinner that tastes anything but basic.

Makes 1 log; 1 cup

8 tablespoons (1 stick) unsalted butter, at room temperature

⅓ cup Gorgonzola, Roquefort, or other blue cheese, at room temperature

3 tablespoons finely chopped and toasted pecans (page 85)

Fine sea salt (optional)

❶ Mash the butter in a small bowl until smooth and slightly fluffy. Add the cheese and pecans. Mix together, mashing with the back of a fork to make sure all the ingredients are incorporated. Taste for seasoning. Add salt only if needed. The cheese should be salty enough. If you do want to add salt, add it slowly, pinch by pinch, because the butter will taste more salty as it sits and the flavors bloom and marry.

❷ Drop the butter in spoonfuls in a row on a piece of plastic wrap or parchment paper. Roll the butter up in the wrap and smooth it out to form a round log about 1½ inches in diameter and about 4 inches long. Twist the wrap to close up the ends.

❸ Refrigerate until firm and easy to cut into pieces. The butter can be made in advance and stored, tightly covered, in the refrigerator for up to 1 week and in the freezer for up to 1 month.

APPLE UPSIDE-DOWN CAKE

WITH CRÈME FRAÎCHE

THE CAKE

This upside-down apple cake is a cross between my Grandmother Odom's Apple Cake (page 108) and the classic French tarte Tatin. Bake it just before your guests arrive so the intoxicating smells of butter, apples, and cinnamon waft from the kitchen and whet everyone's appetite for the evening to come. As a bonus, it will still be warm when you sit down for dessert. If you don't finish it all at dinner, finish it off for breakfast—you'll be in for a treat.

Serves 8

FOR THE TOPPING

8 tablespoons (1 stick) unsalted butter

¼ cup granulated white sugar

Pinch of fine sea salt

4 small Granny Smith apples, peeled, cored, and cut into quarters

FOR THE CAKE

2 cups peeled, cored, and roughly chopped Granny Smith apples (about 2 large apples)

2 cups granulated white sugar

2 large eggs

½ cup neutral vegetable oil, such as Crisco

2 teaspoons pure vanilla extract

3 cups all-purpose flour

1½ teaspoons ground cinnamon

1½ teaspoons baking soda

½ teaspoon fine sea salt

THE MATCHUPS

PROSCIUTTO-WRAPPED FILET
WITH BLUE CHEESE AND PECAN
BUTTER, *page 74*

MARY PAT'S INDIVIDUAL BEEF
WELLINGTONS, *page 86*

BOB'S STEAK AU POIVRE
WITH FRENCH ONION CROUTONS,
page 91

½ to 1 cup black walnut pieces or regular walnut pieces, lightly toasted (see page 85 and Notes)

Homemade Crème Fraîche (recipe follows), for serving (optional)

Pan: 10-inch cast-iron skillet, 10-inch cast-iron braiser, or 10-inch round cake pan

1 Position a rack in the center of the oven and preheat the oven to 350°F.

2 Make the topping: Heat a 10-inch cast-iron skillet, small braiser, or other oven-safe stovetop pan over medium-low heat. Add the butter to the pan, and when it has melted, add the ¼ cup sugar. Stir until the sugar starts to turn brown, 3 to 5 minutes. Be careful not to burn the sugar; it will continue to cook even after you add the apples. Add a pinch of salt to the skillet and stir to combine. Reduce the heat to low and add the quartered apples. Sauté until caramelized and slightly soft, about 5 minutes. Remove the pan from the heat and arrange the sautéed apples neatly on the bottom. If you don't have a 10-inch oven-safe stovetop pan, cook the sugar and butter and fruit and pour into a deep 10-inch round cake pan. I like to use one made of silicone.

3 Make the cake: Mix the 2 cups chopped apples and the 2 cups sugar and set aside.

④ Beat the eggs with the oil in a large bowl just to combine, then add the vanilla. In a separate bowl, whisk together the flour, cinnamon, baking soda, and salt. Mix the flour mixture into the egg mixture a little at a time until all the flour is incorporated and there are no lumps.

⑤ Add the chopped apple mixture and its juices to the flour mixture. Mix well to evenly distribute the apples and sugar into the batter. Stir in the walnuts. Let sit for 15 minutes to extract more juices from the apples. Mix again to incorporate any apple juices. The batter will be very thick, almost like cookie dough. Spoon the batter over the sautéed apples in the skillet and smooth it out so that all the apples are covered. If you have any batter left over, bake it in muffin cups.

⑥ Bake the cake until it pulls away from the side of the pan and a toothpick inserted in the center comes out clean, 90 minutes (see Notes). Let the cake cool in the pan for 15 minutes and then invert it onto a clean cake plate. Serve warm with crème fraîche, if desired.

Notes: If you aren't accustomed to the taste of black walnuts, you may want to start with ½ cup, as they have a very assertive flavor.

Start testing the cake for doneness after 60 to 70 minutes, because all ovens bake slightly differently. This cake takes a full 90 minutes in my oven but takes just over an hour in my mother's oven.

HOMEMADE CRÈME FRAÎCHE

Normandy, France, is famous for crème fraîche, and it is served often with desserts in the same way that we in the United States use whipped cream. I love the slightly sour and tangy thickened cream with any fruit dessert and especially this warm apple cake. I prefer making my own crème fraîche and like the taste better than store-bought. I urge you to make it, but be forewarned that it takes a couple of days to thicken completely before you can use it.

Makes 2 cups

1 pint heavy (whipping) cream

2 tablespoons buttermilk

Pour the cream into a clean large glass jar with a tight-fitting lid. Add the buttermilk, shake gently, and close the lid. Place the jar in the warmest part of your house (for example, on top of the refrigerator) and let sit until thickened, 2 to 3 days. When the cream has cultured, use immediately or store in the refrigerator for up to 1 week.

Note: Some people like the crème fraîche thinner and refrigerate it to stop the thickening process after 12 hours.

VARIATIONS

CRANBERRY-APPLE UPSIDE-DOWN CAKE

Eliminate the apples in the topping and add ¼ cup of packed dark brown sugar to the sugar and butter in the pan. Once the butter and sugar are lightly browned, add a 12-ounce bag of fresh cranberries to the hot butter and sugar mixture and stir to coat well. Follow the rest of the instructions for the Apple Upside-Down Cake.

PEACH UPSIDE-DOWN CAKE

If you make the cake with fresh peaches, use an equal amount of peaches as apples for both the topping and the cake. Decrease the cinnamon to ½ teaspoon and substitute roughly chopped hazelnuts or pecans for the black walnuts. If you can't find fresh peaches, buy 2 cans (29 ounces each) of sliced peaches (you will use one entire drained can for the topping and most of a drained can for the batter), and add the sugar to the egg and oil mixture rather than mixing it with the canned peaches.

Sidecar: An Old-Fashioned Holiday

I love a cocktail, but usually I stick to brown liquor like bourbon and rye, or tequila and maybe a couple of rocks. The reason is simple: I don't like lots of mixtures of unidentifiable alcohols. Not only are they usually overly sweet, but they are a headache—literally!

However, I recently changed my mind when a group of us visited Mike Hudman, Andy Ticer, and Nick Talarico at Hog & Hominy in Memphis, Tennessee. I loved Hog & Hominy before I ever walked through the front door just because of the name, which is an old moniker for the state of Tennessee, as in the Hog and Hominy State.

Once inside, I realized what a special place it is. Everything they do—in their fused-together American Southern and Italian restaurant—they do with care. They don't cut any corners!

First thing, Nick set down a beautiful drink of brown "water" and a great waft of fresh orange oil greeted me before I took my first sip. It was their version of an Old-Fashioned, and there was nothing typically "old-fashioned" about it. By the second sip, I was in love—so much so that I had to learn to make it! Fueled and emboldened by a few of their craft cocktails, I asked for an impromptu class.

What makes this Old-Fashioned so much better for me is that the cherries and their sickly sweet pink syrup are gone. The sweet notes are all natural and perfect for the holidays—orange and vanilla (from the bourbon) and spice. A big strip of orange zest is twisted to release the oils and rubbed all over the inside of the glass, creating the bold citrus aroma. It is removed and then placed in the glass as a garnish once the drink is made.

The inherent vanilla and spice from the best bourbon (you can also use rye, which is purported to be the original spirit) is paramount to the success of this Old-Fashioned. You don't want a fiery hot whiskey for this drink. And two kinds of bitters are essential here: orange bitters to balance out the sweet orange oil and the classic, unmistakable flavor of Angostura bitters.

Just an Old-Fashioned Girl

I adapted this recipe from what I was taught by Nick Talarico and from *Collards & Carbonara*, a cookbook by Andy Ticer and Mike Hudman.

Makes 1 drink

> 1 strip orange zest, about 4 inches long by 1 inch wide
>
> 2 demerara sugar cubes or 1 teaspoon Sugar in the Raw
>
> 3 drops orange bitters
>
> 1 drop Angostura bitters
>
> About 1 teaspoon club soda
>
> 2 ounces favorite best-quality bourbon or rye
>
> Big ice ball or 4 regular ice cubes (see Note)

❶ Twist the orange zest and use it to rub the inside of a rocks glass and around the rim. Place the zest on a plate or napkin and reserve it for garnishing.

❷ Place the sugar cubes or sugar in the bottom of the glass. Add both bitters directly to the sugar. Pour the club soda over the sugar to help dissolve the sugar crystals. Muddle the sugar until melted. Add the bourbon and mix.

❸ When the mixture is smooth, add an ice ball. Slide the reserved orange zest twist into the glass along the side, so it sits between the ice ball and the glass. Serve immediately.

Note: These days "ice balls" are all the rage among the craft cocktail set and serious at-home drinkers. They are generally about 2 inches in diameter, and they literally fill the whole glass. If you don't have a big ice ball or cube, you can use any ice you like, but there are lots of companies that make ice trays for big ice cubes—and ice balls. Find them in kitchenware stores or online.

BEEF TENDERLOIN KEBABS

WITH BACON, SHALLOTS, AND MUSHROOMS

PUMPKIN PALOOZA CAKE WALK

THE STEAK

I came up with this recipe spontaneously one night when a few friends popped in unexpectedly. It was a gorgeous summer night, and we decided that "grilling out" would be infinitely more fun than "going out." Since I had only two filets and four mouths to feed, I cut the filets into chunks. Then I upped the ante by roasting the shallots until they started oozing all that yummy caramelized onion sugar. Before I grilled the kebabs, I wove a slice of slightly cooked bacon through the steak and the mushrooms. Each plate was piled with rare filet, bacon, mushrooms, and roasted shallots. It was a night that remixed the classic song: "Summertime and the grillin' is easy." But it's too good to limit to summer, so make it all fall long.

Serves 4

2 filets mignons (about 8 ounces each and 1½ to 2 inches thick) or 1 pound tenderloin tips

8 slices center-cut bacon

8 shallots, unpeeled

Fleur de sel or kosher salt

Extra-virgin olive oil

Balsamic vinegar

18 whole white mushrooms, cleaned and stemmed

Special equipment: 8 metal skewers or long bamboo skewers, soaked in water for 30 minutes

Grilling Method: Direct/Medium Heat

❶ Preheat the grill with all burners on high. Once preheated, adjust the temperature to medium heat for direct grilling.

❷ Wrap the steaks in paper towels to rid them of excess moisture. Replace the paper towels as needed.

❸ Place the bacon on the grill grate. Cook for 3 minutes to render some of its fat. Set aside.

❹ Place the unpeeled shallots on the warming rack of the grill to roast slowly while you prepare the kebabs. Turn, if necessary, to ensure even cooking. The shallots will take 30 to 45 minutes to caramelize and get soft. Remove them when done. When cool enough to touch, peel off the skins. Place the shallots in a bowl and sprinkle with fleur de sel or kosher salt. Drizzle with the olive oil and a touch of balsamic vinegar. Set aside.

❺ While the shallots roast, make the kebabs: Cut each filet lengthwise into thirds, then cut them horizontally into thirds (like a tic-tac-toe board); you should have 9 pieces per steak, for a total of 18 pieces. Brush the filet chunks and mushrooms lightly with olive oil.

❻ Lay 4 pieces of meat alternating with 4 mushrooms on a clean work surface. Repeat this with the remaining steak and mushrooms for a total of 4 lineups—you will have 2 extra pieces of meat and mushrooms; divide those four pieces among the 4 kebabs.

❼ For each lineup, take 1 slice of bacon and interweave it on the work surface, under the meat and then up and over the mushrooms, until you get to the last piece. Use

THE MATCHUPS

PUMPKIN PALOOZA CAKE WALK, *recipe follows*

BAKED CINNAMON-SUGAR DOUGHNUT PUFFS WITH
DARK CHOCOLATE BOURBON DIPPING SAUCE,
page 25

MY MOTHER'S FRESHLY GRATED COCONUT CAKE,
page 68

a second slice if you run out of bacon before you get to the end of the kebab. (The bacon will be threaded between the mushrooms and meat and will resemble ribbon candy.) Using 2 skewers for each kebab, push them, parallel to each other, through each line of filet, mushrooms, and bacon, forming what looks like a ladder (see box, page 144).

8 Place the kebabs on the grill grate. Cover and cook them until the bacon is crispy and the meat and mushrooms are grill-marked, tender, and cooked, about 7 minutes per side, or 14 minutes in all. Remove the kebabs from the grill and place them on a clean platter. Let rest for 5 minutes. Serve hot with the grill-roasted shallots.

PUMPKIN PALOOZA CAKE WALK

THE CAKE

Pumpkin is all the rage these days! Not only has Starbucks turned it into the number one seasonal coffee enhancer, but Oreos, Pop-Tarts, and basically every grocery category has taken to the autumnal flavor. I say forget all those pumpkin posers that use artificial flavorings to approximate this favorite flavor. Make your own pumpkin palooza with pure pumpkin puree, hazelnuts, cranberries, and even dark chocolate! I make this batter and bake it in Bundts, loaves, and muffin pans. You can serve it bare or drizzled with chocolate ganache, a cinnamon icing, a chocolate icing, a white sugar icing, powdered sugar, or an orange glaze. With all those options, you have an entire pumpkin patch of treats right at your fingertips!

Makes 1 large Bundt cake, 4 small Bundt cakes, or 2 loaves

FOR THE CAKE

Baking spray, for preparing the pans

1 can (15 ounces) pureed pumpkin, preferably Libby's

1¼ cups untoasted hazelnut oil

4 large eggs

¾ cup granulated white sugar

¾ cup (packed) light brown sugar

3 cups all-purpose flour

2 teaspoons baking soda

2 teaspoons baking powder

1 generous teaspoon ground cinnamon

1 teaspoon fine sea salt

¼ teaspoon ground ginger

¼ teaspoon ground nutmeg

2 cups coarsely chopped hazelnuts or walnuts, plus ½ to 1 cup halves and pieces of either nut, lightly toasted (see page 85)

2 cups dark chocolate chips (optional)

1 cup dried cranberries (optional)

FOR THE TOPPING (CHOOSE ONE)

Chocolate Ganache (recipe follows)

Cinnamon Icing (recipe follows)

Chocolate Glaze (recipe follows)

Basic Glaze (page 233)

Orange Glaze (see Note)

Confectioners' sugar

❶ Position a rack in the center of the oven and preheat the oven to 350°F. Spray the cake pan or pans with baking spray.

❷ Make the cake: Beat the pumpkin, oil, eggs, and white and brown sugars together with an electric mixer on medium speed, about 3 minutes. Whisk the flour, baking soda, baking powder, cinnamon, salt, ginger, and nutmeg together in a medium bowl. Add the flour mixture to the egg mixture and mix well. Fold in the 2 cups of chopped nuts, the chocolate chips, and the cranberries, if using. Stop the mixer and scrape down the side of the bowl as necessary.

❸ **If using a large Bundt pan**, place the ½ to 1 cup of nut halves and pieces into the pan and add the batter.

If using small Bundt pans, divide the nut halves and pieces and then the batter among the 4 pans. Lightly tap the Bundt pan(s) down on the counter to make sure the batter is evenly distributed and to remove excess air bubbles.

If using loaf pans, divide the batter equally between the 2 pans, filling each about three-quarters full. Smooth out the tops of each, then lightly tap the pans down on the counter. Decorate the tops of the batter with the ½ to 1 cup of nut halves and pieces. Press them lightly into the batter.

❹ Place the small Bundt pans or loaf pans on a sheet pan to make it easier to pull them out of the hot oven. Bake until the cake pulls away from the side of the

pan and a toothpick stuck in the center comes out clean, 50 to 60 minutes for the large Bundt cake, or 35 minutes for the small Bundts and the loaf cakes.

❺ Let the cake cool for 10 minutes before removing from the pan. Brush or spoon any glaze or other topping onto the cake while it is still warm. If serving plain, let cool for at least 1 hour before slicing into thick chunks.

Note: If you want to make an orange glaze for this cake, use the orange option for the Poppy-Seed Cake glaze on page 94.

SPIKED CHOCOLATE GANACHE

You can make the ganache up to 2 days in advance.

Makes about 1 cup

> ⅓ cup heavy (whipping) cream
>
> 6 ounces bittersweet chocolate (chips or chopped block chocolate)
>
> 2 tablespoons liqueur, such as Kahlúa, Frangelico, or bourbon liqueur
>
> ½ teaspoon pure vanilla extract

Pour the cream into a small saucepan and heat over medium heat to almost boiling. Remove the pan from the heat and let cool several minutes. Add the chocolate and stir until melted and well combined with the cream. Add the liqueur and vanilla, stirring constantly. Cover with plastic wrap and set aside or refrigerate. Drizzle over the cake while the cake is still warm.

CINNAMON ICING

The addition of ground cinnamon to the classic white icing pairs perfectly with the pumpkin for my favorite fall treat.

Makes about ½ cup

> 1¼ cups confectioners' sugar, sifted, plus more if needed
>
> 2 teaspoons ground cinnamon
>
> 1 tablespoon heavy (whipping) cream, plus more if needed

THE MATCHUPS

BEEF TENDERLOIN KEBABS WITH BACON, SHALLOTS, AND MUSHROOMS, *page 80*

AN INDOOR/OUTDOOR TOMAHAWK STEAK, *page 22*

FLATIRON STEAK SMOTHERED IN CARAMELIZED ONIONS, *page 152*

Pinch of fine sea salt

1 teaspoon pure vanilla extract

Place the sugar, cinnamon, cream, and salt in a small bowl. Mix well with a fork until shiny and all of the lumps are out. It should be easy to drizzle over the cake. If the texture is too thick, add a bit more cream. If it is too thin, add a bit more sugar. Taste and adjust as necessary.

CHOCOLATE GLAZE

This chocolate glaze is for milk chocolate lovers. It tastes chocolaty but is much sweeter and less intense than chocolate ganache.

Makes about ¾ cup

2 cups confectioners' sugar, sifted, plus more if needed

1 to 2 ounces unsweetened chocolate, melted

1 tablespoon heavy (whipping) cream, plus more if needed

1 teaspoon pure vanilla extract

Pinch of fine sea salt

Place the sugar, chocolate, cream, vanilla, and salt in a small bowl. Mix well with a fork until shiny and all the lumps are out. It should be easy to drizzle over the cake. If the texture is too thick, add a bit more cream. If it is too thin, add a bit more sugar. Taste and adjust as necessary.

Toasting Nuts

This is one of my kitchen pet peeves: I cringe every time I see someone toasting nuts in a skillet on a stovetop. When you toast nuts this way, the edges of the nuts that make contact with the bottom of the skillet become blackened and the rest of the nut is still raw. Nuts should be toasted in a preheated 250°F oven. They should be on a sheet pan, scattered in a single layer with space between the nuts, and toasted until they are light brown and you can smell them cooking, 10 to 15 minutes.

Melting Chocolate in a Double Boiler

MARY PAT'S INDIVIDUAL BEEF WELLINGTONS

AND

CHOCOLATE-COCONUT CANDY BAR CAKE

THE STEAK

My sister Mary Pat is one of the best steak and cake cooks I know. She was that kid in college who packed up many of our mother's pots and pans and threw dinner parties and brunches featuring dishes made from scratch. One of her specialties is individual beef Wellingtons, which is a riff on our mother's special-occasion beef Wellington, which she made with an entire tenderloin. Instead of the traditional pâté layer, Mary Pat substitutes caramelized onions. With these mini Wellingtons, everyone gets the perfect ratio of crispy crust, beef tenderloin, caramelized onions, and mushroom duxelles. And these little packages also freeze beautifully, which makes them perfect for plan-ahead entertaining.

Serves 4

4 filets mignons (about 6 ounces each and at least 1½ inches thick)

1 tablespoon extra-virgin olive oil

1 teaspoon fine sea salt

½ teaspoon freshly ground black pepper

1 box (17.3 ounces) Pepperidge Farm Puff Pastry Sheets, thawed in the refrigerator

All-purpose flour, for rolling out the puff pastry

Mushroom Duxelles (recipe follows)

Caramelized Onions (recipe follows)

1 or 2 large eggs

2 or 4 teaspoons heavy (whipping) cream

Pan: Sheet pan

Method: Oven

❶ Wrap the steaks in paper towels to rid them of excess moisture. Replace the paper towels as needed.

❷ Line a sheet pan with parchment paper; set aside.

❸ Brush the filets all over with the olive oil and season them on both sides with salt and pepper.

❹ Preheat a heavy sauté pan over medium-high heat. Add the filets and sear them for 1 minute on each side. Transfer to a plate to cool completely.

❺ Roll out the 2 sheets of puff pastry on a lightly floured surface. Cut each sheet in half following the seam of the pastry. Roll each piece a little more to smooth out the edges.

❻ Spread one-quarter of the cooled mushroom duxelles on top of each filet and top the mushrooms with one-quarter of the cooled caramelized onions. Press down lightly to flatten the layers. Center a square of puff pastry over the top of each filet. Flip the filets over by holding your hand over the pastry to make sure the toppings stay in place. You may want to trim the excess puff pastry so that you don't have too much on the bottom when you wrap the filet.

THE MATCHUPS

CHOCOLATE-COCONUT CANDY
BAR CAKE, *recipe follows*

CLASSIC SOUR CREAM
COFFEE CAKE, *page 16*

WILD PERSIMMON CHRISTMAS
FRUIT AND NUT CAKE,
page 241

7 Make an egg wash by beating 1 of the eggs and 2 teaspoons of the cream together.

8 Using a pastry brush or your finger, paint the inside edges of the pastry with egg wash. Fold the pastry over the bottom of the filets as though wrapping a package, and press the edges to seal. Place the packages, seam side down, on the parchment-lined sheet pan and freeze for at least 4 hours or up to 2 weeks. (If you are freezing for longer than 4 hours, wrap very well in plastic wrap and aluminum foil to keep the packets pristine.) If you're going to bake the Wellingtons that same day, place the leftover egg wash in the refrigerator (see Step 9).

9 Preheat the oven to 425°F. If the Wellingtons have been frozen for a more than a day, make a fresh egg wash from the remaining egg and cream.

10 Just before baking, brush the egg wash over the tops and sides of each frozen Wellington. Bake until the pastry is golden brown, about 20 minutes. Then reduce the oven temperature to 350°F and continue cooking for 20 minutes more. The steaks should now be medium-rare. An instant-read thermometer gently inserted through the crust into the center of the steak should register 110°F (see Note). Remove from the oven and let rest for 10 minutes before serving.

Note: This recipe is tricky because it is difficult to test for doneness. The hot duxelles and the golden brown pastry hold in the heat and steam, creating more carryover cooking. It's better to take the Wellingtons out of the oven when they are undercooked and let them continue to cook as they rest than to overcook them.

MUSHROOM DUXELLES

Classic mushroom duxelles is the French preparation of minced mushrooms, shallots, herbs, and butter. Basically, it is a fancy term for mushroom stuffing. I use garlic and red wine in this preparation for a more intense flavor that will balance and complement the layer of caramelized onions.

Makes about 1 cup

2 tablespoons unsalted butter

2 tablespoons minced shallots

½ teaspoon minced garlic

12 ounces button or favorite wild mushrooms, wiped clean, stemmed, and finely chopped

¼ teaspoon fine sea salt

⅛ teaspoon freshly ground white pepper

¼ cup dry red wine

Melt the butter in a medium-size skillet over medium-high heat. Add the shallots and garlic and cook, stirring, to soften, 30 seconds. Add the mushrooms, salt, and white pepper, reduce the heat to medium, and cook, stirring continuously, until all the liquid has evaporated and the mushrooms begin to caramelize, about 12 minutes. Add the wine and cook, stirring to deglaze the pan, until all the liquid has evaporated, about 5 more minutes. Remove from the heat and let cool before using.

CARAMELIZED ONIONS

There is nothing like caramelized onions! Some people call them fried onions, but I think of them as melted onions because you cook them until they are golden brown and limp and literally melting into each other.

Makes about ¾ cup

1 tablespoon unsalted butter

1 tablespoon extra-virgin olive oil

3 large Spanish onions, peeled, halved, and thinly sliced

1 teaspoon kosher salt

¼ teaspoon freshly ground black pepper

Melt the butter in the olive oil in a large skillet over medium heat. Add the onions, season with salt and pepper, and cook slowly, stirring occasionally, until deep golden brown and caramelized, 30 to 40 minutes. Remove from the heat and let cool before using.

CHOCOLATE-COCONUT CANDY BAR CAKE

THE CAKE

My mother's house was the third stop on my national "Steak and Cake tour." Her friends were so excited to be a part of "Cake Week" that they dropped off cake stand after cake stand after cake stand. When we filled them all with cakes, the house looked like a cake shop. Ever the one to raise the stakes, my mother reminded me that her favorite candy bar was Mounds and wondered aloud, "Wouldn't it be great to make a cake that was an homage to the simple but delicious Mounds bar?" With that rhetorical question, we both put on aprons and immediately started baking. The dark chocolate cake we made uses coconut oil instead of butter, and the best part—just like the candy bar—is that the filling is packed with sweet, fluffy white coconut.

Serves 8 to 12

Baking spray, for preparing the pans

1⅔ cups granulated white sugar

⅔ cup coconut oil, such as Nutiva

3 large eggs

2¼ cups cake flour

⅔ cup unsweetened cocoa powder (not Dutch-process)

1¼ teaspoons baking soda

1 teaspoon fine sea salt

½ teaspoon baking powder

1⅓ cups whole milk

1 teaspoon pure vanilla extract

Fluffy White Filling and Frosting (recipe follows)

1 cup Baker's Sweetened Angel Flake Coconut, for sprinkling on the cake (optional)

Pans: Two 9-inch round cake pans

❶ Position a rack in the center of the oven and preheat the oven to 350°F. Spray the cake pans with baking spray.

❷ Cream the sugar and coconut oil together with an electric mixer on medium speed until the sugar is completely integrated (it will be less fluffy than butter and sugar), 2 to 3 minutes.

❸ With the mixer running, add the eggs one at a time, beating well after each addition. Stop the mixer and scrape down the side of the bowl as necessary.

❹ Whisk together the flour, cocoa, baking soda, salt, and baking powder in a large bowl until well combined.

❺ Mix the milk and vanilla together in a small bowl. Add the flour mixture and the milk mixture alternately to the sugar mixture in small batches. Beat well after each addition. Beat on medium-low until smooth, 1 to 2 minutes. Stop the machine and scrape down the side of the bowl as necessary.

❻ Divide the batter equally between the 2 prepared pans. Lightly tap each pan down on the counter to make sure the batter is evenly distributed and to remove excess air bubbles.

❼ Bake until the layers pull away from the sides of the pans and a toothpick inserted in the center comes out clean, 30 to 35 minutes.

❽ Let the layers cool in the pans for 10 minutes, then remove them from the pans onto wire cooling racks. Let cool for a couple of hours before filling and frosting with Fluffy White Filling and Frosting.

⑨ Assemble the cake: Working quickly, carefully trim a thin slice off the rounded tops of each layer to even them out. Turn 1 layer bottom side up and smooth the coconut filling onto the surface. Top with the second layer. Frost the side a scoop of frosting at a time, then smooth a layer of frosting on the top of the cake while the icing is still warm. If desired, sprinkle coconut on the top and sides of the cake.

FLUFFY WHITE FILLING AND FROSTING

This is an old-fashioned filling and frosting that tastes like the best marshmallows.

Makes about 4½ cups, enough to fill and frost a 9-inch round layer cake

- 1½ cups granulated white sugar
- ½ teaspoon cream of tartar
- ½ cup water
- Pinch of fine sea salt
- 3 large egg whites, at room temperature
- 1½ teaspoons pure vanilla extract
- 1 cup Baker's Sweetened Angel Flake Coconut

❶ Place the sugar and cream of tartar in a heavy-bottomed 2-quart saucepan with a lid. Whisk to combine. Add the water and salt and place over medium heat. No need to stir the water and sugar. Bring to a boil, covered, without stirring, until the syrup spins a thin 8-inch thread when poured from a spoon (242°F on a candy thermometer), 3 to 5 minutes.

❷ While the syrup is cooking, beat the egg whites until they're stiff enough to hold a peak, 4 to 5 minutes.

❸ Pour the hot syrup very slowly into the stiff egg whites, beating constantly. Add the vanilla and beat well. The frosting should look very fluffy.

❹ Place one-third of the frosting in a separate bowl, add the coconut, and mix. This will become the filling between layers. The rest will frost the top and sides of the cake.

❺ Assemble the cake as directed, while the frosting and filling are still warm.

THE MATCHUPS

MARY PAT'S INDIVIDUAL BEEF WELLINGTONS, *page 86*

COWBOY STEAK WITH WHISKEY BUTTER, *page 5*

COFFEE-RUBBED TENDERLOIN WITH GARLIC CHEESE GRITS AND REDEYE GRAVY GLAZE, *page 107*

Fresh Grated   Dried Sweetened

BOB'S STEAK AU POIVRE

WITH FRENCH ONION CROUTONS

AND

POPPY-SEED CAKE

WITH LEMON AND ORANGE OPTIONS

THE STEAK

When I first met Bob Blumer, he made me his steak au poivre (aka pepper steak). He was so excited to serve it to me that I didn't have the heart to let him know I didn't like steak au poivre. I am glad I didn't, because one bite told me it was the best version I had ever tasted. Bob simplifies the recipe so that it is as easy as pan-frying a burger, and he uses filet mignon, which is the most tender and lean of all steaks. I love pairing Bob's recipe with Gruyère-topped caramelized onion toasts.

Serves 4

4 filets mignons (6 ounces each and ¾ inch thick)

4 teaspoons coarsely ground black pepper

1 teaspoon kosher salt

1 tablespoon unsalted butter

2 ounces brandy, preferably Cognac

²/₃ cup half-and-half

3 teaspoons Dijon mustard

3 tablespoons drained brined green peppercorns

French Onion Croutons (recipe follows)

Chopped fresh chives, for garnish (optional)

Pan: Sauté pan

Method: Stovetop

❶ Wrap the steaks in paper towels to rid them of excess moisture. Replace the paper towels as needed.

❷ Rub the filets on both sides with pepper and salt.

❸ Heat a dry sauté pan over high heat. When the pan becomes very hot, add the butter. When the butter has melted, add the steaks. Turning the steaks only once, cook to the desired degree of doneness. Insert an instant-read thermometer into the middle of a steak. The temperature should be 135°F for medium-rare (approximately 3 minutes per side, depending on the exact thickness). The high heat will cook this delicate cut of steak fairly quickly.

❹ Turn off the heat, add the brandy to the pan, and let sit for 5 seconds. Make sure there's nothing flammable around, then light a match to the brandy (see box, page 93). The flame should burn out after approximately 10 seconds. If the flame continues to burn, put it out by placing a lid on the pan.

❺ Transfer the steaks from the pan to a warm platter and cover with aluminum foil. Leave the drippings in the pan.

❻ Place the pan over low heat and slowly stir the half-and-half and mustard into the drippings. Add the green peppercorns. Stir and simmer for a couple of minutes until the sauce gains some thickness. Serve the steaks on a bed of the sauce with the French Onion Croutons on the side. Garnish with chives, if desired.

FRENCH ONION CROUTONS

These cheesy onion toasts are reminiscent of the tops of French onion soup—which is the best part of the soup!

Makes 8 croutons

> 1 tablespoon unsalted butter
>
> 2 tablespoons extra-virgin olive oil
>
> 3 large yellow onions, peeled and sliced into rings
>
> 1 teaspoon kosher salt
>
> 1 baguette (16 to 18 inches long)
>
> 1 cup grated Gruyère cheese

❶ Preheat the oven to 300°F.

❷ Melt the butter in the oil in a large, heavy-bottomed skillet over medium heat. When the butter is melted, add the onion rings and salt. Cook, covered, stirring occasionally, until the onions are softened and starting to color, 20 minutes. Remove the cover and cook, stirring occasionally, until the onions are all a deep golden color, about 20 minutes more. (Onions can be cooked up to 2 days in advance and refrigerated in an airtight container until you're ready to make the steak.)

❸ Meanwhile, slice the baguette into 2-inch-thick pieces. You should have 8 slices. Place them on a rack set on a sheet pan and bake until the bread is dried out and lightly toasted, about 20 minutes. Set aside to cool.

❹ When the toasts are cool, remove the rack from the sheet pan and place a silicone baking mat or a sheet of parchment paper on the pan. Space the toasts out evenly on the mat.

❺ Just before serving, preheat the broiler.

❻ Place a generous spoonful of caramelized onions on top of each of the toasts and sprinkle them with Gruyère cheese. Place under the broiler and broil until the cheese is bubbly and melted, about 3 minutes. Serve with steak au poivre.

"Try and Keep the Flames in the Pan!"

Here are Bob's flambé regulations:

1. CLEAR THE DECKS. To keep the flames from burning anything in your kitchen, clear the area of any flammable objects and move your fire extinguisher within easy reach.

2. CAP IT. Tie your hair back, wear a hat, and roll up your sleeves.

3. REDUCE IT. Too much liquid in the pan will dilute the alcohol and prevent it from igniting. Simmer contents until no more than 2 to 3 tablespoons remain before adding alcohol.

4. KEEP YOUR DISTANCE. If you have a gas stove, make sure to turn the burner off before adding the brandy. Spattering particles will likely cause the alcohol to ignite prematurely, as soon as it is poured in the pan.

5. PUT A LID ON IT. Keep a lid within easy reach. If the flames burn too high, or for more than 10 seconds, cover the pan with a lid and they will go out.

THE MATCHUPS

POPPY-SEED CAKE
WITH LEMON AND ORANGE OPTIONS,
recipe follows

LATTE LOAF WITH HAZELNUT GLAZE,
page 34

APPLE UPSIDE-DOWN CAKE WITH CRÈME FRAÎCHE,
page 76

POPPY-SEED CAKE

WITH LEMON AND ORANGE OPTIONS

THE CAKE

My mother made this simple Bundt cake dusted with confectioners' sugar for school picnics and summer get-togethers. I loved the not-too-sweet, almost savory nature of the cake—given the amount of poppy seeds—especially with a cup of coffee. When I was on my "Steak and Cake tour," I made the cake two ways and had my cake testers vote on whether to glaze or not to glaze it. The vote was unanimous—everyone wanted a glaze. I like both lemon and orange, and you can use either or forgo the glaze for a light dusting of confectioners' sugar. This cake is different from a lot of popular poppy-seed cakes in that you use a dense, sweetened poppy-seed filling, not just dry poppy seeds for the visual effect.

Serves 12

FOR THE CAKE

Baking spray, for preparing the pan

1 cup (2 sticks) unsalted butter or margarine, at room temperature

1½ cups granulated white sugar

1 can (12.5 ounces) Solo Poppy Seed Cake & Pastry Filling, or 1 jar (10 ounces) Baker Poppy Seed Filling, or homemade poppy-seed filling (see box, page 96)

4 large eggs, separated

1 cup full-fat sour cream (not light or nonfat)

1 teaspoon pure vanilla extract

1 teaspoon pure lemon or orange extract

2½ cups all-purpose flour

Zest of 1 lemon or orange

1 teaspoon baking soda

1 teaspoon fine sea salt

FOR GLAZING OR DUSTING

Confectioners' sugar

Zest of 1 lemon or orange (if glazing)

3 tablespoons lemon or orange juice, or more if needed (if glazing)

Pinch of fine sea salt (if glazing)

Pan: 12-cup Bundt pan or 10-inch tube pan

❶ Position a rack in the center of the oven and preheat the oven to 350°F. Spray the cake pan with baking spray.

❷ Make the cake: Cream the butter and granulated sugar together with an electric mixer on medium-high speed until light and very fluffy, 3 to 5 minutes.

❸ Add the poppy-seed filling and beat on medium-low just until blended. Add the egg yolks, one at a time, beating well after each addition. Add the sour cream, vanilla, and lemon or orange extract and beat just until blended. Stop the mixer and scrape down the side of the bowl as necessary.

❹ Whisk the flour, zest, baking soda, and 1 teaspoon of salt together in a medium-size bowl until mixed. Add to the poppy-seed mixture gradually, beating well on medium speed after each addition.

❺ Beat the egg whites in a separate bowl with an electric mixer and clean beaters until stiff peaks form. Fold the beaten egg whites into the batter. Do not overmix. You should still see chunks of egg whites. Spoon the batter evenly in the prepared pan. Lightly

tap the pan down on the counter to make sure the batter is evenly distributed and to remove excess air bubbles.

6 Bake until a toothpick inserted in the center comes out clean, 55 to 65 minutes.

7 Meanwhile, if using the glaze, mix 1¼ cups confectioners' sugar, the citrus zest and juice of your choice and a pinch of salt in a small bowl until the glaze is smooth. This is a tart, runny glaze meant to flavor the cake while it is still warm instead of a thicker icing. Add a bit more sugar if it's too thin or a bit more juice if it's too thick.

8 Let the cake cool in the pan on a wire cooling rack for 10 minutes. Remove the cake from the pan, and if it's in a tube pan, flip it so it's top side up.

9 If glazing, cool on the rack for another 20 minutes. The cake should still be warm (not hot). Place a sheet of waxed paper under the cooling rack to catch any

How to Make Your Own Poppy-Seed Filling

Pour 2 cups of boiling water over ⅔ cup of dry poppy seeds. Let sit, covered, for 2 hours and then strain, discarding the water. Add ⅔ cup granulated white sugar to the seeds and mix well. Cover again and let sit at room temperature for 2 hours, stirring occasionally to meld the sugar and poppy seeds. The mixture will keep in an airtight container stored in the refrigerator for about a month.

drips. Spoon the glaze over the top of the warm cake, letting it drizzle down the sides—nudge it toward the edges with the back of the spoon or the brush.

If not glazing, dust the cake with confectioners' sugar once it has cooled completely.

Note: My mother frequently made the poppy-seed cake for covered-dish suppers and picnics. When I asked her why this cake was her go-to cake for a crowd, she said that it was a little unusual for North Carolina—so no one else would be bringing it—and because it baked beautifully, you didn't have to ice it, and it cut into lots of pieces. If you haven't ever had a real poppy-seed cake made with sugar-macerated poppy-seed paste—and you love poppy seeds—this will be your idea of heaven.

THE MATCHUPS

BOB'S STEAK AU POIVRE
WITH FRENCH ONION CROUTONS, *page 91*

CUMIN-RUBBED FLANK STEAK
WITH CHIMICHURRI POTATOES, *page 125*

SIZZLIN' STEAK KEBABS WITH SALSA VERDE,
page 143

SURF AND TURF

LOBSTER WITH HOMEMADE PASTIS CREAM AND STEAK

FARMERS MARKET SUMMER FRUIT AND BERRY CAKE

THE LOBSTER AND STEAK

Surf and turf is beloved—even if it seems a bit old-fashioned! The lobster is traditionally accompanied by a filet mignon, but I think you should feel free to make it with whatever steak you like—and I like a New York strip. My favorite way to serve grilled lobster is to baste it with homemade crème fraîche that has been scented with a dash of pastis, the popular anise-flavored aperitif that is a perfect companion to fresh tarragon.

I can't make this dish without thinking of my dear friends Kirsten and Nat Tessier. Kirsten and Nat met in Chicago and married in his hometown of Uzes in the south of France. I was already a lover of pastis, but after a wedding week in France, when we drank it for days on end, I became a lifelong fan. And this is my favorite way to use pastis, besides drinking it!

Pastis is made with a secret recipe of herbs, spices, and spirits. The combination is reminiscent of tarragon and licorice, so it makes a perfect cooking partner—especially with shellfish and, oddly enough, green vegetables. The most readily available equivalent is Pernod. It isn't a true pastis, but it has similar taste qualities. If you can't find Ricard pastis, you can replace it with Pernod in the recipe, but be aware that its slightly chartreuse yellow color will tint the cream. You can buy crème fraîche in any grocery store, but making your own is a science experiment that you can eat!

Serves 4

4 New York strip steaks
(12 to 16 ounces each and 1½ inches thick)

1 cup Homemade Crème Fraîche (page 78),
plus more for serving

¼ cup pastis or Pernod (Ricard brand)

4 lobster tails (5 to 7 ounces each), thawed if frozen,
and butterflied (see Note)

Extra-virgin olive oil

Kosher salt

4 sprigs fresh tarragon

Special equipment: 4 metal skewers

Grilling Method: Direct/Medium Heat

❶ Preheat the grill with all burners on high. Once preheated, adjust the temperature to medium-high for direct grilling.

❷ Prepare the steaks 101-style (see page 196). Keep warm while you prepare the lobster.

❸ Reduce the grill temperature to medium.

❹ Make the pastis crème by combining the 1 cup crème fraîche and pastis in a small bowl.

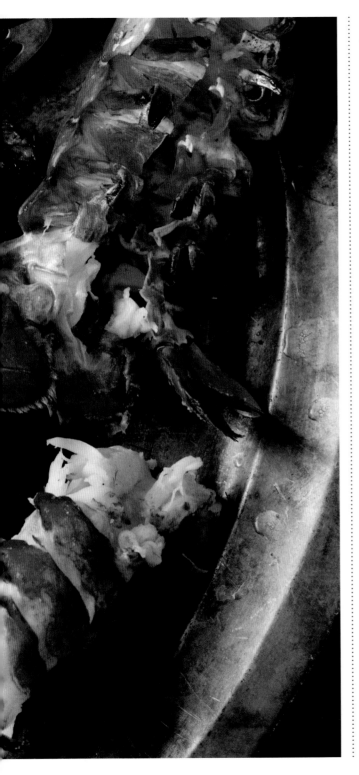

⑤ Brush the lobster tails with olive oil and season with salt (see Note). Set aside.

⑥ Place the lobster on the cooking grate, shell side up. Cover and grill until the shells turn bright red and are just beginning to char, about 4 minutes. Turn the tails over and spoon the pastis crème generously onto the butterflied tails. Continue grilling until the flesh is just cooked through, 2 to 3 minutes more.

⑦ Remove the lobster tails from the grill to plates. Garnish each with a tablespoon of the crème fraîche and top with a sprig of fresh tarragon. Place a steak on each plate and serve at once.

Note: To keep the lobster tails straight during cooking, thread a metal skewer down the center of each tail. Remove them before serving.

THE MATCHUPS

FARMERS MARKET SUMMER FRUIT AND BERRY CAKE, *recipe follows*

ITALIAN CREAM CAKE, *page 63*

CLASSIC KEY LIME CHEESECAKE WITH PECAN CRUST, *page 113*

FARMERS MARKET SUMMER FRUIT AND BERRY CAKE

THE CAKE

My sister Mary Pat loves fresh fruit more than bees love honey. So it wasn't surprising that her wedding cake was a rich butter cake with stabilized whipped cream, decorated with kiwis, raspberries, blueberries, strawberries, peaches, and grated white chocolate. Needless to say, it was beautiful and delicious, and had a welcome freshness at a hot summer wedding.

Last summer, I made the cake in Los Angeles with fresh fruit from the Hollywood farmers market, and it crushed my Instagram account! I received more "likes" for this fresh fruit–decorated cake than any other post. Literally bursting with color, three kinds of raspberries—black, red, and golden—blackberries, wild strawberries, and blueberries adorned the simple square cake. Use whatever fruit is local and in season; be sure to tag me—@elizabethkarmel #steakandcake—in your Instagram post!

Serves 12

Baking spray, for preparing the pan

Assorted fresh fruit, including raspberries, strawberries, kiwis, peaches, and apricots

12 tablespoons (1½ sticks) unsalted butter, at room temperature

1½ cups granulated white sugar

3 large eggs

2¼ cups all-purpose flour

2½ teaspoons baking powder

1 teaspoon fine sea salt

1 cup whole milk

2 teaspoons pure vanilla extract

Stabilized Whipped Cream (page 235)

Pan: 9-inch square pan

❶ Position a rack in the center of the oven and preheat the oven to 350°F. Spray the cake pan with baking spray.

❷ Prepare the fruit: Clean and dry the berries, slicing the strawberries in half or in thinner slices. Clean, dry, and peel the kiwis, peaches, and apricots or other fruits, and slice as desired into halves, quarters, or round or thin slices.

❸ Cream the butter and sugar together with an electric mixer on medium speed until very fluffy, 3 to 5 minutes. Add the eggs one at a time, beating well after each addition until thoroughly mixed.

❹ Whisk the flour, baking powder, and salt together in a medium-size bowl. Pour the milk into a glass measuring cup and add the vanilla.

❺ Add the flour mixture and the milk mixture to the butter mixture alternately in small batches, mixing well after each addition. Stop the machine and scrape down the side of the bowl as necessary.

❻ Pour the batter into the prepared cake pan. Lightly tap it down on the counter to make sure the batter is evenly distributed and to remove excess air bubbles.

❼ Bake until the cake pulls away from the sides of the pan and a toothpick inserted in the center comes out clean, 25 to 30 minutes. Begin testing after 20 minutes.

8 Cool the cake for 10 minutes in the pan. Then remove it from the pan and let cool completely on a wire cooling rack before frosting.

9 Frost the cake generously with the Stabilized Whipped Cream. Decorate the cake attractively with the fruits of choice. Serve with more fresh fruit on the side, if desired.

THE MATCHUPS

SURF AND TURF LOBSTER WITH
HOMEMADE PASTIS CREAM AND STEAK, *page 97*

T-BONE WITH NDUJA BUTTER
AND EASY MUSHROOM TARTS, *page 70*

BACON-WRAPPED BEEF TENDERLOIN WITH
A GREEN PEPPERCORN AND THYME SAUCE,
page 116

THE MATCHUPS

DAVID LEBOVITZ'S ORANGE-GLAZED ALMOND LOAF,
recipe follows

DOUBLE-DUTCH CHOCOLATE GUINNESS BUNDT CAKE
WITH CHOCOLATE GUINNESS GLAZE, *page 133*

MARGARITA TRES LECHES CAKE
WITH STRAWBERRY PAVÉ, *page 150*

FIRST-PLACE SMOKED AND CHARRED TENDERLOIN

WITH GRILLED MEXICAN STREET CORN SALAD

AND

DAVID LEBOVITZ'S ORANGE-GLAZED ALMOND LOAF

THE STEAK

A few years ago, I was invited to participate in a competition between New York City "city" chefs and Long Island "country" chefs called Dan's Taste of Summer GrillHampton. The rule was that each chef had to use one local item. I chose fresh Long Island corn and made a salad with all of the unctuous flavors of Mexican street corn—butter, mayo, cheese, chipotle, and cilantro, plus bacon, garlic, and lime. Since it was a hot summer day, I paired it with a slice of my smoked and charred beef tenderloin. The tenderloin is smoked the day before serving and charred on an open grill just before slicing and plating. It was a hit with the guests and the judges, too, and I took home the first-place trophy.

Serves 8 to 10

1 whole trimmed beef tenderloin (about 5 pounds and 14 inches long)

2 tablespoons coarse pink salt or coarse white sea salt, or 1 tablespoon kosher salt

Extra-virgin olive oil

Grilled Mexican Street Corn Salad (page 178)

Special equipment: 2 cups of wood chips, soaked in water for 3 minutes

Grilling Method: Combo/Low and High Heat

❶ The day before serving, smoke the tenderloin: Wrap the tenderloin in paper towels to rid it of excess moisture. Replace the paper towels as needed.

❷ Preheat the grill with all burners on high. Once preheated, adjust the temperature to low heat (about 250°F) for indirect grilling. If using a gas grill, make sure that the smoker box is filled with soaked wood chips before you preheat the grill. If using a charcoal grill, place the wet wood chips directly on the gray-ashed charcoal just before you add the beef.

❸ Mix the salt with 2 tablespoons of olive oil to make a paste and rub it all over the tenderloin.

❹ Place the tenderloin in the center of the cooking grate, cover, and smoke at a low temperature for about 45 minutes. Remove and let cool. Refrigerate, covered, overnight.

❺ Just before serving, preheat the grill with all burners on high for direct grilling.

❻ Remove the tenderloin from the refrigerator, wrap it in paper towels to remove any moisture, then brush it lightly with olive oil. Using 12-inch tongs, sear the meat on all sides, 1 to 2 minutes per side.

❼ Let the meat rest for 5 minutes. Slice and serve with the Grilled Mexican Street Corn Salad.

DAVID LEBOVITZ'S ORANGE-GLAZED ALMOND LOAF

THE CAKE

David Lebovitz is one of the smartest food people I know. His eponymous blog and his book, *The Sweet Life in Paris*, are smart, original, and hugely popular. I know that any recipe that David gives me, or publishes, not only works but is a cut above, and this cake is no exception. He calls it "Orange-Glazed Polenta Cake," but after I made it, the memory of almonds is what stuck with me, so that is how I think of it. David was the pastry chef at Chez Panisse for many years before he started "living the sweet life," and this cake epitomizes that style of cooking. The cake is simple to prepare and complex in its flavors, being influenced by both Italy and France, and it doesn't need fancy garnishes or adornments to make it stand out.

Makes about 12 slices

FOR THE CAKE

8 tablespoons (1 stick) unsalted butter, at room temperature, plus about 1 tablespoon for preparing the pan

¾ cup yellow cornmeal, plus additional for preparing the pan

Scant 1 cup granulated white sugar

3 large eggs, at room temperature

2 tablespoons orange liqueur, such as Grand Marnier or Cointreau

¾ teaspoon pure almond extract

2 cups almond flour

¼ cup plus 2 tablespoons all-purpose flour

1½ teaspoons baking powder

½ teaspoon fine sea salt

Zest of 1 lemon

FOR THE ORANGE GLAZE

1¼ cups confectioners' sugar, or more if needed

Zest of 1 clementine or small orange

1 tablespoon clementine or orange juice, or more if needed

2 tablespoons orange liqueur, such as Grand Marnier or Cointreau

Pinch of fine sea salt

Pans: 9 x 5 x 3-inch loaf pan; sheet pan

1 Position a rack in the center of the oven and preheat the oven to 350°F. Lightly butter the cake pan with 1 tablespoon of butter. Dust the inside with cornmeal, and tap out any excess.

2 Make the cake: Cream the 8 tablespoons butter and the granulated sugar together with an electric mixer on medium speed until light and very fluffy, 3 to 5 minutes.

3 Add the eggs one at a time, beating well after each addition. Stop the mixer and scrape down the side of the bowl as necessary. Mix in the liqueur and almond extract.

4 Whisk the ¾ cup cornmeal, almond flour, all-purpose flour, baking powder, salt, and lemon zest together in a medium-size bowl until there are no lumps. Gradually add the flour mixture to the butter mixture, beating just until well combined. Do not overmix.

5 Scrape the batter into the pan and smooth the top (see Note). Lightly tap the cake pan down on the counter to make sure the batter is evenly distributed and to remove excess air bubbles.

6 Place the loaf pan on a sheet pan to make it easier to pull it out of the hot oven. Bake the cake until it is golden brown on top, it pulls away from the sides of the pan, and a toothpick inserted into the center comes out almost clean, perhaps with just a few crumbs attached, 45 to 50 minutes.

7 Let the cake cool in the pan on a wire cooling rack for about 30 minutes, then run a knife along the outside of the cake to loosen it from the pan and remove the cake to the rack. Let the cake cool completely before glazing.

8 Meanwhile, make the glaze: Mix the confectioners' sugar with the clementine zest and juice, orange liqueur, and salt in a medium-size bowl until the glaze is thick, but still runny. Add a bit more sugar if it's too thin, or add a bit more liquid if it's too thick.

9 Place a sheet of waxed paper under the cooling rack to catch any drips. Use a spoon to drizzle the glaze over the center of the cake, encouraging it to run down the sides by nudging it toward the edges with the back of the spoon.

10 Serve the cake once the glaze has firmed up. It will keep for up to 5 days, if well wrapped, at room temperature. The cake will be noticeably moister the day after baking due to the oil in the almond flour, which is simply ground almonds. It can be frozen for up to 2 months.

Note: You may have a little bit of batter left over, because the most common loaf pans are 8½ inches instead of 9 inches. (I usually bake a mini loaf, which I eat the day I make it because I can't help myself!)

THE MATCHUPS

FIRST-PLACE SMOKED AND CHARRED TENDERLOIN
WITH GRILLED MEXICAN STREET CORN SALAD,
page 103

STEAK DIANE WITH TWICE-BAKED POTATOES,
page 51

PROSCIUTTO-WRAPPED FILET
WITH BLUE CHEESE AND PECAN BUTTER,
page 74

THE MATCHUPS

GRANDMOTHER ODOM'S
APPLE CAKE, *recipe follows*

WHISKEY BUTTERMILK
BUNDT CAKE, *page 6*

CHOCOLATE-COCONUT CANDY
BAR CAKE, *page 89*

COFFEE-RUBBED TENDERLOIN

WITH GARLIC CHEESE GRITS AND REDEYE GRAVY GLAZE

GRANDMOTHER ODOM'S APPLE CAKE

THE STEAK

Tenderloin is definitely a steak fan favorite. It is tender, as advertised, and adapts well to almost any flavor you pair it with. Another great thing about it is that you can cut it into individual thick filets or cook the whole piece and serve it in thin slices—turning a pricey luxury cut into an economical one. When Nespresso (my favorite coffee system) opened their boutique in Manhattan's Soho, they asked me to create a dish using their coffee. I was inspired to make a dry-rubbed beef tenderloin with ground coffee in the rub and serve it with buttered grits and redeye gravy made with brewed espresso. The resulting recipe is the perfect mash-up of high and low, city and country.

Serves 8 to 10

1 whole beef tenderloin (about 5 pounds and 14 inches long)

3 tablespoons ground espresso coffee beans

2 tablespoons unsweetened cocoa powder

2 tablespoons freshly ground black pepper

2 teaspoons granulated white sugar

2 tablespoons extra-virgin olive oil

Garlic Cheese Grits (page 186)

Redeye Gravy Glaze (recipe follows)

Minced chives, for garnish (optional)

Grilling Method: Combo/Medium-High Heat

❶ Preheat the grill with all burners on high. Once preheated, adjust the temperature to medium-high for direct and indirect grilling.

❷ Wrap the tenderloin in paper towels to rid it of excess moisture. Replace the paper towels as needed.

❸ Mix the coffee, cocoa, pepper, and sugar together in a small bowl. Brush the tenderloin all over with a thin coating of olive oil. Sprinkle the rub mixture evenly over the tenderloin. Gently pat the spices into the meat to adhere.

❹ Place the tenderloin on the cooking grate directly over the heat. Cover and sear for 2 minutes on each side, 6 to 8 minutes total. After all the sides are seared, move to indirect heat and grill until an instant-read thermometer inserted in the thickest part of the meat reads 130°F for the rare side of medium-rare, about 40 minutes more. (If the tenderloin is larger, it will take longer to cook.)

❺ Transfer the meat to a platter and let rest 15 minutes before cutting into thin slices. Place 2 generous spoonfuls of grits in the center of each plate, place 2 thin slices of tenderloin over the grits, and nap with the redeye gravy. Sprinkle the entire dish with minced chives.

REDEYE GRAVY GLAZE

Use dark roast espresso for the best results! Redeye gravy is a classic Southern gravy made with leftover coffee and the little bits of country ham that stick to the skillet when you fry it. The coffee is poured into the hot pan once the ham has been fried, and the reduction is redeye gravy. It is typically made for breakfast and served over grits.

Makes 1 cup

1 ham steak or piece of slab bacon, or several pieces of country ham or thick-cut bacon (about 8 ounces)

¾ cup brewed espresso

½ cup blackstrap molasses

1 tablespoon dark brown sugar

Pinch of fleur de sel

❶ Heat a cast-iron skillet over medium heat. Add the ham steak and cook on both sides until browned and warmed through, about 5 minutes total. Remove the meat from the pan. (If you are using bacon, it will take longer to cook, and you will need to pour out the excess fat—but do leave some in the pan.) Reserve the ham steak or bacon for another meal.

❷ Increase the heat to medium-high, and when the pan is really hot, pour in the espresso. Scrape up all the seasoned ham bits from the bottom of the pan. Stir in the molasses and brown sugar and bring to a simmer. Add the fleur de sel and taste. The glaze should be thick and black. Serve immediately.

GRANDMOTHER ODOM'S APPLE CAKE

THE CAKE

was lucky enough to have my grandmother live with us when I was growing up. She had a real sweet tooth and baked something almost every day. In the fall, when it was apple season, she would bake this very simple, quick apple cake and serve it warm with vanilla ice cream or whipped cream. My mother and I loved this cake and never thought to write down the recipe before my grandmother passed on. We searched and searched her recipe cards without success, until one day many years later I stumbled onto it between the pages of an old notebook. The consistency of the batter is more like cookie dough than cake batter, but don't fret; the natural juice in the apples becomes the liquid in the cake as it bakes. When I made this cake and half a dozen others for a cake tasting, everyone gravitated toward this

one—which showed me once again that warm, homey comfort is what we all crave.

Serves 8 to 10

Baking spray, for preparing the pan

2 cups granulated white sugar

½ cup neutral vegetable oil, such as Crisco

2 large eggs

2 cups all-purpose flour

2 teaspoons ground cinnamon

2 teaspoons baking soda

4 generous cups peeled and coarsely chopped baking apples (about 5; see Notes)

1 cup chopped English walnuts or black walnuts, toasted (see page 85 and Notes)

Pans: 12-cup Bundt pan or 10-inch tube pan; sheet pan

❶ Position a rack in the center of the oven and preheat the oven to 350°F. Spray the cake pan with baking spray.

❷ Beat the sugar and oil together with an electric mixer on medium speed until well combined, 2 to 3 minutes. Add the eggs one at a time, beating well after each addition. Continue beating until the mixture is creamy. (This is the one cake that I have made many times with a bowl and my blending fork—forgoing the mixer—and it still turned out delicious.)

❸ Whisk the flour, cinnamon, and baking soda together in a small bowl. Add the flour mixture to the sugar mixture in 3 batches, beating well on medium-low speed after each addition. Stop the mixer and scrape down the side of the bowl as necessary.

❹ Fold in the chopped apples, then add the walnuts and mix well. The batter is very stiff and you'll need to wait a few minutes for the apples to start releasing their juices before mixing. If you have trouble, use clean hands or a sturdy blending fork.

❺ Pour the batter into the prepared pan and lightly tap it down on the counter to make sure the batter is evenly distributed and to remove excess air bubbles.

❻ Place the pan on a sheet pan and bake until the cake pulls away from the side of the pan and a toothpick inserted in the center comes out clean, 60 minutes.

❼ Cool the cake for 5 minutes in the pan, then remove it from the pan to a cake plate or platter. Serve warm.

Notes: Sometimes my grandmother would make this cake with black walnuts that she gathered and cracked herself instead of traditional English walnuts. If you like black walnuts, you will love them in this cake. For toasting directions, see page 85.

In the past 15 years, Granny Smith apples have become the gold standard for baking apples. I still like baking with them, but sometimes they are less fresh than is needed or desired. If your Granny Smith apples are mealy, look for Pink Lady or Honeycrisp apples. You need a hard, tart variety or it will break down too much during the cooking.

Variation: If you are serving the cake cool, a simple confectioners' sugar glaze spiked with a couple of tablespoons of Calvados and a couple of tablespoons of apple cider dresses it up.

THE MATCHUPS

COFFEE-RUBBED TENDERLOIN WITH GARLIC CHEESE GRITS AND REDEYE GRAVY GLAZE, *page 107*

RED-HOT CAST-IRON STEAK WITH PERFECT CRUST, *page 9*

PRIME NEW YORK STRIP STEAK ROAST WITH BARBUTO-INSPIRED ROASTED POTATOES, *page 36*

GRILLED TENDERLOIN

WITH DECADENT HORSERADISH CREAM AND YORKSHIRE PUDDING

AND

CLASSIC KEY LIME CHEESECAKE

WITH PECAN CRUST

THE STEAK

You know how people sit around and ask each other what their last meal would be? My brother-in-law Karl's request would be grilled tenderloin with horseradish cream and my sister Mary Pat's Key lime pie. You can approximate Karl's last supper by making this "steak for a crowd" dinner and serving the Classic Key Lime Cheesecake on page 113. It hits the spot all year long but makes a perfect holiday meal. During the winter, I love serving it with a big, sizzling hot Yorkshire pudding.

Serves 8

FOR THE RUB

2 tablespoons whole black peppercorns

2 tablespoons dried rosemary

2 tablespoons coarse sea salt or kosher salt

2 tablespoons sweet paprika

2 tablespoons smoked paprika

FOR THE MEAT

1 whole beef tenderloin
(4 to 5 pounds and 12 to 14 inches long)

2 tablespoons extra-virgin olive oil

FOR SERVING

Yorkshire Pudding (page 172)

Decadent Horseradish Cream (recipe follows)

Special equipment: Spice grinder

Grilling Method: Combo/Medium Heat

❶ Preheat the grill with all burners on high. Once preheated, adjust the temperature to medium for direct and indirect grilling.

❷ Make the rub: Combine the peppercorns, rosemary, salt, and both paprikas in a small bowl. Transfer the mixture to a spice (or coffee) grinder and grind until finely blended.

❸ Wrap the tenderloin in paper towels to rid it of excess moisture. Replace the paper towels as needed. When dried, rub the tenderloin all over with the oil and spice mixture.

❹ Place the tenderloin on the cooking grate directly over the heat and sear on all sides, 6 to 8 minutes total. Then move the tenderloin to the unlit part of the grill, cover, and finish cooking, about 30 minutes more for medium-rare (135°F). Let the meat rest for 15 minutes, then slice and serve with Yorkshire Pudding and Decadent Horseradish Cream.

THE MATCHUPS

CLASSIC KEY LIME CHEESECAKE
WITH PECAN CRUST, *recipe follows*

ITALIAN CREAM CAKE, *page 63*

FARMERS MARKET SUMMER FRUIT AND BERRY
CAKE, *page 100*

DECADENT HORSERADISH CREAM

Light and airy, this decadent savory whipped cream is sharp with horseradish and bright with a touch of lemon zest, making it the perfect accompaniment to a prime tenderloin.

Serves 8

> 1 pint heavy (whipping) cream
>
> Zest of ½ lemon

1 tablespoon store-bought white prepared horseradish (not horseradish cream), plus more if needed

Fine sea salt

While the roast rests, pour the cream into a clean stainless-steel bowl. Using an electric mixer, whip on high until the cream forms soft peaks. Add the lemon zest and prepared horseradish. Taste and adjust, adding more horseradish if you like it stronger. Season with sea salt. Serve immediately.

CLASSIC KEY LIME CHEESECAKE

WITH PECAN CRUST

THE CAKE

I have raved about my sister Mary Pat's baking many times in this book, but her Key lime pie is truly legendary. Because Key lime pie is a favorite at steakhouses, but this is a cake—not a pie—cookbook, I took the wonderful flavor of my sister's pie and adapted it to a cheesecake! I've also added a recipe for Key Lime Curd for an all-out, over-the-top extra to dollop on the cheesecake. I think that you will agree that the result will create a new favorite.

Makes 12 slices

FOR THE CRUST

Baking spray, for preparing the pan

1½ cups graham cracker crumbs

¾ cup pecans, chopped

¼ cup granulated white sugar

1 teaspoon ground cinnamon

Pinch of fine sea salt

8 tablespoons (1 stick) unsalted butter, melted

FOR THE FILLING

4 packages (8 ounces each) cream cheese (full-fat version)

1 generous cup granulated white sugar

1 teaspoon pure vanilla extract

Zest of 1 lemon

5 tablespoons Key lime juice, preferably Nellie & Joe's Famous Key West Lime Juice

4 large eggs

Sweetened Whipped Cream, for serving (optional; page 13)

Key Lime Curd (optional; recipe follows)

Pans: 9-inch springform pan; sheet pan

❶ Position a rack in the center of the oven and preheat the oven to 350°F. Spray the cake pan with baking spray.

❷ Make the crust: Mix the graham cracker crumbs and pecans together in a small bowl. Mix the ¼ cup sugar, cinnamon, and salt together in another small

bowl. Add the sugar mixture to the crumb mixture, then pour the melted butter over the crumbs and mix with a fork until all the crumbs are saturated with the butter. Pour the buttered crumbs into the prepared springform pan and press them into the bottom and up the side of the pan. Set aside.

❸ Make the filling: Cream the cream cheese, 1 cup sugar, vanilla, and lemon zest with an electric mixer with the paddle attachment on medium-low speed. Add the Key lime juice a little at a time and mix well after each addition. Add the eggs one at a time, mixing well after each addition. You don't want to overmix because too much air can cause a crack in the baked cheesecake. Stop the mixer and scrape down the side of the bowl as necessary.

❹ Pour the filling into the crust and place the cake pan on a sheet pan to make it easier to transport the cake to and from the oven.

❺ Bake until set, 1 hour and 15 minutes to 1 hour and 25 minutes. Turn off the oven and leave the door cracked. Let cool in the oven for 1 hour. Remove the cake from the oven and let cool on a wire cooling rack to room temperature. Then place in the refrigerator for at least 4 hours.

❻ To serve, run a knife between the side of the pan and the cake and remove the pan's side. Serve sliced with the Sweetened Whipped Cream and/or Key Lime Curd, if desired.

THE MATCHUPS

GRILLED TENDERLOIN
WITH DECADENT HORSERADISH CREAM AND
YORKSHIRE PUDDING,
page 111

AN INDOOR/OUTDOOR TOMAHAWK STEAK,
page 22

SURF AND TURF LOBSTER
WITH HOMEMADE PASTIS CREAM AND STEAK,
page 97

KEY LIME CURD

If you can buy fresh Key limes, use them instead of the bottled Key lime juice.

Makes about 1½ cups

> 4 tablespoons (½ stick) unsalted butter, at room temperature
>
> ¾ cup granulated white sugar
>
> ¼ teaspoon fine sea salt
>
> 4 large egg yolks
>
> ⅔ cup Nellie & Joe's Famous Key West Lime Juice
>
> ¼ cup filtered water
>
> Zest of 1 lime, grated with a Microplane

❶ Cream the butter, sugar, and salt together with an electric mixer on medium speed until light and fluffy, about 2 minutes. Add the egg yolks one at a time, beating well after each addition. Add the lime juice and water and mix until combined.

❷ Pour the mixture into a nonreactive, heavy-bottomed saucepan and cook, stirring frequently, over medium heat until it coats the back of a spoon, 15 to 20 minutes. Don't allow the mixture to boil, or it might curdle.

❸ Remove the curd from the heat and stir in the zest, mixing well. Pour into a glass bowl and chill before using. Place any extra in a glass jar with a tight-fitting lid. It will keep, refrigerated, for up to 2 weeks.

BACON-WRAPPED BEEF TENDERLOIN

WITH A GREEN PEPPERCORN AND THYME SAUCE

AND

OLD VIRGINIA'S BEST POUND CAKE

THE STEAK

I don't remember when my holiday tradition of prime rib changed to a holiday tradition of beef tenderloin, but it is a welcome change. As much as I love prime rib, beef tenderloin is easier to prepare and to carve, and the leftovers are good cold.

The only challenge with beef tenderloin is that it is lean, with little to no fat, and it is best served rare. One year, I wanted to do something that looked a little fancier than plain grilled tenderloin but was just as easy to execute. I remembered one of my favorite ways to prepare filet—bacon-wrapped—and thought, let's see what happens if I wrap the tenderloin in bacon, mummy style!

Finally, since it is the "Christmas beast," I decided to add a rich green peppercorn sauce scented with fresh thyme and a splash of Cognac. This is now my favorite party presentation for beef tenderloin, and I love the mash-up of the bacon wrap with the old-school sauce. It just goes to show you that everything old can be new again!

Serves 6 to 8 or 8 to 10

Pan: Rimmed sheet pan

Method: Oven

> 1 chateaubriand (3 to 4 pounds and about 10 inches long) or a whole trimmed tenderloin (about 5 pounds and 14 inches long)
>
> Extra-virgin olive oil
>
> Fine sea salt and freshly ground black pepper
>
> 1 pound thin-cut bacon, at room temperature
>
> Fresh thyme leaves, for garnish
>
> Green Peppercorn and Thyme Sauce (recipe follows)

❶ Preheat the oven to 325°F.

❷ Brush the tenderloin all over with olive oil and season with salt and pepper. If using a whole tenderloin, tuck the small ends of the tenderloin under each side to make sure that the roast is about the same thickness all over. If roasting a chateaubriand, you won't need to do that.

❸ Beginning at one end, wrap the bacon around the tenderloin, overlapping the strips so they stick to each other. Make sure the ends of the bacon are tucked under.

❹ Place the bacon-wrapped tenderloin on a rack set on a rimmed sheet pan with the ends of the bacon touching the rack so the bacon doesn't unravel.

❺ Roast until the temperature reaches 125°F on an instant-read thermometer inserted into the center of the meat, about 60 minutes. Remove the tenderloin from the oven and let rest for 20 minutes, covered with aluminum foil. If you used thin-cut bacon, it should be crisp, but if you want the bacon to be crispier, you can broil the roast for 1 to 2 minutes before removing from the oven.

❻ Slice and garnish generously with fresh thyme leaves. Serve with the sauce on the side.

GREEN PEPPERCORN AND THYME SAUCE

This old school–style sauce is spiced up with a dash of Tabasco and lots of fresh thyme.

Makes about 1¼ cups

> 2 tablespoons unsalted butter, plus 8 tablespoons (1 stick) cold unsalted butter, cut into cubes
>
> 1 large shallot, peeled and minced (about 2 tablespoons)
>
> 3 tablespoons white wine vinegar
>
> 3 tablespoons brandy, preferably Cognac
>
> 1 tablespoon strong Dijon mustard
>
> ½ cup heavy (whipping) cream
>
> 1 dash Tabasco or other favorite hot sauce (optional)
>
> Fine sea salt and freshly ground white pepper
>
> 2 teaspoons fresh thyme leaves, plus 5 sprigs for infusing
>
> 1 tablespoon green peppercorns, pressed dry

❶ Combine the 2 tablespoons butter, shallot, vinegar, brandy, and mustard in a small saucepan. Bring to a boil over medium heat and cook for 2 minutes. Add 2 tablespoons of the cream and whisk until it is incorporated. This addition of the cream will help prevent the sauce from breaking.

❷ Start adding the butter cubes, one at a time, whisking continuously. When the first cube of butter is almost melted, add another. Repeat until all the butter is incorporated.

❸ Add the rest of the cream, the Tabasco, if using, a pinch of salt, and a few grinds of white pepper. Add the 5 sprigs of thyme and let sit in the hot sauce for 10 minutes.

❹ While the mixture is still warm, strain through a china cap or other fine strainer. Mix in the thyme leaves and peppercorns. Use immediately or keep in a pitcher in a warm water bath. If the sauce breaks, you can reincorporate it with a little heavy cream or by using an immersion blender.

OLD VIRGINIA'S BEST POUND CAKE

THE CAKE

When my mother and I set out to bake the ultimate pound cake, we tried about a dozen recipes before settling on the "Economy Pound Cake," dubbed that by the baker who contributed it to the *Recipes from Old Virginia* cookbook circa 1958. We loved the name—given because it was created using much smaller amounts of ingredients than a standard pound cake, which used a pound of butter, a pound of sugar, and a pound of eggs (about 10, for those of you who are counting!). The "economy" recipe, by contrast, called for only a half pound of butter, 2 cups of sugar, and 4 eggs. The crumb of the economy version was light and moist but dry to the touch—unlike the greasier traditional recipe, of which I am not a fan. And the best part was the slight spiciness and depth of flavor that the cake had because of the addition of mace and nutmeg. To take the flavors one step further, my mother and I added a splash of vanilla extract and doubled the amount of mace and nutmeg. These tweaks helped turn the economy pound cake into the best pound cake that I have ever eaten, and one that hopefully many of you will make for years to come.

In the summer, serve slices of the cake with fresh-picked, vibrant red strawberries that ooze those tart-sweet summer flavors. Or slice and macerate the berries in a little bit of sugar, a pinch of salt, lemon zest, and a splash of Grand Marnier—just enough to bring out the best in the fruit, but not enough to mask it!

Serves 12

- Baking spray, for preparing the pan
- 1 cup (2 sticks) unsalted butter, at room temperature
- 2 cups superfine sugar (see box, page 159)
- 4 large eggs, separated
- 2 teaspoons baking powder
- ½ teaspoon fine sea salt
- ¼ teaspoon ground mace
- ¼ teaspoon freshly grated or ground nutmeg
- 3 cups cake flour
- 1 cup whole milk

Pan: 12-cup Bundt pan

❶ Position a rack in the center of the oven and preheat the oven to 350°F. Spray the cake pan with baking spray.

❷ Cream the butter and sugar together with an electric mixer on medium speed until very light and fluffy, about 4 minutes. Beat the egg yolks in a separate bowl, then add them to the butter mixture and beat until silky. In a separate bowl, with clean beaters, beat the egg whites on medium-high speed until they hold soft peaks, 3 to 4 minutes.

③ Whisk the baking powder, salt, mace, and nutmeg together with the flour in a medium-size bowl. Add the flour mixture and the milk to the butter mixture alternately in batches. Beat until the batter is well mixed. Stop the mixer and scrape down the side of the bowl as necessary. Fold in the beaten egg whites and pour the batter into the prepared pan. Lightly tap the cake pan down on the counter to make sure the batter is evenly distributed and to remove excess air bubbles.

④ Bake until golden in color and a toothpick inserted in the center comes out clean, 55 to 60 minutes.

THE MATCHUPS

BACON-WRAPPED BEEF TENDERLOIN
WITH A GREEN PEPPERCORN AND THYME SAUCE,
page 116

TUSCAN STEAK WITH WHITE ANCHOVY AND
TRUFFLE BUTTER AND GRILLED LEMONS, *page 61*

FLATIRON STEAK SMOTHERED
IN CARAMELIZED ONIONS, *page 152*

⑤ Cool the cake in the pan for 10 minutes before removing it to a wire cooling rack to cool completely.

MY MOTHER'S BEEF STEAK STROGANOFF

ᴀɴᴅ

BAKED RICOTTA CHEESECAKE

WITH McVITIE'S CRUST

THE STEAK

My sisters and I loved when my mother made beef stroganoff. It is hard to believe that a recipe so simple could be viewed as something so special. Stroganoff is definitely a dinner of another era, but even to the uninitiated, one bite will convince you that this throwback deserves to be reintroduced to today's dinner table. My mother adapted this recipe from *The Gourmet Cookbook*. If you are looking to update it as a meatless meal, it is also marvelous when made with only mushrooms.

Serves 4

Pan: 12-inch skillet

Method: Stovetop

> 1 pound tenderloin tips or any tender boneless steak, such as New York strip
>
> Kosher salt and freshly ground black pepper
>
> 8 tablespoons (1 stick) unsalted butter
>
> 1 tablespoon all-purpose flour
>
> 2 cups beef stock
>
> ¼ cup Harveys Bristol Cream sherry (optional)
>
> ¼ cup full-fat sour cream (not light or nonfat)
>
> 2 teaspoons Dijon mustard
>
> 12 ounces white mushrooms, wiped clean and sliced
>
> 1 yellow onion, peeled and thinly sliced
>
> Cooked egg noodles, for serving

1 Cut the beef into 2-inch-wide strips and season all over with salt and pepper. Set aside in the refrigerator until ready to cook.

2 Melt 2 tablespoons of the butter in a large saucepan over medium-low heat. Add the flour and stir to form a thick paste (a roux). Gradually stir in the beef stock and sherry, if using, and bring to a boil. Continue boiling until the sauce thickens, about 2 minutes. Turn off the heat and stir in the sour cream and mustard. Cover the saucepan and set it aside.

3 Melt 2 tablespoons of the butter in a large skillet. Add the meat and cook, stirring occasionally, until browned, 2 to 3 minutes. Transfer the meat and any juices to the sauce and set aside.

4 Melt the remaining 4 tablespoons of butter in the skillet. Add the mushrooms and onion and cook until

THE MATCHUPS

BAKED RICOTTA CHEESECAKE
WITH McVITIE'S CRUST, *recipe follows*

CHOCOLATE LAYER CAKE
WITH COCOA-FRANGELICO FROSTING, *page 38*

ITALIAN CREAM CAKE, *page 63*

the mushrooms are browned but not crispy and the onion has softened, 8 to 10 minutes.

5 Add the meat, mushrooms, and onion to the sauce and warm, if necessary, covered, over low heat. Serve over the hot cooked noodles. (Do not put the meat on the noodles until just before serving; otherwise the noodles will absorb all the sauce and the dish will be dry and the noodles mushy.)

BAKED RICOTTA CHEESECAKE

WITH McVITIE'S CRUST

THE CAKE

One fateful evening when I was seventeen, my mother had a big dinner party, and I volunteered to make dessert—a ricotta cheesecake with a glazed cherry topping. Having labored all afternoon, I was so proud of the finished product—two creamy, not-too-sweet ricotta cheesecakes with a slightly grainy zwieback crust and plump, juicy cherries glistening on top. Once the party was in full swing and all the adults were happily digging into their beef tenderloin, I pulled the cheesecakes out of the refrigerator, set them on the counter, and briefly walked out of the kitchen. Enter McGee, our beloved but ill-behaved German short-haired pointer, who had a penchant for eating food off the countertops. When I reentered the kitchen, I found our dog busily gulping down the last crumbs of one of the cheesecakes, with the cherry juice now dripping from her jowls. I went ballistic, the dog was exiled to the backyard, and my mother calmly noted that at least we had a second cheesecake. The moral to that story is more is better!

Makes about 12 slices

FOR THE CRUST

Baking spray, for preparing the pan

1 package (400 g) McVitie's Digestives biscuits

12 tablespoons (1½ sticks) unsalted butter, melted

2 tablespoons granulated white sugar

Pinch of salt

FOR THE FILLING

1½ pounds (about 3 cups) whole-milk ricotta cheese

4 large eggs

Zest of 1 lemon

1 generous teaspoon fresh lemon juice

1 cup granulated white sugar

1 generous tablespoon cake flour

1 cup heavy (whipping) cream

TOPPING (OPTIONAL)

Fresh strawberries, cut in half

Sweetened Whipped Cream (page 13)

Pans: 9-inch springform cake pan; sheet pan

❶ Position a rack in the center of the oven and preheat the oven to 350°F. Spray the cake pan with baking spray.

❷ Make the crust: Place the biscuits in a food processor and pulse to make crumbs. Add the melted butter, 2 tablespoons sugar, and salt, and pulse to blend. Press the mixture into the bottom and up the side of the prepared pan. Set aside.

❸ Make the filling: With an electric mixer on medium-low speed, beat the ricotta with the eggs, adding them one at a time and beating well after each addition. Add the lemon zest and juice. Whisk the 1 cup of sugar and flour together in a small bowl and add it to the cheese mixture. Blend in the cream. Stop the mixer and scrape down the side of the bowl as necessary. Don't be concerned if the mixture looks liquidy. Some brands of ricotta cheese have more liquid than others, but rest assured that the cake will set up as it bakes.

❹ Pour the cheese filling into the crust. Lightly tap the pan down on the counter to make sure the batter is evenly distributed and to remove excess air bubbles. Place the springform pan on a sheet pan to make it easier to transport the cake to and from the oven.

❺ Bake until firm in the center and slightly puffy, about 1 hour. Turn off the oven and open the door a crack. Let cool in the oven for 1 hour. Remove the cheesecake from the oven and let cool in the pan on a wire cooling rack to room temperature. Refrigerate for at least 4 hours before serving.

❻ To serve, run a knife between the side of the pan and the cake and remove the pan's side. Transfer the cake to a serving plate and top with the strawberries and whipped cream, if using.

THE MATCHUPS

MY MOTHER'S BEEF STEAK STROGANOFF, *page 120*

PERUVIAN STEAK SALAD, *see box, page 63*

STEAK FRITES WITH DIJON BÉARNAISE, *page 155*

CUMIN-RUBBED FLANK STEAK

WITH CHIMICHURRI POTATOES

TEX-MEX CHOCOLATE SHEET CAKE

AND A GERMAN CHOCOLATE VARIATION

THE STEAK

Steak and chimichurri sauce is a classic pairing that is legendary in Argentina. But you don't have to be a gaucho or cowboy to enjoy it. Whether you cook the steak indoors or outdoors, I think this will become one of your favorite meals—I know it's one of mine! And it's quick and easy, to boot! A simple three-ingredient rub is made from spices that you most likely have in your pantry, but it delivers flavor that is anything but simple! Flank steak should be served medium-rare and cut across the grain for maximum tenderness.

Serves 6

1 flank steak (1½ to 2 pounds and about ¾ inch thick)

1 teaspoon granulated garlic

½ teaspoon smoked paprika

½ teaspoon whole cumin seed, toasted on the stovetop in a skillet

Extra-virgin olive oil

Coarse sea salt or kosher salt

Chimichurri Potatoes (page 183), with ¼ cup of the sauce set aside for serving with the steak

Special equipment: 12-inch grill pan with lid (see Note)

Method: Stovetop

❶ Wrap the flank steak in paper towels to rid it of excess moisture. Replace the paper towels as needed.

❷ Mix the garlic, paprika, and cumin seed together in a small bowl until well combined.

❸ Trim the steak of any surface fat. Brush it lightly all over with olive oil. Press the rub into both sides of the steak. Wrap the steak in plastic wrap and refrigerate until ready to cook. (This step can be done the night before cooking.)

❹ Just before cooking, season the steak with salt.

❺ Preheat the grill pan on high until hot, about 2 minutes. Reduce the heat to medium. Place the meat in the grill pan and sear for 1 minute per side with the lid off. Put the lid on the pan and cook for 4 to 6 minutes. Turn the steak with a pair of tongs and sear the second side. Continue cooking with the lid on until done, 3 to 5 minutes more.

❻ Remove the steak and place it on a clean platter. Let rest for 5 to 10 minutes before slicing. Then slice the steak across the grain into thin diagonal slices and sprinkle with a pinch of salt. Serve warm with the Chimichurri Potatoes and the chimichurri sauce.

Steak and Chimichurri

When I visited Buenos Aires, I was surprised that most of the chimichurri sauce in restaurants was made from dried herbs and tasted more of oregano than parsley. And, even though that trip taught me that my recipe is Americanized and not an authentic Argentinean chimichurri, I still prefer it.

The deep green sauce is most commonly served as a condiment for steak, but I toss hot roasted potatoes with the garlicky sauce for a healthy alternative to mashed potatoes that literally bursts with flavor!

Since I love a good chimichurri with steak, the meat in this recipe is still a steak, but a family-friendly, delicious, versatile, and economical flank steak. It can be sliced thin and placed on a slice of toasted or grilled baguette with a dollop of chimichurri sauce for a crowd-pleasing appetizer. One steak will stretch to feed at least 15 to 20 people—and still taste like a luxurious bite. Or it can be served up with chimichurri potatoes for a hearty main course for six. I also sometimes take leftover chimichurri sauce and toss it with hot pasta and chunks of leftover flank steak—it's a leftover that is good enough to plan for!

Note: I find that the steak cooks better if I use a grill pan that has a lid. I like the Staub steam-grill pan that comes with a lid or the Lodge cast-iron 12-inch pan and a 12-inch lid.

THE MATCHUPS

TEX-MEX CHOCOLATE SHEET CAKE AND A GERMAN CHOCOLATE VARIATION, *recipe follows*

CLASSIC SOUR CREAM COFFEE CAKE, *page 16*

POPPY-SEED CAKE WITH LEMON AND ORANGE OPTIONS, *page 94*

TEX-MEX CHOCOLATE SHEET CAKE

AND A GERMAN CHOCOLATE VARIATION

THE CAKE

I f you have never made a cake before and love chocolate, this is the cake that you should bake. Because it is an easy cake for a beginning baker, I sometimes refer to it as the world's easiest chocolate cake—but don't think that it doesn't deliver in the flavor department! The results are spectacular. Plus, this is the cake that I always make for a crowd, as you can cut it into as many as 48 pieces. In this variation on a Texas sheet cake, I've loaded both the cake and the icing with ground cinnamon, giving it a distinctive Tex-Mex flair.

Makes 24 to 48 squares

FOR THE CAKE

Baking spray, for preparing the pan

1 cup (2 sticks) unsalted butter

1 cup sour milk (1 cup fresh whole milk plus 1 teaspoon white vinegar; see Note)

6 tablespoons unsweetened cocoa powder

1½ teaspoons ground cinnamon

2 large eggs

½ cup water

1 teaspoon pure vanilla extract

1 teaspoon baking soda

2 cups all-purpose flour

2 cups granulated white sugar

½ teaspoon fine sea salt

FOR THE ICING

8 tablespoons (1 stick) unsalted butter

6 tablespoons unsweetened cocoa powder

6 tablespoons whole milk

2 teaspoons pure vanilla extract

1 box (1 pound) confectioners' sugar, sifted

1 teaspoon ground cinnamon

Pinch of fine sea salt

Pan: Half sheet pan (aka jelly roll pan)

❶ Position a rack in the center of the oven and preheat the oven to 375°F. Spray the half sheet pan with baking spray.

❷ Make the cake: Place the 1 cup of butter, sour milk, 6 tablespoons cocoa, and 1½ teaspoons cinnamon in a small saucepan over medium-low heat. Bring to just under a boil, stirring to melt the butter and blend the mixture. Beat the eggs with the water, 1 teaspoon vanilla, and baking soda in a small bowl. In a large bowl, whisk the flour, granulated sugar, and ½ teaspoon salt together. Add the egg mixture to the flour, mixing gently until well combined. Add the butter-cocoa mixture and stir well.

❸ Pour the batter into the prepared pan and lightly tap the pan down on the counter to make sure the batter is evenly distributed and to remove excess air bubbles.

❹ Bake until the cake pulls away from the sides of the pan and a toothpick inserted in the center comes out clean, 20 to 25 minutes.

5 While the cake is baking, make the icing, as you will want to spread it on the cake while both are still warm. Place the 8 tablespoons butter, 6 tablespoons cocoa, and whole milk in a small saucepan over medium-low heat. Bring to just under a boil, stirring to melt the butter and blend the mixture. Remove the pan from the heat and add the 2 teaspoons vanilla. Whisk the confectioners' sugar, 1 teaspoon cinnamon, and a pinch of salt together in a separate bowl. Add the butter mixture to the sugar mixture and blend thoroughly.

6 Spoon the warm icing over the warm cake 5 to 7 minutes after it comes out of the oven. Spread the icing using an offset spatula.

7 Let the iced cake cool completely in the pan on a wire cooling rack before cutting into squares.

Note: The consistency of sour milk is the same as the consistency of regular milk with a few little curdles on top. This is what you're looking for.

VARIATION

GERMAN CHOCOLATE SHEET CAKE

German chocolate cake is always a crowd pleaser! I debated whether or not to offer the original German chocolate cake recipe in this book or the recipe that I use when I make it for friends and family. I decided that I would tell the truth and let you in on my German chocolate secret: I always use the Tex-Mex Chocolate Sheet Cake as the base for my German chocolate cake. Depending on my mood and whom I am making the cake for, I either keep the cinnamon in the batter or eliminate it. I like it both ways. The darker, moister sheet cake makes a better cake for this coconut-pecan frosting, but if you prefer a lighter German chocolate cake, you can find the recipe on the Baker's German Chocolate wrapper. Make this in the sheet pan or more traditionally in round cake pans.

1 can (8 ounces) evaporated milk

1 cup granulated white sugar

3 large egg yolks, lightly beaten

8 tablespoons (1 stick) unsalted butter, at room temperature

1 teaspoon pure vanilla extract

Pinch of salt

1⅓ cups Baker's Sweetened Angel Flake Coconut

1 cup chopped pecans

Tex-Mex Chocolate Sheet Cake, warm (cake only, page 127)

1 Place the evaporated milk, sugar, egg yolks, butter, vanilla, and salt in a medium-size heavy saucepan. Mix well like you're mixing a batter. Place the saucepan over medium heat and cook, stirring continuously, until thickened, about 12 minutes. You may notice small particles in the mixture, but don't worry. You will strain them out.

2 Remove the pan from the heat and pour the mixture through a fine sieve set over a large bowl. Stir the mixture vigorously with a fork so that it strains through the sieve. Work quickly so that the icing is still hot when you're finished.

3 Mix in the coconut and chopped pecans. Spread the frosting on top of the warm chocolate sheet cake. Let cool completely in the pan on a wire cooling rack before cutting into squares.

THE MATCHUPS

CUMIN-RUBBED FLANK STEAK WITH CHIMICHURRI POTATOES, *page 125*

SKIRT STEAK WITH CHILE-LIME RUB AND CRUNCHY JICAMA SLAW, *page 138*

SIZZLIN' STEAK KEBABS WITH SALSA VERDE, *page 143*

LUCK OF THE IRISH FLANK STEAK SANDWICH

WITH CHARRED RED ONIONS

AND

DOUBLE-DUTCH CHOCOLATE GUINNESS BUNDT CAKE

WITH CHOCOLATE GUINNESS GLAZE

THE STEAK

As the slogan goes, "Guinness is good for you." And what's good for you is good for your steak. The tangy dry stout adds richness to both savory and sweet recipes, which is why it is an ideal marinade for grilled flank steak and charred onions. For the perfect St. Paddy's Day celebration, pair this steak sandwich and my Double-Dutch Chocolate Guinness Bundt Cake.

Serves 4

> 1 flank steak or London broil (about 2 pounds and at least 1 inch thick)
>
> 1 bottle (14.9 ounces) Guinness beer
>
> 2 large red onions, peeled and cut into ½-inch-thick slices

1 container (5.2 ounces) Boursin cheese

Extra-virgin olive oil

Kosher salt and freshly ground black pepper

8 slices thick sourdough or country bread

Special Equipment: 8 bamboo skewers, soaked in water for 30 minutes

Grilling Method: Direct/Medium Heat

❶ Wrap the flank steak in paper towels to rid it of excess moisture. Replace the paper towels as needed.

❷ Place the steak in a nonreactive container with a lid. Pour the Guinness over the steak. Place the onion slices on top of the steak. Cover the container and marinate in the refrigerator for 1 to 2 hours.

❸ Preheat the grill with all burners on high. Once preheated, adjust the temperature to medium for direct grilling.

❹ Place the Boursin in its packaging in the freezer while the grill is preheating. (Freezing the Boursin will make it easier to shave it into thin slices later on.)

❺ When ready to grill, remove the meat and onions from the marinade and pat dry.

❻ Thread each onion slice through its width with a bamboo skewer. Be sure the skewer goes through each ring (the skewers will look like onion lollipops). Brush both the meat and the onions all over with a thin coating of olive oil and season with salt and pepper.

❼ Place the steak and onions directly on the cooking grate over direct heat and sear. Cover and continue cooking on the first side, 6 to 8 minutes. Uncover, turn the steak and onions with a pair of tongs, and sear the second side. Cover again and continue cooking until done, another 6 to 8 minutes. (Both the steak and the onions will have grill marks on each side.) The steak and onions should take about the same amount of time to grill.

❽ Remove the steak and onions from the grill and put them on a clean platter to rest for 5 minutes.

While the meat is resting, shave the slightly frozen Boursin into thin slices. Spread a thin layer of cheese over the steak. Remove the skewers from the onions and spread a thin layer of Boursin over the tops of them.

9 Spread 1 side of the bread slices with olive oil and grill that side until toasty and grill-marked, 1 to 2 minutes. Remove the bread from the grill and spread the untoasted sides with a thin layer of cheese. Put 2 onion slices on the cheese side of each of 4 pieces of bread and set aside.

10 Thinly slice the steak on the diagonal. Pile the meat on the onion slices and top each sandwich with another slice of bread, grilled side up. Push down to compact the sandwich a little before cutting it in half.

Serve while still warm, or wrap in aluminum foil and refrigerate until ready to eat.

THE MATCHUPS

DOUBLE-DUTCH CHOCOLATE GUINNESS
BUNDT CAKE WITH CHOCOLATE GUINNESS GLAZE,
recipe follows

BAKED CINNAMON-SUGAR DOUGHNUT PUFFS WITH
DARK CHOCOLATE BOURBON DIPPING SAUCE,
page 25

OLIVE OIL CAKE WITH ROSEMARY AND
ORANGE AND A CLEMENTINE SALAD,
page 136

DOUBLE-DUTCH CHOCOLATE GUINNESS BUNDT CAKE

WITH CHOCOLATE GUINNESS GLAZE

———

THE CAKE

This is my go-to chocolate cake. It was inspired by my Aunt Mary Ellen's chocolate pound cake. Back in the day, her cake was legendary at church picnics. It was light brown in color due to her preference for Hershey's cocoa, and the crumb was as fine and reserved as a good Southern Christian. But tastes have changed, and today we want our food to be over-the-top in every respect. I've revised the cake to be much more chocolaty by using a whole cup of Dutch-process cocoa, which creates a deep, rich cake that is almost coal-black in color. The crumb is also moister and more complex with the additions of the heady Guinness and the rich chocolate glaze.

Makes about 12 slices

FOR THE CAKE

Baking spray, for preparing the pan

1 cup (2 sticks) unsalted butter, at room temperature

2½ cups granulated white sugar

4 large eggs

2½ cups all-purpose flour

1 cup cocoa powder, preferably Dutch-process

½ teaspoon baking powder

½ teaspoon baking soda

½ teaspoon fine sea salt

⅛ teaspoon freshly ground nutmeg

1 tablespoon pure vanilla extract

½ cup half-and-half

½ cup Guinness beer, at room temperature

FOR THE CHOCOLATE GUINNESS GLAZE

2 generous cups confectioners' sugar

3 generous tablespoons Dutch-process cocoa powder

3 tablespoons Guinness beer

2 tablespoons half-and-half or heavy (whipping) cream

½ teaspoon pure vanilla extract

Pinch of fine sea salt

Pan: 12-cup Bundt pan

❶ Position a rack in the center of the oven and preheat the oven to 325°F. Spray the cake pan with baking spray.

❷ Make the cake: Cream the butter and granulated sugar together with an electric mixer on medium speed until light and very fluffy, 3 to 5 minutes. Add the eggs one at a time, beating well after each addition.

❸ Whisk the flour, 1 cup cocoa, baking powder, baking soda, ½ teaspoon salt, and nutmeg together in a large

---

THE MATCHUPS

LUCK OF THE IRISH FLANK STEAK SANDWICH WITH CHARRED RED ONIONS, *page 130*

RED-HOT CAST-IRON STEAK WITH PERFECT CRUST, *page 9*

CLASSIC NEW YORK STEAKHOUSE STRIP WITH BEEFSTEAK TOMATOES AND SIZZLING THICK BACON AND ONIONS, *page 41*

---

bowl. Mix the 1 tablespoon of vanilla, ½ cup half-and-half, and ½ cup Guinness together in a separate bowl.

④ Add the cocoa mixture and the Guinness mixture to the butter mixture alternately in batches, beating well after each addition. Stop the mixer and scrape down the side of the bowl as necessary.

⑤ Pour the batter into the prepared pan. Tap the pan down on the counter to make sure the batter is evenly distributed and to remove excess air bubbles. Bake until the cake pulls away from the side of the pan and a toothpick inserted in the center comes out clean, 1 hour and 10 minutes.

⑥ Meanwhile, make the glaze: Whisk the confectioners' sugar and 3 tablespoons cocoa together in a medium-size bowl. Mix the 3 tablespoons Guinness,

2 tablespoons half-and-half, ½ teaspoon vanilla, and a pinch of salt together in a separate bowl. Add the Guinness mixture to the sugar mixture and stir with a heavy-duty fork until completely mixed and smooth.

⑦ Let the cake cool in the pan on a wire cooling rack for 5 minutes. Place a sheet of waxed paper under the rack to catch the dripping glaze, then remove the cake from the pan and set it on the rack.

⑧ Poke the top of the cake all over with a toothpick. Spoon the glaze over the top and wait until it seeps into the holes. Cover the holes with more glaze until the holes are full and let set for 10 minutes or so. Pour the remaining glaze over the top of cake and let it run down the sides. Let the cake cool completely before slicing.

LONDON BROIL

WITH ROASTED CHERRY TOMATOES ON THE VINE AND BURRATA CHEESE

AND

OLIVE OIL CAKE

WITH ROSEMARY AND ORANGE AND A CLEMENTINE SALAD

THE STEAK

London broil is a North American beef dish made by marinating beef, grilling or broiling it, then cutting it across the grain and on the diagonal into thin strips. The origin of the name is unknown. Although American butchers may label a cut of meat "London broil," the term does not refer to a specific cut of meat but to a method of preparation and cookery. Butchers may label a sirloin roast, flank steak, or a top round steak as London broil. I prefer a sirloin London broil and urge you to ask your butcher for one. You can also substitute tri-tip or flank steak for the London broil in this recipe.

The marinade is inspired by my favorite steak rub of espresso and black pepper. Although I love the rub, it is a little strong for some. I created this rich marinade to impart the same flavors, but in a milder form. It is equally good on any cut of steak, from the more expensive and marbled big prime ribeye to the leaner "value" cuts like flatiron or flank steak. The more tender the cut, the less time you want to let it soak before cooking. And remember to salt your steaks just before grilling.

Serves 4; makes 2½ cups marinade

THE MATCHUPS

OLIVE OIL CAKE WITH ROSEMARY AND
ORANGE AND A CLEMENTINE SALAD,
recipe follows

GINGERBREAD WITH ORANGE MARMALADE
AND GRAND MARNIER GLAZE, *page 11*

HOUSTON BANANA LOAF CAKE, *page 31*

1 sirloin London broil, tri-tip, or flank steak (1½ to 2 pounds)

1 cup brewed espresso or very strong black coffee

1 cup full-flavored red wine, such as cabernet sauvignon, Shiraz, or zinfandel

4 cloves garlic, peeled and grated

2 tablespoons Dijon mustard

2 tablespoons dark brown sugar

1 tablespoon Worcestershire sauce

½ cup extra-virgin olive oil, plus extra for brushing the steaks

2 teaspoons coarsely ground black pepper

1 teaspoon cinnamon chips or 1 cinnamon stick (about 3 inches long), broken into pieces

Fine sea salt

Roasted Cherry Tomatoes on the Vine and Burrata Cheese (page 179)

Special Equipment: 12-inch grill pan with lid (see Note, page 126)

Method: Stovetop

❶ Wrap the steak in paper towels to rid it of excess moisture. Replace the paper towels as needed.

❷ Whisk together the espresso, wine, garlic, mustard, sugar, Worcestershire sauce, ½ cup oil, pepper, and cinnamon chips in a medium-size nonreactive bowl until well blended. (The marinade will keep, tightly covered, in the refrigerator for up to 2 days.)

❸ Add the steak to the marinade and marinate for 30 to 40 minutes. Blot dry with paper towels to remove the surface marinade. Brush the steak all over with olive oil and season with salt.

4 Preheat the grill pan on high until hot, about 2 minutes. Reduce the heat to medium. Place the meat in the grill pan and sear for 1 minute per side with the lid off. Put the lid on the pan and cook for 4 to 6 minutes with the lid on. Lift the lid and check the bottom for doneness after 4 minutes. If it still needs more time, replace the lid and continue cooking another 2 minutes. Uncover and turn the steak with a pair of tongs. Replace the cover and cook the second side until done, 3 to 5 minutes more.

5 Remove the steak and place it on a clean platter. Let rest for 5 to 10 minutes before slicing against the grain and on the diagonal. Serve with Roasted Cherry Tomatoes on the Vine and Burrata Cheese.

OLIVE OIL CAKE

WITH ROSEMARY AND ORANGE AND A CLEMENTINE SALAD

THE CAKE

This light, almost savory cake is a nice change of pace, especially after a heavy meal. People in the United States don't usually think of olive oil and dessert together, but in Italy it is very common to use olive oil in cakes—just as it is common for us to use vegetable oil. The cake batter is very loose, but don't worry because it bakes up beautifully—and the addition of cornmeal likens it to a sweet version of cornbread. The supremed clementines make a gorgeous garnish.

Serves 9 to 12

- Baking spray, for preparing the pan
- 3 large eggs
- 1 cup granulated white sugar
- 1¼ cups half-and-half
- 1 cup good-quality extra-virgin olive oil
- ¼ cup Grand Marnier
- Juice and zest of 1 large orange (about ¼ cup juice)
- 1½ cups all-purpose flour
- ⅓ cup yellow cornmeal
- ½ teaspoon baking powder
- ½ teaspoon baking soda
- ¼ teaspoon dried rosemary leaves, crumbled
- Pinch of fine sea salt
- Confectioners' sugar, for garnish
- Clementine Salad, for serving (recipe follows)
- Sweetened Whipped Cream, for garnish (page 13)

Pan: 9-inch square pan or 9-inch round pan

1 Position a rack in the center of the oven and preheat the oven to 350°F. Spray the cake pan with baking spray.

2 Whisk the eggs and sugar together in a large bowl until well blended and light in color. Add the half-and-half, olive oil, Grand Marnier, and juice and mix well.

3 Whisk the flour, orange zest, cornmeal, baking powder, baking soda, rosemary, and salt together in another large bowl. Add the egg mixture to the flour mixture, stirring until just blended (the batter will be slightly lumpy; do not overmix).

④ Pour the batter into the prepared pan. Lightly tap the pan down on the counter to make sure the batter is evenly distributed and to remove excess air bubbles.

⑤ Bake until the cake pulls away from the sides of the pan and a toothpick inserted in the center comes out with only a few crumbs, 45 to 50 minutes. Place the pan on a wire cooling rack to cool completely.

⑥ When the cake has cooled, run a knife around the perimeter of the pan and invert the cake onto a serving plate. Dust with confectioners' sugar, cut into pieces, and serve with the Clementine Salad and Sweetened Whipped Cream.

CLEMENTINE SALAD

If you make this salad when clementines are out of season, feel free to substitute your favorite orange or tangerine. There is little more to it than supreming the oranges. Supremed citrus is the "meat" of the segments with the membranes removed. If you have never supremed a clementine (or other citrus fruit) before, it is much simpler than it sounds.

6 to 8 clementines or oranges

Pinch of salt

Pinch of granulated white sugar

① To supreme a clementine, slice a thin piece off the bottom of the fruit so that it sits flat. Place the clementine on the cut bottom and remove the peel, the white pith, and the outer membrane in strips. Go around the whole clementine trimming until you can see the bare fruit. Cut off the remaining top cap of peel and pith. Holding the fruit in the palm of your hand, carefully slice between each membrane with a small sharp knife, and remove the clean fruit segments, dropping them into a bowl. Squeeze any juice from the remaining clementine "skeleton" over the segments.

❷ When the clementines are all supremed, sprinkle with a pinch of salt and a pinch of sugar. Toss gently to combine and serve.

THE MATCHUPS

LONDON BROIL WITH
ROASTED CHERRY TOMATOES ON THE VINE
AND BURRATA CHEESE,
page 134

CARNE ASADA WITH
AVOCADO AND TOMATO SALAD,
page 18

TUSCAN STEAK WITH WHITE ANCHOVY
AND TRUFFLE BUTTER AND GRILLED LEMONS,
page 61

SKIRT STEAK

WITH CHILE-LIME RUB AND CRUNCHY JICAMA SLAW

AND

EASY LEMON LOAF

THE STEAK

I associate skirt steak with my favorite steak tacos from a little hole-in-the-wall taco joint in Tulum, Mexico. Skirt steak is so rich and flavorful, and I like to grill it up and serve it with a crunchy, refreshing jicama slaw and beautiful fuchsia-colored pickled onions.

Serves 4 to 6

FOR THE CHILE-LIME RUB

½ cup granulated white sugar

2 tablespoons unsweetened limeade mix, such as Kool-Aid

1 tablespoon New Mexico or ancho chile powder, or other pure chile powder such as chipotle chile powder for those with a hotter palate

1 tablespoon garlic powder

1 tablespoon onion powder

2 teaspoons finely ground black pepper

1 teaspoon celery seeds

1 teaspoon ground cumin

1 teaspoon ground cayenne pepper, or to taste

FOR THE STEAKS

2 skirt steaks (about 1 pound each)

Extra-virgin olive oil

Kosher salt

Crunchy Jicama Slaw (page 180)

Grilling Method: Direct/Medium-High Heat

THE MATCHUPS

EASY LEMON LOAF,
recipe follows

TEX-MEX CHOCOLATE SHEET
CAKE AND A GERMAN CHOCOLATE
VARIATION, *page 127*

MARGARITA TRES LECHES CAKE
WITH STRAWBERRY PAVÉ,
page 150

① Combine all the rub ingredients in a bowl and stir to mix. Transfer to a covered jar. Store in a cool, dry place. You'll have about 1 cup of rub, and it will keep for several months. (This rub doesn't have salt, so you must remember to salt before cooking anything that is seasoned with it.)

② Preheat the grill with all burners on high. Once preheated, adjust the temperature to medium-high for direct grilling.

③ Wrap the meat in paper towels to rid it of excess moisture. Replace the paper towels as needed.

④ Just before grilling, brush the steaks all over with olive oil and sprinkle both sides evenly with the rub. Sprinkle one side of each steak with about ½ teaspoon kosher salt just before placing them on the grill.

⑤ Place the steaks, salted side down, on the cooking grate. Cover and grill until the meat begins to brown and shrink, 4 minutes. Salt the top of each steak, turn them over, and grill for 4 to 5 minutes more for medium-rare.

⑥ Let the meat rest for 10 minutes before slicing it across the grain and serving with the Crunchy Jicama Slaw.

EASY LEMON LOAF

THE CAKE

This lemon tea loaf is easy to whip up at the last minute—and no one but you will know just how easy it is. I gave a loaf to my friends Terry Kidder and Shawn Peacock, and when they got home, they decided to have "just a sliver." Well, sliver after sliver, it was soon gone in one sitting, and they dubbed it Lem-yum Loaf. The best thing is that you can substitute any citrus that you have on hand, or use a combination of lemons and limes or lemons and oranges. And if you can get your oven mitts on Meyer lemons, blood oranges, or kaffir limes, so much the better!

Serves 8

FOR THE CAKE

Baking spray, for preparing the pan

12 tablespoons (1½ sticks) unsalted butter, at room temperature

¾ cup granulated white sugar

½ teaspoon pure vanilla extract

3 large eggs

1¼ scant cups self-rising flour

Zest of 2 lemons

⅓ cup fresh lemon juice (from 2 large lemons)

FOR THE LEMON SYRUP

Zest and juice of 2 lemons

⅓ cup granulated white sugar

Pinch of fine sea salt

Pans: 9 x 5 x 3-inch loaf pan; sheet pan

① Position a rack in the center of the oven and preheat the oven to 350°F. Spray the loaf pan with baking spray.

② Make the cake: Cream the butter and ¾ cup sugar together with an electric mixer on medium-high speed until light and very creamy, 3 to 5 minutes. Add the vanilla and the eggs, one at a time, beating well after each addition.

③ Whisk the flour and the zest of 2 lemons together in a small bowl. Add the flour mixture and the ⅓ cup of lemon juice to the butter mixture alternately in batches. Stop the mixer and scrape down the side of the bowl as necessary.

④ Spoon the batter into the prepared loaf pan and lightly tap the pan down on the counter to make sure the batter is evenly distributed and to remove excess air bubbles.

⑤ Place the loaf pan on a sheet pan to make it easier to pull it out of the hot oven. Bake until the cake starts to pull away from the sides of the pan and a toothpick inserted in the center comes out clean, about 50 minutes. Remove the cake from the oven and let cool in the pan for 5 minutes before removing it from the pan and letting it cool on a wire cooling rack.

⑥ Meanwhile make the lemon syrup: Mix the juice of 2 lemons, ⅓ cup of sugar, and salt in a microwavable bowl and heat in the microwave on high until the mixture boils and the sugar is dissolved, 1 minute or so. Stir in the zest of 2 lemons. Spoon or brush the syrup over the cake while the cake is still warm and let cool completely before serving.

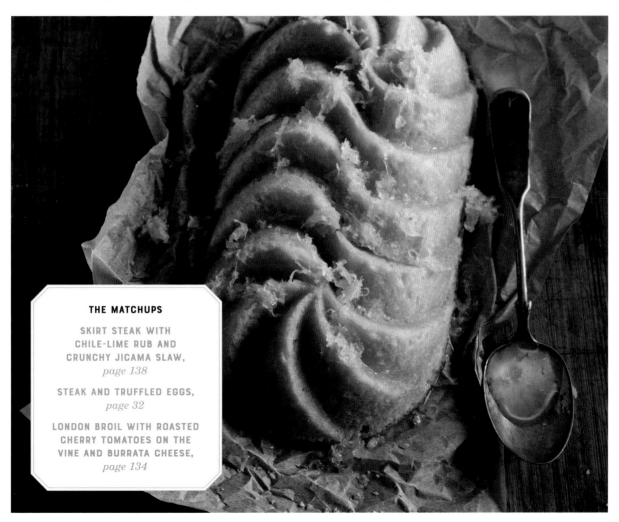

THE MATCHUPS

SKIRT STEAK WITH
CHILE-LIME RUB AND
CRUNCHY JICAMA SLAW,
page 138

STEAK AND TRUFFLED EGGS,
page 32

LONDON BROIL WITH ROASTED
CHERRY TOMATOES ON THE
VINE AND BURRATA CHEESE,
page 134

THE MATCHUPS

PECAN-STUDDED RUM CAKE,
recipe follows

POPPY-SEED CAKE WITH
LEMON AND ORANGE OPTIONS,
page 94

TEX-MEX CHOCOLATE
SHEET CAKE AND A GERMAN
CHOCOLATE VARIATION,
page 127

SIZZLIN' STEAK KEBABS

WITH SALSA VERDE

PECAN-STUDDED RUM CAKE

THE STEAK

These party-friendly kebabs deliver all your favorite taco flavors on a stick. The beauty of the recipe is that everything is cooked on the grill and assembled after cooking for easy serving—and easy eating. You can make the Salsa Verde (aka Houston Salsa) and roast the poblano peppers up to one day in advance.

Serves 8

> 1 skirt steak (about 2 pounds)
>
> 2 poblano peppers
>
> Extra-virgin olive oil
>
> 1 red onion, peeled and cut into quarters
>
> Kosher salt
>
> 1½ cups Salsa Verde (recipe follows)
>
> Tortillas, warmed, for serving (optional)

Special equipment: 16 bamboo skewers (12 inches long), soaked in water for 30 minutes

Grilling Method: Direct/High and Medium-High Heat

❶ Preheat the grill with all burners on high.

❷ Wrap the meat in paper towels to rid it of excess moisture. Replace the paper towels as needed.

❸ Rinse and dry the peppers. Place them directly on the cooking grate. Cover and cook, turning occasionally, until the skin blackens and blisters all over, about 5 minutes. Remove the peppers from the grill and immediately put them in a paper bag or sealed plastic container until cool to the touch. Skin and seed the peppers (the skins will slip off easily). Cut into strips and set aside.

❹ Reduce the grill heat to medium-high.

❺ Lay the skirt steak horizontally on a cutting board. Notice that the grain of the steak runs from top to bottom. Cut the steak into segments along the grain of the meat, 6 to 8 inches long. Cut each piece into thin strips, about 2 inches wide.

❻ Place the steak slices in a nonreactive bowl. Toss with olive oil. Toss the onion quarters with olive oil, too.

❼ Using 2 skewers per piece of meat (see box, page 144), thread the meat onto the skewers using an up-and-under weave and leaving about ½ inch between skewers. Stretch the meat flat and season with salt.

❽ Skewer the onion quarters using 2 skewers per quarter, 1 on each side of the quarter, sort of like ladder rails, with the onion as the rungs. Season with salt and place the onions on the cooking grate. Cover, and when they start to wilt and char around the edges, 3 to 4 minutes, place the meat skewers on the cooking grate.

❾ Grill both the meat and the onions until well marked and the meat is cooked to medium-rare, about 4 minutes for the meat, 6 to 8 minutes total for the onions. Turn the meat once halfway through the cooking time.

❿ Once the meat is cooked, serve it on the skewers immediately with the grilled red onion, roasted poblanos, Salsa Verde, and tortillas, if using.

SALSA VERDE (AKA HOUSTON SALSA)

The first time that I ever had this salsa was in Houston, when my sister first moved there. I loved how the avocado smoothed out the rough edges of the tomatillos, garlic, and chiles. For years I made this for grilled shrimp, until one day I tried it with beef and I was sold! This recipe is different from a lot of other versions because you do not need to char the chiles or roast the tomatillos. I like the fresher, bright flavors you get from the raw ingredients.

Makes about 1½ cups

1 can (12 ounces) whole tomatillos, drained, or about ¾ pound small tomatillos, husks removed

1 avocado, cut in half, pitted, peeled, and cut into chunks

1 serrano pepper, stem removed and chopped

4 cloves garlic

¼ cup fresh cilantro leaves

Zest and juice of ½ lime

Fine sea salt, to taste

Layer the tomatillos and all the remaining ingredients in a blender and puree until smooth. Transfer to a bowl and serve.

Double-Skewer It, aka the Ladder Method

Skewering makes grilling chunks of vegetables and meats very simple. It eliminates the possibility of small pieces falling through the grate and makes the food easier to turn.

But how many times have you skewered a chunk of food down the middle only to have it twirl around and around on the skewer like a wheel on an axle? My solution is to double-skewer it. I like to use inexpensive bamboo skewers that I've soaked in water for about 30 minutes. This step is necessary, or your skewers will burn. Using a piece of tenderloin tip as an example of the double-skewer kebab method, I suggest the following: For each kebab, lay out 2 skewers and thread the tenderloin chunk through 2 sides of the meat instead of the middle. The skewers end up looking like a meat ladder (thus my nickname for the method) and hold the meat so it cooks evenly on both sides. Now all you have to do is place the kebab ladder on the cooking grate and turn once halfway through the cooking time.

PECAN-STUDDED RUM CAKE

THE CAKE

Everywhere you go in the Bahamas, you see storefronts lined with tins of rum cake. People go nuts for it, and for good reason—it's incredibly moist and decadent. Years ago, I was lucky enough to learn the "secret" recipe from a distant cousin of a famous rum-distilling family. I was surprised that it was made with a packaged yellow cake mix with pudding. I tried again and again to make it from scratch, but it never was the same. At the end of the day, even though I'm a "from-scratch" kind of gal, I had to give it up to the mix. It's just that much better. I've tweaked the recipe a bit and added the pecans to the batter, which I like so much more than encrusting the outside. I also prefer Don Q Gold rum, because it is both smooth and flavorful.

When I teach this cake in a class, it is—without fail—the one recipe that people make over and over again. I find that this cake is even better the second and third day after you make it because the rum glaze is more fully absorbed by the cake. If you like piña coladas, bake the cake with Don Q Coco rum instead of the Gold rum.

Serves 8 to 10

FOR THE CAKE

Baking spray, for preparing the pan

1 package (18.5 ounces) yellow cake mix with pudding or 1 package (18.5 ounces) yellow cake mix plus 1 package (3.4 ounces) vanilla pudding mix (see Notes)

4 large eggs

½ cup cold water

½ cup neutral vegetable oil, such as Crisco

½ cup rum, preferably Don Q Gold or Don Q Coco

2 cups chopped pecans

FOR THE RUM GLAZE

8 tablespoons (1 stick) unsalted butter

1 cup granulated white sugar

¼ cup water

½ cup rum, preferably Don Q Gold or Don Q Coco

Pinch of fine sea salt

Pan: 12-cup Bundt pan or 10-inch tube pan

❶ Position a rack in the center of the oven and preheat the oven to 325°F. Spray the cake pan with baking spray.

❷ Make the cake: Place the cake mix (plus pudding, if you're using a separate mix), eggs, cold water, oil, and ½ cup rum in a large bowl and stir to mix. Fold in the chopped pecans. Pour the batter into the prepared pan. Lightly tap the pan down on the counter to make sure the batter is evenly distributed and to remove excess air bubbles.

❸ Bake until the cake pulls away from the side of the pan and a toothpick inserted into the center comes out clean, 1 hour.

❹ While the cake is baking, make the glaze: Melt the butter in a heavy saucepan over medium heat. Stir in the sugar and ¼ cup water. Bring the mixture to a boil and cook, stirring continuously, until the sugar has melted and the mixture is syrupy, 5 minutes. Remove from the heat and add the ½ cup rum and salt.

❺ Once the cake is done, allow it to cool in the pan on a wire cooling rack for 10 minutes. Invert it onto a serving plate or cake platter and prick the top and sides all over with a toothpick. Then, slowly drizzle some of the glaze over the cake.

❻ Allow the cake to absorb the glaze before adding more, repeating until all of the glaze is used. Let the dripping glaze collect on the bottom of the plate.

❼ Allow the cake to cool completely before serving.

Notes: Buy a cake mix that already has the pudding in the mix; I prefer the Betty Crocker brand. This cake is best made the day before you serve it, so the glaze is fully absorbed by the cake.

THE MATCHUPS

SIZZLIN' STEAK KEBABS WITH SALSA VERDE,
page 143

STEAK DIANE WITH TWICE-BAKED POTATOES,
page 51

SURF AND TURF LOBSTER
WITH HOMEMADE PASTIS CREAM AND STEAK,
page 97

STEAK TACOS

WITH 1-2-3 GUACAMOLE, CARROT-JALAPEÑO RELISH, AND CHIPOTLE CREMA

MARGARITA TRES LECHES CAKE

WITH STRAWBERRY PAVÉ

THE STEAK

Nothing beats a steak taco! And my favorite taco combines both tangy and acidic toppings with richer, creamy ones—and, of course, guacamole. This is an easy steak dinner since everything except the steak can be made up to a day in advance and set out for assembly just before serving. The 1-2-3 Guacamole is the best guacamole that I have ever had. The secret is in my friend Rick Bayless's tomatillo salsa, which is now marketed as Frontera Original Guacamole Mix.

Serves 4 to 6

> 2 skirt steaks (about 1 pound each)
>
> Extra-virgin olive oil
>
> Kosher salt
>
> 8 to 12 flour or corn tortillas, warmed
>
> 1-2-3 Guacamole (recipe follows)
>
> Elizabeth's Carrot-Jalapeño Relish (page 170)
>
> Chipotle Crema (recipe follows)

Grilling Method: Direct/Medium-High Heat

❶ Preheat the grill with all burners on high. Once preheated, adjust the temperature to medium-high for direct grilling.

❷ Wrap the meat in paper towels to rid it of excess moisture. Replace the paper towels as needed.

❸ Brush the steaks all over with olive oil. Sprinkle with kosher salt just before placing them on the grill.

❹ Place the steaks on the cooking grate and grill for 4 to 5 minutes. Turn and cook for 4 to 5 minutes more for medium-rare. Remove the steaks from the grill and place on a clean platter. Let the meat rest for 5 minutes before slicing it against the grain, on the diagonal, and serve with tortillas and taco condiments.

1-2-3 GUACAMOLE

I first made this recipe for a very large event at the Culinary Institute of America Worlds of Flavor conference. I was daunted by the task of making guacamole for 500, but my friends at Frontera Foods suggested that I try their easy recipe, made with tomatillo salsa. Well, it was so good that it was the hit of the event, and I couldn't stop eating it myself! Since I tried this recipe, I've never made guacamole any other way.

Makes about 2 cups

> 3 ripe Hass avocados
>
> 1 cup store-bought tomatillo salsa or Frontera Original Guacamole Mix
>
> ¼ cup chopped fresh cilantro leaves
>
> Kosher salt

Cut the avocados in half, remove the pits, scoop the soft flesh into a bowl, and mash. Leave some small chunks of avocado in the mash. Stir in the tomatillo salsa and the cilantro; add salt to taste. Refrigerate with an avocado pit in the center of the guacamole for up to 5 hours (the pit will help keep the guacamole from browning).

CHIPOTLE CREMA

This sauce comes together instantly in a blender. Start with 1 chipotle and taste after each addition for spiciness. Add according to your taste.

½ cup mayonnaise, preferably Hellmann's or Best Foods

½ cup full-fat sour cream

1 to 3 canned chipotles in adobo sauce

Place the mayonnaise and sour cream in a blender with 1 chipotle and some of the adobo sauce from the can. Puree and taste for spice. Add another chipotle or two if desired.

THE MATCHUPS

MARGARITA TRES LECHES CAKE WITH STRAWBERRY PAVÉ, *recipe follows*

MY SISTER'S FAVORITE LEMON-BLUEBERRY BUNDT CAKE, *page 20*

BANANA PUDDING ICE CREAM CAKE, *page 162*

Try a Mango Margarita

I recently had the pleasure of traveling to Mexico to learn how to make tequila. Tequila is made by hand and reflects both the terroir of the highlands (the valley soil in which the blue agave plant is grown) and the heart and soul of the distillers. It is a fascinating industry that combines old-fashioned, traditional methods and new science and technology in equal parts. And, of course, tequila is delicious and fun to drink.

While I was in Jalisco—the state that almost all tequilas come from—I visited the Patrón distillery. As I tasted, it occurred to me that their liqueur might be a great substitute for the Grand Marnier that I usually use in a margarita. My thought was that the liqueur would add just the tiniest amount of sugar and a fruity component to complement the tequila and citrus juice. So, the skinny margarita would be a little smoother than the traditional tequila and lime juice version, with no need to add agave syrup or sugar. I couldn't wait to test my theory, so that night, I asked Oscar, the bartender at the distillery, to help me make skinny margaritas with the four flavors of the Patrón liqueurs: orange, lime, mango, and pineapple.

He happily agreed and made four margaritas, the only difference being the flavor of the liqueur. A group of us tasted them all blind, and the overwhelming winner was the mango liqueur. When I came home, I made a batch of the margaritas using Meyer lemons, because they are sweeter than a traditional lemon or lime, so the juice would highlight, not overpower, the delicate mango flavor.

The results were even better than what I envisioned, and I hope you'll agree. This new margarita is my choice for a Cinco de Mayo celebration and the summer months. The drink is refreshing and smooth without being sweet at all. You can taste the real Ataulfo (aka Champagne) mangoes that the liqueur is made with, and the sweet-tart Meyer lemon juice is just sour enough to make it a margarita.

When I thought about how to garnish the margarita, I decided to incorporate a tip from the master tequillier of Cazadores. Tania Oseguera is one of the few female tequilliers, and her favorite accompaniment to sipping tequila is a cut orange whose edge has been dipped in ground cinnamon. This beats the heck out of the lime and salt tradition and complements the rich, fresh flavors of the tequila. Even though it was designed for a glass of neat tequila, I decided to try it with my mango margarita. I used a slice of the Meyer lemon, since I already had one cut, but you could use Tania's favorite, the orange. Both work well for this cocktail. Cheers!

Skinny Mango Margarita

Makes 2 drinks

  Ice cubes

  2 ounces (¼ cup) fresh-squeezed Meyer lemon juice

  1½ ounces favorite silver tequila

  1 ounce Patrón Mango Liqueur

  Crushed ice

  Ground cinnamon

  Meyer lemon or orange slice, cut in half for garnish

Fill a cocktail shaker with ice cubes. Add the lemon juice, tequila, and mango liqueur and shake to combine. Strain into two short rocks glasses filled with crushed ice. Spread a thin layer of cinnamon on a small plate. Dip the side of each half lemon or orange slice into the cinnamon and use them to garnish the glasses. I make a cut in the center of the slice with a paring knife so that it slips over the rim of the glass more easily.

Note: 1 ounce is equal to 2 tablespoons. If you don't have an ounce measure, you can use a tablespoon. Enjoy!

MARGARITA TRES LECHES CAKE

WITH STRAWBERRY PAVÉ

THE CAKE

res leches is a popular Mexican cake that is soaked in three milks (*tres leches*) after it is baked. The milk-soaked cake lends itself to lots of flavors, and in my version, the bright lime-orange of a classic margarita is the perfect counterpoint to the sweet milks. There are lots of different recipes for *tres leches* cake, so my sister Mary Pat and I had a *tres leches* cake-off. The short story is that she won! Being the good loser that I am, I congratulated her, then immediately took the best of what she did (as sisters are wont to do) and rolled it into my recipe. One thing that distinguishes my sister's version is that all the liquid is poured on the cake at once, and it absorbs overnight in the refrigerator. I never thought that would work. But it works beautifully. I've added the spirits from my favorite margarita, which cut the sweetness of the milks, and a layer of pavé strawberries because they add a colorful burst of fresh fruit to the presentation. Just remember that the cake has to be made the day before you serve it.

Serves 12 to 16

FOR THE CAKE

Baking spray, for preparing the pan

1 cup all-purpose flour

1½ teaspoons baking powder

¼ teaspoon fine sea salt

5 large eggs, at room temperature

1 cup granulated white sugar

⅓ cup whole milk or half-and-half

1 generous teaspoon pure vanilla extract

FOR THE SOAKING LIQUID

1 can (14 ounces) sweetened condensed milk

1 can (12 ounces) evaporated milk

½ cup heavy (whipping) cream

Pinch of fine sea salt

2 tablespoons tequila (optional)

2 tablespoons orange liqueur, such as Cointreau, or zest of 1 orange

FOR THE TOPPING

1½ cups heavy (whipping) cream

1 tablespoon orange liqueur, such as Cointreau, or zest of 1 orange

2 tablespoons confectioners' sugar

½ teaspoon pure vanilla extract

Zest of 1 lime

1 pound fresh strawberries, trimmed and thinly sliced

Pan: 9 x 13-inch glass or porcelain baking dish

❶ Position a rack in the center of the oven and preheat the oven to 350°F. Spray the baking dish with baking spray.

❷ Make the cake: Whisk together the flour, baking powder, and salt in a medium-size bowl. Separate the eggs, putting the whites in a second medium-size bowl and the yolks in the bowl of an electric stand mixer (or a large mixing bowl).

3 Beat the yolks and ¾ cup of the granulated sugar with the mixer on medium speed until the mixture is pale and creamy, about 2 minutes. Add the milk and 1 teaspoon vanilla and beat until combined, about 1 minute more. Transfer the yolk mixture to a large bowl and set aside. Thoroughly wash and dry the mixer bowl and beaters.

4 Pour the egg whites into the mixer bowl and, using the whisk attachment, whisk on medium-low, gradually increasing the speed to medium-high, until the whites reach soft peaks, 2 to 3 minutes. Add the remaining ¼ cup sugar gradually, continuing to beat on medium-high, until you see firm peaks, 1 to 2 minutes more.

5 Slowly add the flour mixture to the yolk mixture and mix by hand until thoroughly combined. Gently fold in the egg whites by hand, in 3 separate batches.

6 Pour the batter into the prepared pan and lightly tap the pan down on the counter to make sure the batter is evenly distributed and to remove excess air bubbles.

7 Bake until a toothpick inserted in the center comes out clean, 30 to 35 minutes. Let the cake cool completely in the pan on a wire cooling rack.

8 Make the soaking liquid: Stir together the condensed milk, evaporated milk, ½ cup cream, salt, tequila (if using), and 2 tablespoons orange liqueur or orange zest until well blended. Pour into a 4-cup measuring cup or a bowl with a lip.

THE MATCHUPS

STEAK TACOS WITH 1-2-3 GUACAMOLE, CARROT-JALAPEÑO RELISH, AND CHIPOTLE CREMA, *page 147*

COWBOY STEAK WITH WHISKEY BUTTER, *page 5*

SKIRT STEAK WITH CHILE-LIME RUB AND CRUNCHY JICAMA SLAW, *page 138*

---

9 With a toothpick, poke the cake all over, going all the way to the bottom, making holes about ¼ inch apart. Pour the soaking liquid slowly over the whole cake, starting at the edges and pausing to let it soak in before adding more. Cover loosely with plastic wrap and refrigerate overnight.

10 Just before serving, make the topping: Beat the 1½ cups cream with an electric mixer on medium speed. When it begins to thicken, slowly add the 1 tablespoon orange liqueur, confectioners' sugar, and ½ teaspoon vanilla, and continue to beat just until it holds firm peaks, 3 to 4 minutes—do not overbeat. Spread the whipped cream all over the top of the cake and sprinkle the lime zest over it. Add the sliced strawberries in an overlapping fashion. Serve immediately.

Making Tres Leches to Suit Your Taste

Tres leches is one of those cakes that easily adapts to your taste. I like to think of it as the cake version of ice cream. Like ice cream, the delicate milks, and the sweet cake, too, lend themselves to all your favorite flavors. I particularly like orange—like a Creamsicle—and coffee. Try coconut and substitute a can of coconut milk for the evaporated milk. Or use mango, chocolate, rich vanilla, banana, strawberry, raspberry, almond, hazelnut . . . even pumpkin. You can take the basic recipe and customize it to your taste and to the seasons. And, don't forget to flavor the whipping cream as well.

FLATIRON STEAK

SMOTHERED IN CARAMELIZED ONIONS

AND

ANTHONY'S GRANDMOTHER'S "EARTHQUAKE CAKE"

THE STEAK

When I was at the offices of Certified Angus Beef in Wooster, Ohio, I broke down a side of beef with their team of steak whisperers. We set certain pieces aside and cooked them, tasting them along the way. The last steak of the day was a flatiron steak that I cooked in the rain on one of their many Weber grills. Despite the weather, it was the best bite of the day! The full flavor of flatiron steak is often described as slightly "livery"—which may help explain why it is so delicious when served smothered in caramelized onions.

Serves 4

2 flatiron steaks (about 12 ounces each)

Extra-virgin olive oil

1 teaspoon kosher salt

1 teaspoon whole black peppercorns, coarsely ground

Caramelized Onions (recipe follows)

Grilling Method: Direct/Medium-High Heat

❶ Preheat the grill with all burners on high. Once preheated, adjust the temperature to medium-high heat for direct grilling.

❷ Wrap the meat in paper towels to rid it of excess moisture. Replace the paper towels as needed.

❸ Just before grilling, brush both sides of the steaks with oil and season with salt and pepper.

❹ Place the steaks on the cooking grate over medium-high heat for about 4 minutes. Turn the steaks and continue cooking for 3 to 4 more minutes for medium-rare.

❺ Remove the steaks from the grill and allow them to rest for at least 5 minutes but no longer than 10.

❻ Top the steaks with the Caramelized Onions and serve.

Butcher Tip

The flatiron steak is cut from the chuck. Its official name is shoulder top blade steak. It is cut in a way that eliminates the connective tissue that normally runs through the center; each half resembles a flank steak in shape. These pieces are then cut crosswise into individual steaks. (See the Steak Primer Grid, page 204, for more information.)

CARAMELIZED ONIONS

These can be made up to two days in advance and refrigerated in an airtight container until you are ready to make the steak.

Makes 1 cup

1 tablespoon unsalted butter

2 tablespoons extra-virgin olive oil

3 large yellow onions, peeled and sliced into thin rings

1 teaspoon kosher salt

Melt the butter in the oil in a large, heavy-bottomed sauté pan over medium heat. Add the onion rings and salt and cook, covered, for 20 minutes, stirring occasionally. Remove the cover and cook, stirring occasionally, until the onions are all a deep golden color, about 20 minutes more. Turn off the heat and leave the onions in the pan until ready to serve. When ready to serve, turn the heat back on to warm through.

THE MATCHUPS

ANTHONY'S GRANDMOTHER'S "EARTHQUAKE CAKE," *recipe follows*

OLD VIRGINIA'S BEST POUND CAKE, *page 118*

THE ORIGINAL PB&J CUPCAKES, *page 167*

ANTHONY'S GRANDMOTHER'S "EARTHQUAKE CAKE"

THE CAKE

When my friend and Texas native Anthony Underwood mentioned his grandmother's Earthquake Cake, the name instantly hooked me. Anthony went on to explain that "the cake gets its name from its craggy, cavernous appearance. During baking, the cake rises to the top, the cream cheese mixture sinks to the middle, and the coconut and pecans create a delicious, crust-like bottom layer. When you take it out of the oven, the cake looks like it was caught in an earthquake! And, naturally, she would serve it with Blue Bell vanilla ice cream to cut the richness." One of Anthony's most prized possessions is his grandmother's hand-written recipe card for Earthquake Cake. According to the faded card, "Mama" (as he called her) used a cake mix. My instinct was to see if I could improve on it by starting with a from-scratch cake, but I found that I actually liked the cake mix version better—which proves once again that Mama always knows best!

Serves 18

Butter, for preparing the pan

2 scant cups chopped pecans

2 scant cups sweetened dried coconut, such as Baker's Sweetened Angel Flake Coconut

1 box Betty Crocker German Chocolate Cake mix (or use the German Chocolate Sheet Cake recipe on page 128)

1½ cups water

3 large eggs

½ cup vegetable oil

8 tablespoons (1 stick) butter, melted

1 teaspoon pure vanilla extract

8 ounces cream cheese, at room temperature

1 box (1 pound) confectioners' sugar

Pan: 9 x 13-inch cake pan

❶ Position a rack in the center of the oven and preheat the oven to 350°F. Generously butter the baking pan. Sprinkle the chopped pecans and coconut around the bottom of the baking pan, evenly distributing both.

2 Mix the cake batter according to box instructions, using the 1½ cups water, eggs, and vegetable oil. Pour the batter over the layer of coconut and pecans.

3 Combine the melted butter, vanilla, and cream cheese in the bowl of an electric mixer fitted with the paddle attachment. Beat on a low speed until the butter and cream cheese are smooth—the mixture will look curdled at first but will eventually become smooth, 2 to 3 minutes. Add the confectioners' sugar a little at a time. Beat on low so the sugar doesn't go flying. The mixture should look smooth and creamy. Stop the machine and scrape down the side of the bowl as necessary.

4 Dollop the cream cheese mixture over the cake batter. Using a butter knife, gently swirl the mixture into the chocolate batter to create a marbling effect (do this sparingly; you don't want to create an entirely marbled cake).

5 Bake until the cake pulls away from the sides of the pan and a toothpick inserted in the center of the chocolate batter comes out clean, 50 to 60 minutes.

6 Let cool in the pan on a wire cooling rack for at least 1 hour before serving. It can be served warm, at room temperature, or chilled. Store leftover cake, covered, in the refrigerator.

THE MATCHUPS

FLATIRON STEAK SMOTHERED
IN CARAMELIZED ONIONS, *page 152*

CECE'S CAST-IRON LEMON STEAK, *page 28*

NEW YORK STRIP WITH RED WINE BUTTER AND
SPINACH ARTICHOKE CASSEROLE, *page 47*

STEAK FRITES

WITH DIJON BÉARNAISE

AND

BROWN SUGAR POUND CAKE

WITH SAUTÉED APPLES AND CALVADOS WHIPPED CREAM

THE STEAK

Steak Frites will never go out of style! It is a marriage of everyone's favorite foods. I make this most often with hanger steak, known as *onglet* in France, because it delivers a delicious rich and beefy flavor. When paired with *frites*, it is truly *magnifique*!

Serves 4

> 2 hanger steaks (about 1 pound each and 12 inches long)
>
> Extra-virgin olive oil
>
> 1 teaspoon kosher salt
>
> 1 teaspoon whole black peppercorns, coarsely ground
>
> Grilled Frites with Dijon Béarnaise (page 184) or Dijon Butter (page 185)

Grilling Method: Direct/Medium Heat

1 Preheat the grill with all burners on high. Once preheated, adjust the temperature to medium heat for direct grilling.

2 Wrap the meat in paper towels to rid it of excess moisture. Replace the paper towels as needed.

❸ Brush both sides of the steaks with olive oil and season with salt and pepper.

❹ Place the steaks on the cooking grate over medium heat for about 5 minutes. Turn the steaks and continue cooking for 4 to 5 minutes more for medium-rare.

❺ Remove the steaks from the grill and allow them to rest at least 5 minutes but no longer than 10 before serving. Serve with the Grilled Frites with Dijon Béarnaise or Dijon Butter.

Note: The hanger steak "hangs" from the diaphragm of the cow and has a delicious rich and beefy flavor. If the steak is trimmed into two thin, round pieces and served medium-rare, it is both tender and full of

flavor. Sometimes known as the butcher's cut, it must be sliced against the grain just like a flank steak. If you can't find hanger steak, or it is too assertive for you, use your favorite steak and adjust the timing.

THE MATCHUPS

BROWN SUGAR POUND CAKE WITH SAUTÉED APPLES AND CALVADOS WHIPPED CREAM, *recipe follows*

TURTLE BROWNIE BITES, *page 58*

BAKED RICOTTA CHEESECAKE WITH McVITIE'S CRUST, *page 121*

BROWN SUGAR POUND CAKE

WITH SAUTÉED APPLES AND CALVADOS WHIPPED CREAM

___

THE CAKE

This lovely fall dessert has a fancier presentation than a homey apple cake but all the same great flavors. It can also be beautifully baked in some of the smaller shaped pans that Nordic Ware makes, my favorite of which is the ribbed square pan.

Serves 12

Baking spray, for preparing the pan

1 cup (2 sticks) unsalted butter, at room temperature

1 cup (packed) light brown sugar

4 large eggs

1 teaspoon vanilla bean paste or pure vanilla extract

1 tablespoon Calvados or other apple brandy

1¾ cups all-purpose flour

½ teaspoon baking powder

¼ teaspoon fine sea salt

¼ teaspoon ground cardamom

Sautéed Apples (recipe follows)

Calvados Whipped Cream (recipe follows)

Pan(s): 9 x 5 x 3-inch loaf pan or 10-cup Bundt pan; sheet pan, if using a loaf pan

1 Position a rack in the center of the oven and preheat the oven to 350°F. Spray the cake pan with baking spray.

2 Cream the butter and sugar together with an electric mixer at medium-high speed until light and very fluffy, 3 to 5 minutes. Add the eggs one at a time, beating well after each addition. Add the vanilla and Calvados.

3 Whisk the flour, baking powder, salt, and cardamom together in a small bowl. Add the flour mixture to the butter mixture in batches, beating well after each addition. Stop the mixer to scrape down the side of the bowl as necessary.

4 Pour the batter into the prepared pan. Lightly tap the cake pan down on the counter to make sure the batter is evenly distributed and to remove excess air bubbles.

5 If using a loaf pan, place it on a sheet pan to make it easier to pull it out of the hot oven. Bake until the cake pulls away from the sides of the pan or a toothpick inserted in the center comes out clean, 30 to 35 minutes in a loaf pan, 50 to 60 minutes in a Bundt pan. Begin testing for doneness at 40 minutes.

6 Cool in the pan for 5 minutes before removing from the pan to a wire cooling rack to cool completely. Serve thick slices with the Sautéed Apples and Calvados Whipped Cream.

Note: You can turn this cake into Bourbon Brown Sugar Pound Cake by substituting bourbon for the Calvados.

___

THE MATCHUPS

STEAK FRITES WITH DIJON BÉARNAISE,
page 155

CECE'S CAST-IRON LEMON STEAK,
page 28

ELIZABETH'S STEAK BURGER WITH ROASTED SHALLOT AND BACON MARMALADE,
page 164

SAUTÉED APPLES

Sautéing tart, crunchy fall apples in butter with a little cinnamon sugar transforms them into one of the best bites on Earth. They have all the flavors of apple pie, minus the crust! Add a slice of brown sugar pound cake and whipped cream, and you've got fall on a plate.

Makes about 3 cups cooked apples

> ¼ cup granulated white sugar
>
> 2 teaspoons ground cinnamon
>
> Pinch of fine sea salt
>
> 5 cups peeled and sliced Granny Smith or other favorite apples
>
> 4 tablespoons (½ stick) unsalted butter
>
> 1 tablespoon fresh lemon juice
>
> 1 tablespoon Calvados or other apple brandy

1 Mix the sugar, cinnamon, and salt together in a large bowl and toss with the apples. Let sit for 2 to 3 minutes, until the apples begin to give up some of their juices.

2 Melt the butter in a heavy-bottomed saucepan over medium heat. Stir in the apples with the sugar mixture and juices, then add the lemon juice and Calvados and bring to a boil, stirring frequently. Reduce the heat to low and let simmer until the apples are slightly softened, 5 minutes.

3 Serve the apples while hot with slices of the pound cake and dollops of whipped cream.

CALVADOS WHIPPED CREAM

Adding Calvados to the whipped cream rounds out the apple flavors in this comforting fall dessert. In case you aren't familiar with Calvados, it is apple brandy from the Calvados region of Normandy. The apples are pressed into a cider, which is fermented and distilled. It is aged in oak casks for 2 years before being bottled and sold as Calvados.

Makes about 2 cups

> 1 pint heavy (whipping) cream, chilled
>
> 1 tablespoon superfine sugar (see box)
>
> Pinch of fine sea salt
>
> 1 to 2 tablespoons Calvados or other apple brandy

1 Place a large bowl and electric mixer beater blades (preferably the whisk attachment) in the freezer for a minimum of 15 minutes.

2 Pour the chilled cream and the sugar into the cold bowl and beat on medium-high until soft peaks form, 2 to 3 minutes.

3 Sprinkle in the salt and add the Calvados in a steady stream, beating constantly until stiff peaks form, another 2 to 3 minutes. Refrigerate until ready to serve.

What Is Superfine Sugar?

I prefer using superfine sugar here because it dissolves more quickly than regular granulated sugar. You can buy superfine sugar or make your own by placing sugar in a food processor and processing for a few seconds, until the sugar is of a finer texture. This is a good trick to know if you love Sugar in the Raw, as I do, and want to use it instead of granulated white sugar. The finer the grain, the more quickly it will dissolve. This is not the same as confectioners' sugar, which is processed until it is powder and has added cornstarch.

HANGER STEAK

WITH GARLIC SMASHED POTATOES

AND

BANANA PUDDING ICE CREAM CAKE

THE STEAK

My Garlic Smashed Potatoes are the one side dish in this book that I make over and over again all year long. My friend David Lineweaver requests them every time I make steak. And they make an appearance at nearly every dinner party because it is the dish that gets the most requests for seconds . . . and thirds! I love the way the fluffy baked potatoes and crispy, salty skin are mixed together with fragrant garlic, sharp green extra-virgin olive oil, and fresh basil into a creamy smash-up exploding with flavor.

A grilled hanger steak is a favorite pairing because the assertiveness of the steak stands up to the rich flavor of the potatoes.

Serves 4 to 6

2 hanger steaks or other favorite steak (about 1 pound each)

Extra-virgin olive oil

Kosher salt and freshly ground black pepper

Salted butter, at room temperature

Chopped fresh parsley, for garnish (optional)

Garlic Smashed Potatoes (page 185)

Grilling Method: Direct/Medium Heat

❶ Preheat the grill with all burners on high. Once preheated, adjust the temperature to medium for direct grilling.

❷ Wrap the meat in paper towels to rid it of excess moisture. Replace the paper towels as needed.

❸ Lightly brush both sides of the steaks with olive oil and season both sides with salt and pepper, pressing the spices lightly into the meat.

❹ Place the steaks on the cooking grate over direct heat for 4 to 5 minutes. Turn the steaks and grill for 4 to 5 minutes more for medium-rare; an instant-read thermometer will read 135°F.

❺ Remove the steaks from the grill to a clean platter. Allow to rest for 5 minutes. Serve the steaks warm, with the butter spread on top. For a restaurant touch, garnish with chopped parsley, if desired. Serve with a big bowl of the Garlic Smashed Potatoes.

THE MATCHUPS

BANANA PUDDING ICE CREAM CAKE, *recipe follows*

CHOCOLATE LAYER CAKE WITH
COCOA-FRANGELICO FROSTING, *page 38*

THE ORIGINAL PB&J CUPCAKES, *page 167*

BANANA PUDDING ICE CREAM CAKE

THE CAKE

I created this cake in one of my classes at ICE (the Institute of Culinary Education). I was lucky enough to have two amazing assistants there, Andrew Lavenski and Vanessa Feliu, who both went on to help me open Hill Country Barbecue Market. Andrew still helps me at events, and Vanessa was one of Hill Country's opening pastry chefs. During the class, Andrew and Vanessa challenged me to make my famous banana pudding into a banana pudding ice cream cake. This is the result of that challenge. It has all the flavor of a from-scratch banana pudding in an ice cream cake—and it will feed a crowd!

Serves 20 to 24

3 pints best-quality vanilla ice cream

Ice cubes

1 cup (2 sticks) unsalted butter

¾ cup (packed) dark brown sugar

1 teaspoon pure vanilla extract

½ teaspoon freshly grated nutmeg

Pinch of fine sea salt

8 ripe bananas, peeled and thinly sliced

¼ cup plus a little more (generous pour) dark rum, preferably Cruzan Single Barrel

1 tablespoon 99 Bananas liqueur

2 cups heavy (whipping) cream

1 tablespoon confectioners' sugar (optional)

1 large box (about 11 ounces) Nilla Wafers

Pan: 9 x 13-inch cake pan

❶ Let the ice cream sit in the refrigerator for 30 minutes to soften—but you don't want it to reach a liquid state.

❷ Prepare an ice bath: Choose a bowl that's large enough to hold another large bowl. Fill the first large bowl with ice and add enough water to make the ice begin to melt. Set it aside.

❸ Melt the butter and brown sugar together in a large skillet over medium heat. When the mixture is bubbly, add the vanilla, nutmeg, and salt. Stir to combine. Add the bananas and sauté, stirring to coat them with the butter mixture. Don't worry if the butter and sugar appear to separate. When the bananas are warmed through and beginning to soften, turn off the burner and add the rum. Because it might flambé, be sure there is nothing flammable around the skillet (roll up your sleeves, tie your hair back). If it doesn't flambé, that's fine too. Using a fork, mash the bananas, leaving some pieces whole and some larger than others.

❹ Transfer the bananas to the second large bowl and cool them down by placing the bowl in the ice bath. When cool, mix the bananas with the softened ice cream. Remove 3 cups and set it aside in the refrigerator. Place the remaining mixture in the bowl in the freezer until partially frozen, about 1 hour.

❺ Meanwhile, add the banana liqueur to the cream and whip the cream until it holds soft peaks. Taste, and if you like things sweeter, add 1 tablespoon of confectioners' sugar. Continue whipping until the cream holds very stiff peaks; set aside in the refrigerator.

❻ Measure out 1 cup of Nilla Wafers and place them in a food processor. Process the cookies until you have crumbs. Set the crumbs aside. Line the bottom and sides of the cake pan with the remaining whole wafers.

⑦ When the ice cream–banana mixture has been in the freezer for about 1 hour, fold the whipped cream into the reserved *refrigerated* 3 cups of ice cream–banana mixture and set aside for topping. Spoon the *frozen* ice cream mixture over the wafers. Smooth it out to the edges and top with a layer of the whipped cream mixture. Smooth that out.

⑧ Top with the cookie crumbs and place back into the freezer until ready to serve, but at least 3 hours.

THE MATCHUPS

HANGER STEAK WITH GARLIC SMASHED POTATOES,
page 161

CLASSIC NEW YORK STEAKHOUSE STRIP
WITH BEEFSTEAK TOMATOES AND SIZZLING THICK
BACON AND ONIONS, *page 41*

STEAK TACOS WITH 1-2-3 GUACAMOLE,
CARROT-JALAPEÑO RELISH, AND CHIPOTLE CREMA,
page 147

ELIZABETH'S STEAK BURGER

WITH ROASTED SHALLOT AND BACON MARMALADE

AND

THE ORIGINAL PB&J CUPCAKES

THE STEAK

You can make this steak burger with hanger steak and dry-aged ribeye or a combination of chuck and sirloin. My basic burger is enhanced with Worcestershire sauce and dry mustard, making the burger taste meatier.

Serves 6

1⅓ pounds ground hanger steak and ⅔ pound ground dry-aged ribeye, or 2 pounds of your favorite blend

1 tablespoon Worcestershire sauce (optional)

1 teaspoon Colman's dry mustard (optional)

About ½ teaspoon kosher salt

About ½ teaspoon freshly ground black pepper

Extra-virgin olive oil

6 soft potato rolls, toasted

Roasted Shallot and Bacon Marmalade (page 170) and other favorite condiments, as desired

Grilling Method: Direct/Medium Heat

Special Equipment: Lodge cast-iron sizzle platter or a large cast-iron skillet

❶ Place the ground meats in a large bowl. Add the Worcestershire sauce and dry mustard, if using, and the salt and pepper. Mix just until combined. Be careful not to overwork the meat.

❷ Gently shape the meat into 6 burgers of equal size and thickness (about ¾ inch thick). Brush all over with a thin layer of olive oil. Make an imprint in the center of each burger with your thumb. Place on a platter, cover with plastic wrap, and refrigerate for at least 15 minutes or until ready to grill. (I like to make sure that the meat is cold because I'm placing it on a hot cast-iron platter.)

❸ Place the cast-iron sizzle platter or cast-iron skillet on the cooking grate and allow it to preheat with the grill. Preheat the grill with all burners on high. Once preheated, adjust the temperature to medium for direct grilling.

❹ When ready to grill, place the burgers on the sizzle platter (6 good-size burgers will fit on the platter). Cook until the meat is deeply crusted on the outside and medium-rare on the inside, 8 to 10 minutes, turning once halfway through the grilling time.

❺ Let rest 2 to 3 minutes and then serve on toasted potato rolls with the Roasted Shallot and Bacon Marmalade and other condiments of your choice.

THE MATCHUPS

THE ORIGINAL PB&J CUPCAKES,
recipe follows

RETRO CHOCOLATE CUPCAKES
WITH A SWEET MASCARPONE CENTER,
page 53

BANANA PUDDING ICE CREAM CAKE,
page 162

The Perfect Burger Blend

In advance of a recent dinner party that I was hosting with my friend Pete, I decided to test multiple combinations of ground beef to create the ultimate steak burger. (The burger blends that I had relied on for years were as simple as half sirloin and half chuck and as complex as a combination of sirloin, brisket, hanger steak, and dry-aged ribeye trimmings.) Pete and I ground seven different cuts of beef, some fresh and some dry-aged. We tested various combinations before settling on the blend of two-thirds hanger steak and one-third dry-aged ribeye. Grinding our own meat and testing the different blends were fun, but the best finding of the night was discovering that grilling the burgers on a preheated Lodge cast-iron sizzle platter resulted in an outstanding crust and a juicy, medium-rare interior. Whether you grind your own blend or buy your burger meat already ground, be sure to cook the burgers on a preheated cast-iron sizzle platter or a cast-iron skillet for steakhouse results.

THE MATCHUPS

THE ORIGINAL PB&J CUPCAKES

THE CAKE

Without braggadocio, I can say with full confidence that I created the PB&J cupcake. It was in 2006, when, as the executive chef, I developed the menu for Hill Country Barbecue Market in New York City. In fact, one of my partners at the restaurant loved saying that the PB&J cupcake was going to be my culinary legacy. I'm not sure about that, but when we opened in 2007, Hill Country was known for my PB&J cupcakes as much as it was known for barbecue. Countless customers bought them for weddings, birthdays, anniversaries, and every other special occasion. Now you can make them at home and brag about it too.

Makes 12 jumbo cupcakes or 24 regular cupcakes

11 tablespoons unsalted butter, at room temperature

1½ cups granulated white sugar

3 large eggs

2⅓ cups all-purpose flour

2½ teaspoons baking powder

1 teaspoon fine sea salt

1 cup whole milk

1½ teaspoons pure vanilla extract

1 small (9.5 ounce) jar grape jelly, preferably Welch's

Peanut Butter Icing (recipe follows)

Reese's Pieces, for decoration (optional)

Salted and roasted peanuts, chopped, for decoration (optional)

Pan(s): 1 jumbo Texas-size 12-cup cupcake tin or four 6-cup cupcake tins; cupcake liners

Special equipment: Piping bag with small round tip and extra-large star tip

1 Position an oven rack in the center of the oven and preheat the oven to 350°F. Line the cupcake cups with paper liners.

2 Cream the butter and sugar together with a handheld mixer on medium-high speed until very fluffy, 3 to 5 minutes. Then add the eggs one at a time, beating well after each addition.

3 Whisk the flour, baking powder, and salt together in another bowl. In a third bowl, stir the milk and vanilla together. Add the flour and the milk to the butter mixture alternately in batches mixing until the batter is smooth and silky in texture. Stop the mixer and scrape down the side of the bowl as necessary.

4 Fill each prepared cupcake cup about half full with batter. This makes the baked cupcakes flatter and easier to decorate with the icing.

5 Bake until the tops are golden brown and a toothpick inserted in the center comes out clean, 20 to 25 minutes. If you are using a jumbo Texas-size cupcake tin, they will take a little longer to bake. Remove the tins from the oven and let cool for 5 minutes in the tin. Then remove the cupcakes to wire cooling racks and let cool completely, about 20 minutes.

6 Stir the jelly while it's still in the jar with a fork or spoon to loosen it up. Pour the jelly into a piping bag fitted with a small round tip. Gently push the tip into a cupcake and gently squeeze the bag to fill the cupcake with 1 to 2 teaspoons of jelly, depending on the size of your cupcakes. Repeat with the remaining cupcakes. The cupcakes can be frozen at this point; if not freezing, ice the cupcakes.

7 Fill a piping bag fitted with an extra-large star tip with the icing. Pipe the icing decoratively on the cupcakes. Or, alternatively, spoon a heaping tablespoon of Peanut Butter Icing on each cupcake and spread it out to cover the top. Decorate with Reese's Pieces and chopped peanuts, if using.

PEANUT BUTTER ICING

Please don't substitute freshly ground peanut butter (such as is often sold at health food stores) for the Skippy in this recipe. The emulsified peanut butter is far superior in terms of taste and texture for the icing—in fact, the freshly ground kind will separate out and you will have a mess.

Makes enough to frost 12 jumbo (Texas-size) or 24 regular-size cupcakes

1 cup (2 sticks) unsalted butter, at room temperature

Generous ½ cup Skippy Smooth Peanut Butter

2 cups confectioners' sugar, sifted

1½ teaspoons pure vanilla extract

⅛ teaspoon fine sea salt, or more if needed

Cream the butter and peanut butter together with a handheld mixer on medium-high speed until smooth, about 5 minutes. Add the confectioners' sugar a little at a time. Stir in the vanilla and salt. Taste and add more salt, if necessary. Continue beating until the mixture is pale brown and very fluffy, another 3 to 5 minutes. You will notice that the color changes the longer you whip. Use the icing to top the cupcakes.

SOMETHING ON THE SIDE

ROASTED SHALLOT AND BACON MARMALADE

Although this savory jam takes a little while to make, you'll be glad you have it on hand to top a quick grilled burger or steak or to serve with your favorite cheeses. It is also great spread over grilled bread, with or without a little butter! *Makes about 4 cups*

2 pounds shallots (about 24), peeled

Extra-virgin olive oil

Kosher salt

6 ounces garlic (30 to 40 cloves), peeled

1 cup turbinado sugar, such as Sugar in the Raw

¼ cup honey

2 cups red wine vinegar

1 cup spring water

2 tablespoons distilled white vinegar

2 tablespoons Cognac

Leaves from 4 sprigs fresh thyme or 2 teaspoons dried thyme

2 pounds (or closest equivalent if buying packaged) thick-cut smoked bacon, diced, cooked, and drained (see Note)

❶ Preheat the oven to 400°F.

❷ Coat the shallots in olive oil and sprinkle them generously with salt—about 1 teaspoon. Lay them on a wire rack set on a sheet pan.

❸ Place a double layer of large sheets of aluminum foil on your work surface. Make a second set of layered foil. Divide the garlic cloves between the 2 sets of foil and drizzle each with oil and sprinkle each with about ¼ teaspoon salt. Toss to make sure each clove is oiled and seasoned. Close up the foil to make packets (the garlic doesn't have to be in a flat layer), making sure the top and ends are tightly sealed. Place both the pan of shallots and the garlic in the foil packets in the oven and roast until both the shallots and garlic

are well caramelized but not mushy, 30 to 45 minutes, checking occasionally to make sure that they aren't burning. Stir if necessary.

❹ Meanwhile, mix the sugar, honey, red wine vinegar, water, white vinegar, Cognac, 1 tablespoon salt, and thyme in a large, heavy-bottomed, nonreactive saucepan. Set the pan over medium heat. Stir to make sure the salt and sugar are dissolved. Add the roasted shallots and garlic and stir gently. Bring to a boil, then reduce the heat and simmer, stirring occasionally, until the shallots are translucent and soft enough to smash, about 2 hours. Smash the shallots and garlic; it will look like a soft and chunky jam. Add the cooked bacon and let simmer for 5 minutes more.

❺ Taste and adjust the seasoning, if necessary, with a splash of vinegar. Remove from the heat and let cool. Once cool, stir well and serve, or transfer to glass Mason jars with tight-fitting lids. The jam will keep in the refrigerator for about 2 weeks.

Note: The easiest way to cook this amount of diced bacon is in a large skillet over low heat, stirring occasionally. Once cooked, remove to several layers of paper towels to drain.

ELIZABETH'S CARROT-JALAPEÑO RELISH

I love this relish with any grilled or roasted meat, including beer-can chicken, but I have also been known to top a block of cream cheese with it, making a quick and crave-able appetizer. Serve with whole wheat crackers and your favorite libation. Like me, you may like it so much that you keep it on hand year-round. *Makes about 4 cups*

3 pounds carrots, peeled and coarsely grated

1 cup thinly sliced shallots (about 6 shallots)

6 to 10 jalapeños or assorted hot peppers, seeded and sliced into thin rings

3 cups distilled white vinegar

Pickling Spice

2 cups granulated white sugar or Sugar in the Raw

2 tablespoons kosher salt

2 teaspoons pickling spice

2 teaspoons red chile pepper flakes (optional)

1 teaspoon whole cloves

1 teaspoon whole black peppercorns

Special equipment: 3 pint-size or 2 quart-size canning jars and lids, sterilized and ready for canning (see Note)

❶ Place the carrots, shallots, and jalapeños in a large stockpot and set aside.

❷ Combine the vinegar, sugar, salt, pickling spice, chile flakes (if using), cloves, and peppercorns in a separate, heavy-bottomed stockpot and bring to a boil over high heat. When the vinegar mixture is boiling, pour it over the vegetables and stir continuously with a long-handled wooden spoon. Be careful not to let the boiling vinegar splash, because it could cause a burn. The boiling vinegar should cook the vegetables enough; you want them to be brightly colored and crunchy. Cool the vegetables in the vinegar to room temperature.

❸ When the vegetables have cooled, divide them among the prepared canning jars, leaving a 3-inch headspace in each. Bring the remaining liquid to a boil again and divide it among the jars. You want there to be a high liquid-to-relish ratio. Make sure that the liquid level is about ½ inch above the relish and leave another ½-inch space below the top seam of the jar.

④ Place the canning lids and rings on the jars and tighten them. Turn the hot jars upside down so that all the heat is on the seals. Turn them back upright when the jars are completely cool. As they cool, you will hear a popping noise as they seal. After the relish cools, you can start to use it immediately. Store in the refrigerator for up to 6 months.

Note: I wash and sterilize my jars, lids, and rings in the dishwasher, timing it so the cycle is done and the jars are hot when I am ready to pack them.

SAVORY ROSEMARY SHORTBREAD

The rosemary scent makes this Scottish staple into a buttery savory biscuit that is more cracker than cookie. Try it as a side with any of your favorite steak preparations and a nice glass of Scotch on the rocks. *Makes about 24 shortbreads*

- 1 cup (2 sticks) butter, at room temperature
- ½ cup (packed) light brown sugar
- 2 tablespoons poppy seeds
- 1 teaspoon Maldon flaky sea salt
- 1 teaspoon dried rosemary
- ¼ teaspoon dried thyme
- 2 to 2¼ cups all-purpose flour, plus flour for the work surface

❶ Preheat the oven to 325°F. Lightly flour a work surface.

❷ Cream the butter and brown sugar together in a large bowl with an electric mixer until light and fluffy, 3 to 5 minutes. Add the poppy seeds, salt, rosemary, and thyme and mix well. Add 1¾ cups of the flour and mix again.

❸ Remove the dough from the bowl to the prepared work surface. Knead the dough for 5 minutes, adding enough of the remaining flour to form a soft dough.

❹ Flour the work surface again and roll the dough out to ½ inch thick. Cut into strips. Place the strips 1 inch apart on ungreased baking sheets. Prick the strips all over with a fork.

❺ Bake until the shortbread is lightly browned and fragrant, 20 to 25 minutes. Let sit on the baking sheet for 5 minutes before moving to a wire cooling rack. Store extra shortbread in an airtight container for up to 1 week.

YORKSHIRE PUDDING

This giant popover is known "across the pond" as Yorkshire pudding and is served most often to accompany rich, beefy roasts. In England, it is traditionally made with the beef drippings, but if you are grilling, you won't be catching the drippings—and I prefer the taste of butter any way. *Serves 8*

- 1 cup all-purpose flour
- ½ teaspoon fine sea salt
- Pinch of freshly grated or ground nutmeg
- 4 large eggs
- 1 cup whole milk
- 8 tablespoons (1 stick) unsalted butter

Pan: 9 x 13-inch porcelain, glass, stainless-steel, or cast-iron casserole pan or baking dish or popover pan for individual Yorkshire puddings

❶ Preheat the oven to 450°F.

❷ Stir together the flour, salt, and nutmeg in a small bowl.

❸ Beat the eggs and milk together in a medium-size bowl until light and foamy. Add the flour mixture and blend just until incorporated.

❹ Place the butter in the pan. Put the pan in the oven until the butter is melted and the pan is sizzling hot, 5 minutes.

❺ Carefully take the pan out of the oven and swirl the pan to coat the bottom with the butter. Slowly pour in

the batter. Put the pan back in the oven immediately and cook until the batter is crisp and crunchy on the edges and golden, puffed, and custardy in the center, 15 to 20 minutes. Serve immediately.

SUPER CELERY SALAD

This crunchy celery salad elevates the much maligned "rabbit food" to gourmet status. The secret is in slicing the celery paper-thin. The basic recipe is made great by a lemon vinaigrette and ribbons of hard cheese. It is also a perfect foundation for add-ins; depending on my mood or what I can find at the market, I fancy it up with fennel, mushrooms, apples, pears, beets—all thinly sliced—and/or walnuts, hazelnuts, or pomegranate seeds—even mâche. Try any other ingredients that suit your fancy. Just keep the three main ingredients consistent.

Serves 4

8 ribs celery, cleaned and trimmed

2 bars (2 ounces each) hard cheese, such as Manchego and/or Parmigiano-Reggiano

Juice of 1 to 2 lemons (about ⅓ cup)

⅔ cup extra-virgin olive oil

Kosher salt and freshly ground white pepper

White mushrooms, fennel, apples, pears, beets, walnuts, hazelnuts, pomegranate seeds, mâche, or mint (optional)

Special Equipment: Mandoline

❶ Slice the celery very thin, using a very sharp knife, mandoline, or food processor. Transfer the slices to a large bowl.

❷ Using a vegetable peeler, slice 18 to 24 "ribbons" off the bars of cheese and set aside.

❸ Make a dressing by whisking together the lemon juice and olive oil. Season to taste with salt and pepper.

❹ Toss the celery with just enough dressing to coat. Divide the salad among 4 plates and top each with 3 to 4 ribbons of cheese and any other optional ingredients, thinly sliced or chopped, depending on the ingredient. Add more dressing if needed. Serve immediately with more ground pepper at the table.

CLASSIC CAESAR SALAD

Some days, I literally crave a garlic-rich, pungent Caesar salad, and I know that I am not alone! More people download this recipe than any other on my website, proving that sometimes it doesn't pay to reinvent the wheel. If you want to put a spin on the classic, add leftover steak, slivers of sun-dried tomatoes, and niçoise olives when you toss the lettuce in the dressing. *Serves 2 to 4, depending on appetite*

> 1 large head romaine lettuce
>
> 1 teaspoon fine sea salt, or more if needed
>
> 1 teaspoon freshly ground black pepper, or more if needed
>
> 3 large or 5 small cloves garlic, or to taste, minced
>
> 1 to 2 anchovies or 2 teaspoons anchovy paste
>
> 1 tablespoon strong Dijon mustard
>
> Juice of 1 lemon
>
> 2 teaspoons Worcestershire sauce
>
> ½ to ⅔ cup extra-virgin olive oil
>
> ½ cup freshly grated Parmigiano-Reggiano cheese, plus more for garnish
>
> 1 cup croutons, preferably homemade

❶ Rinse the lettuce leaves and spin dry in a salad spinner or pat dry with paper towels. Cut the leaves into 1-inch pieces and set aside.

❷ Make the dressing by placing the salt, pepper, garlic, anchovies, and Dijon mustard in a bowl and mashing them together into a paste with the back of a spoon. Add the lemon juice and Worcestershire sauce and mix well. Slowly whisk in ½ cup of the olive oil until smooth and creamy, adding more oil if needed. Taste and add more salt and pepper, if needed. You can also make this dressing in a blender or a small food processor by combining the ingredients and pulsing until emulsified.

❸ To assemble the salad, toss the lettuce with enough dressing and cheese to coat the leaves. Divide among plates and top with croutons and a sprinkling of cheese. Serve immediately.

GRILLED HEARTS OF ROMAINE WITH HOMEMADE BLUE CHEESE DRESSING

This is the ultimate steakhouse wedge salad, created for blue cheese lovers! Grilled hearts of romaine are paired with the classic combination of a homemade blue cheese dressing and crispy applewood smoked bacon. The magic of the grill wilts and caramelizes the lettuce, intensifying the flavor and adding a wisp of smoke. The texture becomes crispy on the edges and silky inside. Mix that with the rich and slightly pungent blue cheese and the salty, smoky bacon and you've got a salad that eats like a main course. Make the dressing a day in advance and let it sit overnight to allow the garlic, shallots, and blue cheese to mellow and marry. *Serves 4*

FOR THE BLUE CHEESE DRESSING

> 1 cup mayonnaise, preferably Hellmann's or Best Foods
>
> ½ cup sour cream
>
> 4 to 8 ounces crumbled blue cheese, depending on taste
>
> 1½ tablespoons grated shallot
>
> 1 tablespoon fresh lemon juice
>
> 2 cloves garlic, peeled and grated with a Microplane
>
> Kosher salt and freshly ground black pepper, to taste

FOR THE SALAD

- 2 hearts romaine lettuce, cut in half lengthwise

- Extra-virgin olive oil

- Kosher salt and freshly ground black pepper

- 4 slices applewood smoked bacon, diced and cooked

Grilling Method: Direct/Medium Low Heat

❶ Make the dressing: Combine the dressing ingredients and refrigerate for at least 3 hours or preferably overnight (this lets the flavors develop). Store, covered, in the refrigerator until ready to use. This recipe will make 2 cups and keeps for 2 weeks in the refrigerator.

❷ Preheat the grill with all burners on high. Once preheated, adjust the temperature to medium-low heat for direct grilling.

❸ Lightly brush the lettuce all over with olive oil, taking care not to break the leaves. Sprinkle with salt and pepper. Using a pair of tongs, place the lettuce directly on the cooking grates, cut side down, for 2 to 3 minutes. Do not grill longer; the lettuce should be slightly raw and crunchy in the center. Move to a clean platter and let sit 5 minutes.

❹ Place half a heart of romaine on each plate, drizzle with blue cheese dressing, and sprinkle with bacon bits. Serve immediately.

Note: This blue cheese dressing can be used as a dip—and is the quintessential dip for wing lovers.

BLOODY MARY SALAD WITH HORSERADISH VINAIGRETTE

I f you love a Bloody Mary loaded with garnishes, you will love this salad! Pickled okra can be found in the condiment aisle of most grocery stores, or order it from Amazon or another favorite online grocer. The sharp and sweet horseradish dressing turns the garnishes into an official salad! Freshly grated horseradish can be found in small jars in the refrigerated case in

FOR THE HORSERADISH VINAIGRETTE

- ⅓ cup white wine vinegar

- 2 tablespoons drained freshly grated or prepared horseradish

- 1 tablespoon honey

- 1 teaspoon mayonnaise, preferably Hellmann's or Best Foods

- Pinch of sea salt and freshly ground black pepper

- ⅓ cup hot chili oil or ⅓ cup olive oil mixed with 1 teaspoon Tabasco

- ⅓ cup extra-virgin olive oil

FOR THE SALAD

- 2 dill pickles or pickled okra, cut into julienne strips

- 1 small shallot, peeled and sliced into thin rings

- 2 tablespoons brine from jar of pickles or okra

- 1 pound ripe small tomatoes (about 14), preferably Campari, cut into quarters

- 1 to 2 ribs celery, sliced thin

- 1 large carrot, peeled and sliced into ribbons with a vegetable peeler

- 1 generous tablespoon vodka (optional)

- Zest of 1 lemon

- 5 pimento-stuffed olives, cut in half lengthwise

❶ Make the vinaigrette: Whisk together the vinegar, horseradish, honey, mayonnaise, salt, and pepper in a small bowl. Slowly whisk in the chili oil, then the olive oil, making sure they are emulsified. Adjust the seasoning to taste with salt and pepper and use immediately or store in the refrigerator in a tightly sealed container for up to 5 days.

❷ Assemble the salad: Toss the pickles and shallot together with the pickle brine and let sit for at least 5 minutes.

3 Layer the tomatoes, celery, and carrot in a bowl and add the vodka, if using. Toss the vegetables with the vodka. Sprinkle the lemon zest over the base of the salad and top with the pickle-shallot mixture. Top that with the olives and vinaigrette. Toss and serve immediately.

AVOCADO AND TOMATO SALAD

Buy an assortment of cherry tomatoes to vary the taste and look of the salad. *Serves 4*

1 ripe avocado, preferably Hass

1 pint cherry tomatoes, cut in half

Juice of 2 limes (about 2 teaspoons)

1 tablespoon Roasted Garlic Paste (recipe follows)

¼ cup extra-virgin olive oil

Fine sea salt (optional)

6 sprigs fresh oregano

1 to 3 cups baby arugula, clover, microgreens, or mâche

❶ Pit, peel, and dice the avocado and place it in a large bowl. Add the cherry tomatoes and toss gently.

❷ Mix the lime juice and Roasted Garlic Paste together until smooth. Slowly add the olive oil and whisk until well mixed and emulsified. Taste for seasoning and add salt if necessary. Add the leaves from 2 sprigs of oregano and mix again.

❸ Divide the arugula or other greens among 4 plates and drizzle with the roasted garlic dressing. Top with the avocado-tomato mixture, garnish each plate with a sprig of fresh oregano, and serve.

Roasted Garlic Paste

Roasting garlic brings out its sweetness, and it is a welcome addition to salad dressings, blended butters, soups, and any number of meat and poultry dishes. Roasted garlic will keep for 2 days in an airtight container in the refrigerator. *Makes about ½ cup*

> 3 heads garlic
>
> 3 tablespoons extra-virgin olive oil, plus extra for drizzling
>
> Kosher salt

❶ Preheat the oven to 400°F.

❷ Remove the outer layer of papery skin from the garlic heads. Slice off ¼ inch from the pointy tops. Place each head on a separate sheet of aluminum foil, cut side up. Drizzle with olive oil and season with salt. Wrap each head in the foil, place on a sheet pan, and roast until the cloves are golden brown and soft, about 1 hour. Remove and let cool.

❸ Remove the roasted cloves from their skin and place them in a bowl by squeezing the whole head from the bottom. Using a fork, vigorously mix the garlic and the 3 tablespoons of oil together. Taste and add a pinch of salt, if needed.

BEEFSTEAK TOMATO AND VIDALIA ONION SALAD WITH STEAK SAUCE DRESSING

Peter Luger Steak House may be more famous for this simple salad than it is for its steaks—it is all about the Steak House Old-Fashioned Sauce. If you live near New York City, you can buy the sauce at most grocery stores; if not, look for it on Amazon. However, I have made my version of the sauce based on taste memory. Be sure to make it at least a day ahead of serving to let all the flavors meld. *Serves 4 to 6*

FOR THE DRESSING

> ¼ cup extra-virgin olive oil
>
> ¼ cup minced onion
>
> 3 cloves garlic, peeled and grated
>
> ⅓ cup red wine vinegar
>
> ¼ cup (packed) dark brown sugar
>
> 1 tablespoon Worcestershire sauce
>
> 1 teaspoon coarsely ground black pepper
>
> 1 cup canned crushed tomatoes

FOR THE SALAD

> 3 ripe beefsteak tomatoes, sliced ½ inch thick
>
> 1 large Vidalia onion, peeled and sliced ½ inch thick
>
> Fine sea salt
>
> 2 tablespoons chopped fresh herbs, such as basil, tarragon, and/or parsley, for garnish (optional)

❶ Make the dressing: Heat 2 tablespoons of the oil in a small saucepan over medium heat. Add the minced onion and garlic and sauté until translucent, about 10 minutes.

❷ Stir in the vinegar, brown sugar, Worcestershire sauce, and pepper. Allow the sugar to dissolve in the vinegar and the liquids to come to a low boil. Add the crushed tomatoes and bring to a boil. Remove the sauce from the heat and whisk in the remaining oil.

Purée with an immersion blender, if desired. Let the dressing cool. When cold, pour it into a glass jar, cover, and refrigerate. It's best served the next day when the flavors have even more of a chance to blend together.

❸ Assemble the salad: Arrange the sliced tomatoes and Vidalia onion on a serving platter. Season both lightly with salt.

❹ Shake the cold dressing and pour it over the tomatoes and onion. Garnish with chopped fresh herbs, if desired.

GRILLED MEXICAN STREET CORN SALAD

This dish has all of the flavors of popular street corn in an easy-to-eat salad and can be made up to 1 day in advance. I grill some of the corn in the husk for a sweeter, more steam-grilled flavor, and some of the corn out of the husk for a more intense smoky flavor. I think that combination creates the best balance of sweet and smoky corn. *Serves 4 to 6*

6 large ears corn, 3 with husks and silks removed, 3 still with husks and silks intact

1 tablespoon extra-virgin olive oil

4 tablespoons (½ stick) unsalted butter, melted

Generous ½ cup mayonnaise, preferably Hellmann's or Best Foods

¼ cup minced fresh cilantro leaves

Zest and juice of 1 lime (about 2 tablespoons juice)

2 garlic cloves, peeled and grated with a Microplane

½ teaspoon chipotle chile powder

Maldon sea salt or kosher salt and freshly ground black pepper

½ cup grated queso añejo or 3-cheese blend of Pecorino Romano, Parmesan, and Asiago cheese, plus a little more for garnish

6 slices Nueske's or favorite applewood-smoked bacon, fried crisp and crumbled

1 sprig fresh cilantro, for garnish

1 lime, cut into small wedges, for serving (optional)

Grilling Method: Direct/Medium-High Heat

❶ Preheat the grill with all burners on high. Once preheated, adjust the temperature to medium-high for direct grilling.

❷ Soak all 6 ears of corn in water to cover for 10 minutes. Remove the corn from the water and pat dry with paper towels. Brush the shucked corn on all sides with the olive oil and leave the other corn in the husk.

❸ Grill all the corn, turning occasionally, until the shucked corn is well browned and charred in places and the husks of the unshucked corn are dried out and charred in places, about 10 minutes.

❹ Remove all the corn from the grill and let rest until easy to handle, about 5 minutes. When you can handle the corn comfortably, shuck the unshucked cobs. Then, stand a cob on its flat end on a cutting board. Holding the cob steady, take a sharp knife and carefully cut the kernels off, sliding the knife down the cob from top to bottom. Rotate the cob, cutting off a section at a time. I usually do 5 turns per cob. Repeat with the remaining corn. Discard the cobs, transfer the kernels to a bowl, and mix with the melted butter.

❺ In a separate bowl, stir the mayonnaise, minced cilantro, lime zest and juice, garlic, chile powder, and a pinch of salt and pepper together until well mixed. Stir in the cheese and toss the buttered corn with the dressing. Taste and adjust the seasonings. Garnish with a little more grated cheese. Serve warm or cold; either way, reserve topping with the bacon crumbles until just before serving, or they will get limp. Garnish with the cilantro sprig and the lime wedges, if desired.

ROASTED CHERRY TOMATOES ON THE VINE AND BURRATA CHEESE

The first time that I saw tomatoes on the vine roasted whole was at the Los Angeles restaurant Mozza. I was entranced by the simple and beautiful presentation and started making them right away. In the restaurant, they place the vine-attached cherry tomatoes on a sizzle platter and place the platter in their wood oven. Here, I have taken their lead and roast the vine on a shallow bed of salt. The warm cherry tomatoes are the perfect accompaniment for fresh burrata, best-quality extra-virgin olive oil, and a smattering of basil leaves. For those new to burrata, it tastes like the best fresh mozzarella cheese that you have ever eaten. In reality, it is its own designated cheese made from fresh mozzarella cheese that is wrapped around a center of creamy cheese curds, giving it a rich, buttery taste and soft texture. *Burrata* means "buttered" in Italian, and thus its name reflects its flavor. *Serves 4*

4 stems cherry tomatoes on the vine
(5 tomatoes per stem)

1 cup kosher salt

Best-quality extra-virgin olive oil

4 balls (4 ounces each) burrata

Crunchy sea salt and freshly ground black pepper

16 to 20 fresh baby basil leaves

Crusty bread, for serving

❶ Preheat the oven to 400°F.

❷ Rinse the tomatoes gently, making sure they stay on the vine. Spread the kosher salt on the bottom of a half sheet pan (small cookie sheet). Place the tomatoes gently on the salt bed.

❸ Roast until the tomato skins begin to collapse but the tomatoes are still firm, about 7 minutes. Remove them from the oven and, while still warm, carefully divide them among 4 salad plates so that the tomatoes don't fall off the vine. Then drizzle the tomatoes with olive oil.

❹ Just before serving, add a ball of burrata to each plate, drizzle with olive oil, sprinkle with salt and freshly ground pepper, and scatter with basil leaves. Serve with crusty bread.

CRUNCHY JICAMA SLAW

love the crunchy, fresh texture of jicama subbed for cabbage in this slaw. Jicama looks somewhat like a flattish, smooth, oval onion; it should be firm, and its skin should be blemish-free and look shiny, very similar to fresh ginger. Jicama comes in sizes from apple to small cabbage, yet the taste is not affected by size. A good jicama should be very crunchy to the bite—if it's dry or soft and mealy with brown spots, discard it. *Serves 4 to 6*

1 jicama (1½ to 2 pounds, the size of a small grapefruit)

1 papaya

3 navel oranges

Juice of 2 limes, plus 4 to 6 lime wedges

1 batch Pickled Red Onions (recipe follows)

Leaves from 3 or 4 sprigs fresh cilantro

½ cup pumpkin seeds (pepitas), toasted (see page 85)

Pinch of Chile-Lime Rub (page 138) or cayenne pepper (optional)

❶ Peel the jicama with a sharp vegetable peeler or paring knife. (The skin is too thick for a standard potato peeler.) To steady the jicama for peeling, cut off a slice from the top and bottom. Set the jicama cut side down on a cutting board and cut off the rest of the peel like you would the peel of an orange, from top to bottom.

❷ Cut the peeled jicama into ⅛- to ¼-inch-thick slabs, and then cut the slabs into French fry–like sticks. If the strips are very long, cut them in half. Alternatively, you can shred the jicama in a food processor or with a mandoline.

❸ Peel, seed, and cut the papaya into matchstick strips (julienne).

❹ Peel the oranges in the same manner as the jicama. Cut out each orange section from between the membranes, retaining as much juice as possible. Give the leftover membranes a squeeze with your hand to collect any remaining juice.

❺ Mix the collected orange juice with the lime juice. Arrange the jicama, papaya, and orange wedges on a platter or on individual plates. Top with the Pickled Red Onions; pour the orange and lime juice over them; garnish with cilantro leaves, lime wedges, and pumpkin seeds; and sprinkle the rub over all, if desired.

Pickled Red Onions

A quick pickled onion scattered about the slaw adds welcome acidity that is the perfect counterpoint to rich, beefy skirt steak. *Makes about 2 cups*

1 large red onion, peeled and thinly sliced into rings (about ⅛ inch thick)

Kosher salt

¼ teaspoon cumin seeds

2 cloves garlic, peeled and cut in half

¼ cup cider vinegar

Juice of 2 limes

❶ Place the onion rings in a heavy-bottomed saucepan. Cover with salted water and bring to a boil; boil for 1 minute. Immediately remove the pan from the heat and drain the onion rings. Return the onion rings to the saucepan.

❷ Coarsely grind the cumin seeds in a mortar with a pestle or in a spice grinder. Add them to the saucepan along with the garlic, vinegar, lime juice, and ¼ teaspoon salt. Pour in just enough water to cover the onions, bring to a boil over medium heat, and let boil for 3 minutes. Remove from the heat and pour into a small nonreactive bowl. Let stand for 3 hours to let the flavors meld. Drain the liquid and use the onions immediately or refrigerate, covered, for up to 2 weeks.

BARBUTO-INSPIRED ROASTED POTATOES

The New York City restaurant Barbuto is famous for deliciously craggy fried potatoes. The grated Pecorino cheese adds a sophisticated salty note and the rosemary makes them super savory—and the perfect steak potato! Plan on one potato per person, adding more as needed. *Serves 6*

1½ pounds baby new potatoes, such as Yukon Gold or red new potatoes, unpeeled

Extra-virgin olive oil

3 sprigs fresh rosemary

Peanut oil for frying (24 ounces, if using a 4-quart pot; 48 ounces, if using an electric fryer)

Coarse sea salt and freshly ground black pepper

¼ cup grated Pecorino Romano cheese

❶ Preheat the oven to 350°F.

❷ Scrub the potatoes and dry them with paper towels. Brush them all over with a thin coat of the olive oil and prick them with a fork in a few places.

❸ Place the potatoes in the oven and bake until they are tender when pierced with a knife, about 45 minutes. Set the potatoes aside to cool. This step can be done up to a day in advance. If making in

advance, store the cooled potatoes, covered, in the refrigerator.

❹ When ready to proceed with the recipe, break the potatoes into pieces by hand. Sprinkle them all over with the leaves from 2 sprigs of fresh rosemary.

❺ Pour the peanut oil into a heavy 4-quart pot or deep fryer and preheat to 325°F. You know that the oil is hot enough when you drop a cube of bread into the oil and it instantly begins to brown. Place the cold potatoes in the hot oil and cook until they're golden brown and crispy, 3 to 4 minutes.

❻ Remove the potatoes and rosemary from the oil using the fry basket if using a deep fryer or with a slotted spoon if frying in a pot. Drain well. Place on a serving platter, season with salt and pepper, and scatter the fresh Pecorino all over. Garnish with the remaining rosemary sprig. Serve immediately.

The Perfect Baked Potato

My friends and I have an ongoing debate about how to bake potatoes; many people are in the "foil" camp and a few others like me are in the "no foil" camp. My mother baked potatoes using the "no foil" method, and that is where I learned it and why I am partial to it. But I decided for the sake of potato science to test both methods at the same time.

I washed and dried two russet potatoes, about the same size. I coated one in Crisco and pricked it with a fork. I did the same thing to the other potato but wrapped it in aluminum foil. I put both potatoes in a preheated 350°F oven for 1 hour and 20 minutes. The "no foil" potato was perfectly done, and it had a fluffy, snowy interior. The foil-covered potato was still hard. So, I am forever sticking with my method, which produces a better potato.

CHEESY TWICE-BAKED POTATOES

This potato is the very definition of crave-able! It is not difficult to make at home and can be prepped up to 2 days in advance and refrigerated, making it the ideal potato dish for a crowd. I always bake at least one extra potato to make sure that I have ample filling for all of the shells that I want to turn into twice-baked potatoes. *Makes 4 twice-baked potatoes*

> 5 large baking (russet) potatoes (about 8 ounces each)
>
> 1 tablespoon extra-virgin olive oil or solid vegetable shortening, such as Crisco
>
> 2 tablespoons heavy (whipping) cream
>
> 4 tablespoons (½ stick) unsalted butter, melted
>
> ½ cup sour cream
>
> ½ cup cream cheese with chives
> (or 2 teaspoons chives mixed into ½ cup cream cheese)
>
> 8 ounces sharp Cheddar cheese, grated (about 2 cups)
>
> 2 tablespoons finely chopped scallions or chives
>
> Kosher salt and freshly ground black pepper

❶ Preheat the oven to 350°F.

❷ Scrub the potatoes and pierce them all over with a fork. Rub the potatoes with the olive oil or Crisco. Place them directly on an oven rack and bake until a fork passes easily through one, 70 minutes to 1 hour and 20 minutes. Leave the oven on.

❸ Remove the potatoes from the oven and let cool for 10 minutes. Cut them in half lengthwise and place them on a baking sheet.

❹ When the potatoes are cool enough to handle, scoop out the potato flesh into a large mixing bowl, leaving enough flesh around the skin to keep the potato from falling apart. Choose the worst-looking potato and remove all of the flesh. (You baked one extra potato so that you could fill each potato half and have the top mound over.)

5 While the potato flesh is still hot, add the heavy cream, melted butter, sour cream, cream cheese with chives, 1½ cups of the Cheddar cheese, and scallions. Mix until creamy and season to taste with salt and pepper. Divide the mixture equally among the potato shells. Sprinkle the remaining Cheddar cheese over the tops. Return the potatoes to the oven on the baking sheet. Bake until they are hot and the Cheddar topping is melted, lightly browned, and bubbling, 20 to 25 minutes. Remove from the oven and serve immediately.

CHIMICHURRI POTATOES

I describe chimichurri sauce as "parsley pesto" to people who have never had it before. I prefer using curly parsley over flat-leaf for its fresh grassy-green flavor. Flat leaf tastes a little like cilantro to me and is less versatile. *Serves 6*

FOR THE POTATOES

> 2 pounds red or other small potatoes, cleaned and cut in halves or quarters or left whole, depending on size
>
> Extra-virgin olive oil
>
> Kosher salt

FOR THE CHIMICHURRI SAUCE

> 4 cups lightly packed chopped fresh curly parsley (about 1 nice bunch)
>
> 4 cloves garlic
>
> 1 teaspoon fine sea salt
>
> ½ teaspoon freshly ground black pepper
>
> ½ teaspoon red pepper flakes
>
> 2 tablespoons minced shallot or onion
>
> ¾ cup extra-virgin olive oil
>
> 3 tablespoons sherry wine vinegar or red wine vinegar
>
> 1 tablespoon fresh lemon juice

1 Position a rack in the center of the oven and preheat the oven to 350°F.

2 Toss the potatoes in just enough olive oil to coat all sides. Sprinkle them with salt and toss to evenly season them.

3 Place the potatoes one by one on a rack set into a sheet pan. Place the pan in the oven and roast until the potatoes look dry and "puffy" and a fork or paring knife can be inserted easily, 30 to 40 minutes, depending on size. You will not need to turn the potatoes as they roast; they should be crispy on the outside and soft and tender on the inside when done.

④ While the potatoes roast, make the chimichurri sauce: Place all the sauce ingredients in a blender and pulse until well chopped and combined. It will have a beautiful green color and will look like parsley pesto.

⑤ If serving the potatoes with steak, set aside ¼ cup of sauce to spoon on the steak. Toss the potatoes with the remaining sauce (or all of it) while they are still warm so that they will absorb all the flavors.

⑥ Serve the potatoes warm, room temperature, or even cold. They are good served at all three temperatures. Just be sure to toss them again before serving.

GRILLED FRITES WITH DIJON BÉARNAISE

When I lived in France, I picked up the habit of dipping my French fries in *très forte* (super strong) Dijon mustard. While I admit that it is an acquired taste, albeit delicious, there is nothing better than a Dijon mustard–scented Béarnaise to go with a French steak and fries. My recipe here is for grill-baked fries, which are easier to prepare, but if you have a deep fryer—fry away! *Serves 4*

> 4 large baking potatoes, scrubbed, with skins on
>
> Extra-virgin olive oil
>
> Fine sea salt and freshly ground black pepper
>
> Blender Dijon Béarnaise or Dijon Butter (recipe follows)

Special Equipment: Resealable plastic bag

Grilling Method: Direct/Medium-Low Heat or Oven Method

❶ Set up a grill for direct grilling and preheat to medium-low, or preheat the oven to 400°F. Prepare a large bowl of ice water.

❷ Cut the potatoes into ½-inch-thick log shapes that resemble thick-cut French fries. Soak them in the ice water for 15 minutes. This soak removes some of the excess starch and prevents them from sticking to each other. Drain the potatoes and pat dry with paper towels. Place them in a resealable plastic bag and

drizzle with just enough oil to coat all surfaces of the potatoes. Seal the bag and massage the contents to ensure a thorough, even coating. Transfer the potatoes to a large dry bowl and sprinkle with salt and pepper.

❸ If grilling, place the fries crosswise across the grill grate so they won't fall through. Grill for 12 to 16 minutes, turning occasionally so both sides have good grill marks. When done, you should have grill marks on all sides of the potatoes and they should be tender on the inside. If the potatoes are marked before they are tender, move them to the warming rack or another place of indirect heat to finish cooking without burning.

If oven roasting, place the fries on a rack set on a sheet pan and roast until golden brown on the outside and tender on the inside, about 20 minutes.

❹ Serve immediately with the Blender Dijon Béarnaise or Dijon Butter as a dipping sauce.

Blender Dijon Béarnaise

Bill Barrick and Tony Kemp are dear friends who own a charming inn located in Galena, Illinois. One morning, I watched Bill make a perfect "blender" hollandaise. It was so brilliant—fool- and fail-proof! And Bill's trick to making it creamy is a little hot water. No more breaking hollandaise! I've adapted his technique for my dinnertime Dijon Béarnaise. Once you make it, you'll wonder why you waited so long to try it—especially as a dip for fries and a sauce for steak. *Makes 2 cups*

> 7 large egg yolks
>
> 1 cup (2 sticks) unsalted butter
>
> ¼ cup fresh lemon juice
>
> ¼ teaspoon ground cayenne pepper
>
> ½ to 1 tablespoon hot water, as needed
>
> 1½ teaspoons Dijon mustard
>
> 1 tablespoon chopped fresh tarragon leaves
>
> ½ teaspoon tarragon vinegar

❶ Place the egg yolks in a blender and whip until creamy and light in color.

❷ Place the butter in a small saucepan and melt over low heat—do not clarify. Add the lemon juice and cayenne to the melted butter. Bring the butter mixture slowly to a boil.

❸ Pour the hot butter mixture slowly over the egg yolks while the blender is running at medium speed. When smooth, add up to 1 tablespoon of hot water so that the mixture is creamy but pourable. Mix in the Dijon mustard, chopped fresh tarragon leaves, and the tarragon vinegar. Serve right away if not making in advance (see Note).

Note: You can make the Béarnaise in advance. It will hold, covered, in the refrigerator for 1 week. Warm in the top of a double boiler over simmering water. If it is too thick, reconstitute with a small amount of hot water—up to 1 tablespoon.

Dijon Butter

Make this if you prefer a compound butter over a classic sauce. It's quick and easy and so good. It tastes like Béarnaise without all the fuss! I've added the Dijon mustard to make it taste like the Blender Dijon Béarnaise. Place generous slices of the butter atop a hot steak. Once melted, it also makes a great dip for French fries. *Makes 1 log; about ½ cup*

> 8 tablespoons (1 stick) unsalted butter, at room temperature
>
> 4 teaspoons minced fresh parsley
>
> 2 teaspoons granulated garlic
>
> 2 teaspoons dried tarragon
>
> 1 generous teaspoon Dijon mustard

❶ Combine the butter, parsley, garlic, and tarragon in a small bowl. Add the Dijon mustard and blend well.

❷ Drop the butter in spoonfuls in a row on a piece of plastic wrap. Roll up the butter in the wrap and smooth it out to form a log. Twist the ends to seal the wrap and refrigerate until the butter is hard, at least 2 hours.

This recipe will make more than you need, but if it is well wrapped, it will keep in the refrigerator for up to 1 week and in the freezer for 1 month.

GARLIC SMASHED POTATOES

I like these potatoes better than mashed because they are full of texture and flavor. The grilled red potatoes are "smashed" with good green extra-virgin olive oil, basil, and raw garlic and can stand up to a smoked and charred ribeye. *Serves 4*

> 16 baby red or Yukon Gold potatoes or 4 russet potatoes, quartered
>
> 7 to 8 tablespoons extra-virgin olive oil
>
> Kosher salt
>
> ⅓ cup minced fresh basil leaves
>
> 4 cloves garlic, peeled and minced
>
> Freshly ground black pepper

Grilling Method: Indirect/Medium-High Heat or Oven Method

❶ Preheat the grill with all burners on high. Once preheated, adjust the temperature to medium-high for indirect grilling, or preheat the oven to 400°F.

❷ Toss the potatoes with 2 tablespoons of the olive oil in a large bowl. Season with salt.

❸ **If grilling**, place the potatoes in the center of the cooking grate over indirect heat or on the grill's warming rack. Grill, turning occasionally, until cooked through and super crispy on the outside, about 30 minutes.

If oven roasting, place the potatoes in a single layer on a rack set on a sheet pan. Roast the potatoes until cooked through and super crispy on the outside, about 30 minutes.

❹ While the potatoes are cooking, place 5 tablespoons of the oil and the basil and garlic in a serving bowl.

❺ Add the potatoes to the oil mixture and toss them thoroughly so they are coated with oil and herbs.

Smash the potatoes, but not so much that they wind up mashed. Add the remaining 1 tablespoon oil, if needed, and season to taste with salt and pepper.

GARLIC CHEESE GRITS

I can't make these garlic cheese grits without thinking about my dear friend and CarolinaCueToGo.com partner David Lineweaver. He loves grits morning, noon, and night and, like me, prefers coarse-ground white grits. We sell white grits that have been milled on a 300-year-old, water-propelled grist mill and they are the best grits that we have ever eaten—if we do say so ourselves! *Serves 8*

> 5½ cups cold water, plus more if needed
>
> 2 cups heavy (whipping) cream, plus more if needed
>
> 3 cups coarse-ground white grits, preferably Carolina Cue brand (of course!)
>
> 4 tablespoons (½ stick) unsalted butter (optional)
>
> 8 ounces white Cheddar cheese, freshly grated
>
> 8 ounces Parmigiano-Reggiano cheese, freshly grated
>
> 2 teaspoons kosher salt, or to taste
>
> 1 teaspoon granulated garlic or garlic powder
>
> 2½ teaspoons freshly ground black pepper
>
> Tabasco sauce, to taste

❶ Place the water and cream in a medium-size saucepan and bring to a gentle boil over medium-high heat. Stir in the grits, reduce the heat, and simmer, continuing to stir occasionally, with the lid alternating on and off every 15 minutes, until soft but still with a little resistance (not mushy), about 1 hour. The grits can be cooked with the lid off the whole time, but that will take twice as long. If the grits get too stiff, add more cream or water.

❷ Stir in the butter (if desired), cheeses, salt, granulated garlic, pepper, and Tabasco. Adjust seasonings to taste—both cheeses have a lot of natural salt, so be careful when adding salt. Serve piping hot.

WILD MUSHROOM SAUTÉ

I love making this with the harder-to-find chanterelles and morels, but the garlic, shallot, thyme, and sherry dress up even everyday mushrooms like baby bellas and white button mushrooms, making them just as good a choice—the decision is yours. *Makes about 2 cups*

> 1 pound assorted fresh mushrooms, such as chanterelles, king oysters, baby bellas, cremini, morels, and other favorites
>
> 2 tablespoons extra-virgin olive oil
>
> 2 tablespoons unsalted butter
>
> 2 cloves garlic, peeled and grated with a Microplane (about 1 teaspoon)
>
> 1 small shallot, peeled and grated with a Microplane (about 1 teaspoon)
>
> 1 teaspoon fresh thyme leaves or ¼ teaspoon dried ground thyme
>
> ¼ teaspoon kosher salt
>
> ½ cup cream sherry
>
> ½ cup crème fraîche (see page 78)
>
> 1½ teaspoons best-quality truffle oil
>
> Fine sea salt and freshly ground black pepper (optional)
>
> Fresh thyme leaves, for garnish

❶ Clean the mushrooms with a damp paper towel or a mushroom brush; trim and discard the ends. Slice the mushrooms into large pieces. Be creative; you want to be able to see the shape of the mushrooms—some of them will lend themselves to slices and others will be easier to cut into chunks.

2 Heat a large cast-iron skillet or heavy-bottomed sauté pan over medium heat. Add the olive oil and butter, and once the butter has melted, stir to combine. Add the garlic, shallot, thyme, and kosher salt to the pan and stir. Let cook without stirring for 2 minutes. Add the mushrooms, increase the heat to medium-high, and sauté, stirring occasionally, until well caramelized all over, 7 to 10 minutes.

3 When the mushrooms are done, pour in the sherry and stir to deglaze the pan. Cook until the liquid has reduced a bit and the mushrooms have absorbed the sherry, 3 to 4 minutes. Remove the pan from the heat and quickly stir in the crème fraîche and truffle oil. Taste for seasoning and add fine sea salt and pepper, if desired. Garnish with fresh thyme leaves and serve immediately.

EASY MUSHROOM TARTS

Delicious with a T-bone or porterhouse steak. If you can't find porcinis, use your favorite mushroom. *Makes 4 tarts*

 2 cloves garlic, peeled and grated with a Microplane

 5 tablespoons extra-virgin olive oil

 1 sheet Pepperidge Farm Puff Pastry Sheets or 8 ounces Dufour Classic Puff Pastry Dough, thawed in the refrigerator

 All-purpose flour, for rolling out the puff pastry

 2 medium Vidalia onions, peeled and very thinly sliced

 1¼ pounds fresh whole porcini or other favorite mushrooms, cleaned, caps evenly sliced ½ inch thick, stems cut in half

 3 tablespoons unsalted butter

 Kosher salt

 ½ cup walnut halves, coarsely chopped and lightly toasted (see page 85)

 1 teaspoon fresh thyme leaves, plus 1 teaspoon for garnish (optional)

 Freshly ground black pepper

Special equipment: Silicone baking mat or parchment paper

1 Combine the garlic and 3 tablespoons of the olive oil in a small bowl and let stand for 1 hour. Strain the oil, discarding the garlic; set the oil aside.

2 Roll out the pastry dough to ⅛ inch thick on a lightly floured surface. Using a 5-inch round or square cutter, cut 4 disks from the pastry and transfer the disks to a baking sheet lined with a silicone baking mat or parchment paper. Pierce the disks repeatedly with the tines of a fork, then refrigerate on the baking sheet.

3 Combine the onions, mushroom stems, 1 tablespoon of butter, the remaining 2 tablespoons of olive oil, and a pinch of salt in a medium-size saucepan. Cook over medium heat, stirring occasionally, until the onions are lightly browned and caramelized and the mushroom stems are cooked, about 15 minutes.

4 Add the walnuts and cook, stirring continuously, for 2 minutes more. Transfer the mixture to a food processor and process to a smooth paste. Add 1 teaspoon of thyme leaves and taste for seasoning. Add more salt if necessary. Transfer to a bowl, cover, and refrigerate.

5 Heat a heavy-bottomed sauté pan over medium heat. Add the remaining 2 tablespoons of butter and when it has melted, add the sliced mushroom caps.

Sauté, stirring occasionally, until the mushrooms begin to get limp but are not completely cooked, 2 to 3 minutes. Remove from the heat and let cool. These slices will decorate the top of the tart, so you want them to be pretty and uniform.

6 Preheat the oven to 425°F.

7 Remove the pastry from the refrigerator and spread one-quarter of the cooled onion paste over each disk, leaving a ½-inch border around the sides. Top each with mushroom slices and season with salt and pepper.

8 Brush each pastry border and the mushroom slices with the garlic oil and bake until the pastry is golden and the mushrooms are lightly browned, 15 to 20 minutes.

9 Brush the mushrooms again with garlic oil as soon as they come out of the oven. Serve the tarts immediately, garnished with a few of the remaining thyme leaves, if desired.

LOW-AND-SLOW CABBAGE

This is a favorite of the barbecue circuit, and it is one of those recipes that tastes much better than it sounds. The slow cooking process "melts" the cabbage, transforming it into a silky, sweet, smoky treat. The real trick is to cook it until it is so tender that you can pluck a leaf from the center without any resistance.

Of course, everyone on the barbecue circuit has a version of this recipe. Because I truly believe that less is more, I like this simple, pared-down version that I created, but that's me and might not be you. Some people I know add barbecue sauce during the last hour of cooking time; some add cream cheese to the butter; some sprinkle the cabbage with grated cheese; and I even met a team whose secret ingredient was grape jelly! So, if you feel like adding your own personal touch, go right ahead; you are in good company! *Serves 4 to 6*

> 1 medium whole green cabbage
>
> 4 tablespoons (½ stick) butter, cut into small pieces
>
> 1 tablespoon barbecue spice rub, preferably homemade (see Tri-Tip Santa Maria, page 56), or kosher salt and freshly ground black pepper

Grilling Method: Indirect/Medium Heat

1 Preheat the grill with all burners on high. Once preheated, adjust the temperature to medium heat for indirect grilling.

2 With a sharp paring knife, remove the core of the cabbage, leaving a hole about 3 inches deep. Turn the cabbage upside down so that the hole faces up. Gently loosen the cabbage leaves from the inside cavity. Spread pieces of the butter in the cavity and between the cabbage leaves. Sprinkle the cavity with the barbecue spice rub or salt and pepper. Wrap the cabbage in heavy-duty aluminum foil so that only the hole is exposed. Make a ring from crumbled aluminum foil about as wide as the bottom of the cabbage.

3 Place the foil ring in the center of the cooking grate, away from the heat, and place the cabbage on it. Cover and cook until very tender and the leaves can be plucked from the core with little resistance, 2 to 3 hours. Baste the exposed top occasionally with the butter that's melted in the cabbage core.

4 Unwrap the cabbage and eat by pulling the leaves from the center, or cut into wedges and serve.

SPINACH AND ARTICHOKE CASSEROLE

This is a favorite recipe that we make for family celebrations. It is always served at holiday time, and I often make it for steak parties, as it is easy to make in advance and is a great substitute for creamed spinach. *Serves 8*

2 tablespoons extra-virgin olive oil

1 pound white button mushrooms, trimmed and sliced

2 cans (14 ounces each) artichoke hearts in water, drained and cut in half

4 to 6 boxes (9 ounces each) frozen chopped spinach, preferably Green Giant, thawed, squeezed dry, and microwaved for 1 to 2 minutes

1 can (10.5 ounces) condensed cream of mushroom soup, preferably Campbell's (not light)

1 tablespoon Pernod (optional)

¼ teaspoon granulated garlic

¼ teaspoon fine sea salt

½ cup full-fat sour cream

½ cup mayonnaise, preferably Hellmann's or Best Foods

½ teaspoon fresh lemon juice

Special Equipment: Large (4-quart) soufflé dish

❶ Preheat the oven to 350°F.

❷ Heat the oil in a large skillet over medium heat. Add the mushrooms and sauté until soft and nicely browned around the edges, about 10 minutes.

❸ Place half the artichoke halves in the bottom of the baking dish. Mix the warm spinach, condensed soup (do not thin with liquid), Pernod (if using), garlic, salt, and mushrooms together in a bowl. Spread half of the spinach mixture over the artichokes. Cover with the remaining artichokes, followed by the remaining spinach.

❹ Mix the sour cream, mayonnaise, and lemon juice together in a small bowl and spread it over the spinach, covering the casserole completely. If making in advance, cover with aluminum foil and refrigerate for up to 2 days.

❺ Bake until bubbling and slightly browned on top, 30 minutes. The casserole can be made up to 2 days ahead. Refrigerate, covered, and reheat at 350°F for 15 minutes. Serve immediately.

STEAKHOUSE SPINACH

I could eat this spinach dish every night, all year long. It is my version of creamed spinach, although unlike most versions, it is mostly spinach with just a touch of half-and-half. If you prefer a looser dish, feel free to add more half-and-half. The real secret to this recipe is using frozen spinach that is sold in sealed bags, such as Green Giant. The sealed flash-freezing prevents the spinach from getting frostbite or picking up off flavors in the freezer. It tastes much better than fresh and is easier to use to boot! *Serves 8*

4 packages (9 ounces each) frozen chopped spinach, preferably Green Giant, cooked, drained in a strainer, and cooled

2 tablespoons unsalted butter

2 shallots, peeled and minced

1 tablespoon Pernod or Ricard pastis, plus 2 teaspoons for drizzling

1 tablespoon all-purpose flour

½ to ⅔ cup half-and-half or cream

Pinch of freshly grated or ground nutmeg

Fine sea salt or fleur de sel and freshly ground black pepper

❶ Preheat the oven to 375°F.

❷ With the cooled spinach still in the strainer, remove as much additional water as possible by pressing down on it with the back of a spoon. Set aside.

3 Melt the butter in a skillet over medium heat. Add the shallots and cook until soft and slightly caramelized, about 10 minutes. Stir in 1 tablespoon of Pernod, then add the flour. Whisk until the flour is slightly browned (this eliminates the raw flour taste), 2 to 3 minutes. Stir in ½ cup of half-and-half and the spinach. Cook until the mixture is heated through. Add the remaining half-and-half if the spinach seems too dry. Season with a pinch of nutmeg and salt and pepper to taste, and drizzle with the remaining 2 teaspoons Pernod. Mix well.

4 Place the spinach in an oven-proof casserole dish and bake in the oven until hot and bubbly, about 30 minutes.

Note: This dish can be made a day in advance and stored, covered, in the refrigerator. Reheat just before serving.

STEAK PRIMER

Cooking Steak at Home

If you eat meat, there's a good chance you love steak. And making steak at home is very satisfying and easy. Statistically, steak is the number one favorite food to grill—hands down, male or female, young or old. So you'll notice there's a lot more grilling in this book than indoor cooking. I'm a griller at heart and by profession, and I believe that it is the best way to cook a steak. If you've never done it before, grilling is a little more complicated than cooking on the stovetop or in an oven. This is mostly because you're cooking the meat over an open flame, whereas indoors it is always protected by a pan. But the good news is that it isn't difficult to become a master steak griller, and I will help you become one! But first . . .

How to Buy Steak

Buying a steak can be daunting, and that often deters home cooks. But it's really quite simple and begins with knowing what kind of steak you like. I am not a butcher or a meat industry expert, but I am an expert at cooking meat. So, I'm writing this from the perspective of an expert steak cook.

First, how do you figure out your preferences? A steak is not a steak is not a steak, and the different cuts taste very different. The amount of intramuscular fat, aka marbling, changes the flavor enormously. For example, a lean filet mignon has very little flavor, but the muscle is very tender. A well-marbled New York strip has more chew, but you are rewarded with a juicier, more flavorful steak. Skirt steak and flank steak have to be sliced across the grain or else they are too tough to chew, but the rich flavor explodes with every bite, especially with skirt steak.

After the cut, you really only have one decision to make: whether you want to buy Prime grade or Choice grade beef. If you aren't sure which to buy, your safest bet is to buy Certified Angus Beef (CAB), which is always a high Choice to low Prime grade even if it only says Choice on the label (see the box on the facing page).

I asked several of my friends who are in the food business how they choose the steaks that they buy. None of them are in the meat business, but they all love steak and have varying experience with buying it and cooking it. These conversations drew me to create my Steak Primer Grid (see page 204). In talking with them, I realized that there are three considerations that inform how you buy a steak:

- Flavor

- Texture

- Point of reference/emotional perception

The flavor is subjective; the texture is less subjective and easier to communicate in a concrete fashion; and the third consideration is completely subjective. The point of reference/emotional perception is how you view the steak. For example, Rachel is a friend of mine who grills steak once a week at home. She generally buys and grills a New York strip but when she goes to a steakhouse, it is almost always for a special occasion and she orders a filet mignon every time. When I asked her if she liked the flavor better, she replied, "No, but I associate special occasions with filet mignon." That is the point of reference/emotional perception aspect of the decision. But more on that later. Let's start with a little glossary of beef terms that should help with the shopping process. I compiled it using information from the USDA, Certified Angus Beef (CAB), the National Cattleman's Association, and universities with meat science programs like Texas A&M.

GRADING BEEF—WHAT DO THE GRADES OF BEEF MEAN?

The US Department of Agriculture (USDA) **grade shields** are generally regarded as symbols of safe, high-quality American beef.

Beef is evaluated by certified USDA meat graders using both a subjective assessment process and electronic instruments to measure meat characteristics. These characteristics follow the official grade standards developed, maintained, and interpreted by the USDA's Agricultural Marketing Service.

Beef is graded in two ways:

1. QUALITY GRADES for tenderness, juiciness, and flavor;

2. YIELD GRADES for the amount of usable lean meat on the carcass.

Prime beef is produced from young, well-fed beef cattle. It has abundant marbling (the amount of fat interspersed with lean meat) and is generally sold to restaurants and hotels. Prime roasts and steaks are excellent for dry-heat cooking, such as pan-frying, roasting, or grilling.

Choice beef is high quality but has less marbling than Prime. Choice roasts and steaks from the loin and rib will be very tender, juicy, and flavorful and are suited for dry-heat cooking.

Select beef is very uniform in quality and normally leaner than the higher grades. It is fairly tender, but, because it has less marbling, it may lack some of the juiciness and flavor of the higher grades. Only the tender cuts should be cooked with dry heat. Other cuts should be marinated before cooking or braised to obtain maximum tenderness and flavor.

VISUAL CLUES

COLOR: Beef has a dark purplish hue when it is freshly butchered and before exposure to oxygen turns it cherry red, like the meat you see in most supermarkets and butcher shops. If you buy vacuum-sealed meat and it is purple instead of red, this is a good thing, as it will turn red once it is exposed to the air for 15 minutes. The "red" liquid in packaging with the beef is not blood. All meat is drained of blood before packaging. The "red" liquid is natural water-like fluids and protein that is reddish in color. If the

Certified Angus Beef (CAB)

Angus beef is everywhere these days, but buying Angus beef doesn't mean you're buying quality. I didn't know that until I met the folks at Certified Angus Beef, CAB for short. It turns out many brands use the word "Angus," but it's the CAB label that guarantees quality Angus beef. I had thought that CAB was solely a marketing program; I didn't realize that it was really a quality program. But after spending several days at its headquarters in Ohio and breaking down a cow into steaks with its top meat scientist, I'm a believer. If you don't have a local butcher or a favorite local beef source, look for the CAB label at your grocery store, and you can rest assured that you've purchased good-quality meat.

The CAB brand is based on ten extremely high standards by which all its beef is measured. All ten must be met for tenderness, juiciness, and flavor, which are the same three points that the USDA uses to grade meat, but CAB grades to more exacting standards, according to the CAB website.

How did those standards come into being? In 1978, getting a great steak at home or even at a restaurant was hit or miss. The CAB founders were determined to create a set of uncompromising standards for taste and then find the best Angus ranchers to help them raise beef cattle that would meet those standards. Decades later, the vision to be "the best of the best" remains. Despite everything that has changed since 1978, CAB is still dedicated to producing beef of the highest quality.

meat is brown or is sticky to the touch, it is no longer good.

MARBLING: The flecks of white fat interspersed in the muscle are called *marbling,* and it's what makes the steak juicy, flavorful, and tender. Evidence of this marbling is the best visual clue you have for good meat.

SMELL: If the meat has no smell or a clean, neutral smell, it is fine. If it smells off, it is probably not good any more.

AIR IN THE BAG: If the vacuum pouch looks like it has air trapped in it, it is most likely a gas created by the meat breaking down. If there is enough of this to make the previously flat and tight vacuum-sealed plastic inflate like a balloon, the meat is no longer good.

HOW MUCH TO BUY

Some general guidelines:

SLICED: Plan on 3 to 5 ounces of steak per person if you slice the steak and serve it family style.

WHOLE: Plan on 5 to 6 ounces for light eaters and 10 to 12 ounces for steak lovers with average appetites. Hard-core carnivores will eat the whole steak, even if it is 16 or more ounces. Most individual steaks that you can buy will be between 12 and 16 ounces.

How to Cook Steak

When you drill down, there are really only a few ways I would recommend you cook a steak, and once you learn what you like, there may be only one way that you like to cook a steak.

OUTDOOR GRILL

There are three ways to grill a steak using an outdoor grill.

DIRECT GRILLING: The first way is what I call "Steak 101." It is very simple: Build a single-layer charcoal fire and preheat it to high, letting the coals develop a gray

Bringing Meat to Room Temperature Before Cooking

When I was learning how to cook meat, I always heard and read that you need to bring meat to room temperature. It *was* my secret that I rarely did it myself, but I used to write all my recipes to include that as the first step.

The reason that I rarely followed my own rule to take the meat out and let it come to room temperature is because it is easier to get a medium-rare interior when the steak is still cold. It is also a potential health hazard to leave raw food out without refrigeration—30 minutes won't hurt anyone, but if 30 minutes turns into 3 hours, that could be a different story. It is more sanitary and a better food safety practice to keep the meat refrigerated until you are ready to prep and cook it. Besides, new cooking studies have shown that the time out of the refrigerator doesn't lower the temperature enough to affect cooking times anyway.

The most important steps are to dry the steak of all surface moisture with paper towels, oil the meat, and salt it just before cooking.

ash, or preheat a gas grill to a high direct heat. Then, adjust the heat to the temperature called for in the recipe. Cook the steak for about 5 minutes on each side over direct heat, turning once halfway through the cooking time. This is assuming that the steak is about 1 inch thick and you start with a cold steak and want a medium-rare interior.

Note that you never want to use a heat higher than 500°F. High direct heat can easily burn instead of caramelize the steak, and some people think that it also shocks the meat, causing it to toughen and taste bitter.

INDIRECT GRILLING: This method uses a heat source positioned on either side of the cooking food, not directly under it.

COMBO GRILLING: The third method is the technique used by most advanced grillers. I call it the combo method because it is a combination of direct and indirect heat: You sear the steak over medium-high direct heat and then move it to a medium indirect heat to finish cooking. A gentler indirect heat helps the steak cook evenly and prevents flare-ups and burning. This is especially effective with any steak that is 1½ inches thick or more. You can approximate this technique indoors using a grill pan to sear the steak and finishing it in a preheated oven.

When deciding whether to use direct or indirect heat, remember this simple rule of thumb:

- If the food takes less than 20 minutes to cook, use the *direct method*.

- If the food takes more than 20 minutes to cook, use the *indirect method*.

The combo method can be used for food that takes any amount of time to cook. The combo method is my favorite.

Flare-Ups: Covering the Grill

The quickest way to extinguish flare-ups is to close the lid on the grill. The lid will reduce the amount of oxygen that feeds the fire, thus limiting or snuffing out the flare-ups.

Don't be tempted to use a water bottle to extinguish flare-up flames. When the water hits the hot cooking grate and the flames, it can splatter, causing burns and/or cracking the porcelain enamel finish on your grill.

If you already have a large fire, follow these steps:

1. Remove the food.

2. Turn off the grill.

3. Extinguish the flames with kosher salt or baking soda.

Elizabeth's Trilogy of Olive Oil, Salt, and Pepper

The story of the holy trilogy of cooking and grilling (or Elizabeth's Trilogy, for short) is a simple one. Years ago, I developed this technique to use in my grill trainings for chefs and food writers. I wanted to showcase the inherent flavors of grilled food not masked by rubs, marinades, or sauces. I decided to focus on teaching the techniques of grilling without the flourishes (of other flavors).

I am a firm believer that a little bit of oil is essential to great grilled food (more on that below), so I added olive oil. I still wanted the food to taste good and knew that salt was essential to the taste and caramelization process, so I added salt. Finally, I added salt's companion, pepper, to add a subtle dimension to the food. That was the genesis of the holy trilogy of grilling.

What I discovered was that, assuming you buy the best-quality raw ingredients (a given) and use the trilogy principles, everything that you grill will be guest-ready and delicious. Remember, in most cases—in life and in cooking—less is more, and the grilling trilogy is the epitome of that!

OLIVE OIL

Oil the food, not the grates! Brushing your steak (or any other food) with olive oil is the secret to great cooking whether you are grilling, oven roasting, or pan-frying. It is absolutely essential, and you don't need to use very much oil for it to be effective. Coat all the outside surfaces with a thin layer of olive oil. I prefer olive oil for everything, but you can use any kind of oil except butter (because it burns easily).

And remember: Grilling is intrinsically low-fat and healthy because you aren't frying or sautéing in loads of oil or butter. We want the juices to stay inside the meat so it is tender and juicy when we serve it, and a light coating of oil keeps the juices inside, promotes great grill marks, and prevents sticking. *If you don't oil the food, it will dry out and become tasteless.*

I use extra-virgin olive oil for everything. I only have two kinds of olive oil in my pantry: a good extra-virgin olive oil for everyday cooking needs and the best extra-virgin olive oil for finishing dishes and dressing salads.

I generally buy a good green olive oil because that is the flavor that I like. There are many good brands, from as close as California and as far away as the Middle East. I like California Olive Ranch, Monini, Lucini, and some of the Trader Joe's choices for my everyday cooking, brushing food, and sautéing. I also keep a bottle of the best-quality olive oil that I can find, like Laudemio, for drizzling on cooked food and making vinaigrettes.

SALT

Likewise, salt is very important. It is a natural mineral. Used in moderation, I think it is the most important ingredient for great taste. There are a few things to keep in mind when cooking with salt. Season food with salt just before it goes on the grill; otherwise it will draw the juices to the surface of the meat, and a dry surface always results in better sear marks and a more caramelized exterior. Start with a little salt and add to taste. There is a fine line between just right and too much—it's much easier to add than take away.

I recommend seasoning *uncooked* food with kosher salt because it has a cleaner taste and an irregular surface that sticks to the food better than table salt. Kosher salt can be found in any grocery store. Morton is my preferred brand of kosher salt for grilling because it is harder and coarser and doesn't melt on the surface as easily as Diamond Crystal. This quality is preferable for steak cooking in particular because the coveted crust and great grill marks can only happen when the surface of the meat is dry. Being able to see the salt also prevents oversalting.

I recommend seasoning *cooked* food with fleur de sel or another coarse sea salt like Maldon to add both the final salt note and a nice crunchy texture.

SALT PRIMER

TABLE SALT, or granular salt, is produced by a vacuum-pan evaporation process that produces dense, bouncy crystals of sodium chloride that are packaged with additives to keep them from clumping.

IODIZED SALT is table salt to which sodium or potassium iodine has been added to reduce the incidence of goiter, which is caused by iodine deficiency. It is especially important for people who do not eat seafood.

KOSHER SALT is coarser and contains no additives. It is produced by one of several methods that produce larger, lighter, flakier granules. Chefs often choose to use kosher salt because it sticks to the surface of foods better than the small, bouncy granules of table salt and has a purer flavor. There are two major brands of kosher salt: Morton and Diamond Crystal. I use Morton when grilling or cooking meat and vegetables because it is harder and coarser and doesn't dissolve easily. Diamond Crystal is better for baking and for making sauces, brines, and marinades, where you want the salt to melt and merge into the mixture.

SEA SALT usually has large granules produced by surface evaporation. Its crystals can be a variety of different colors, depending upon the additional minerals present. Sea salts, including fleur de sel and Maldon, have more flavor and texture, and they vary from one to another. I use fine-grain sea salt in all my baking.

PEPPER

Pepper is the companion to salt. It is said to add a depth of flavor, although I'm not sure about that. But it does add a peppery, almost bitter bite that rounds out the salt. And, most importantly, we have become accustomed to tasting them together.

Pepper is the most popular spice in the world. It is harvested at different stages to produce the three types of berry: green, black, and white. Green peppercorns are picked underripe. They are soft and generally packed in brine, although they are sold dehydrated and dry as well. The brined variety have a mild, fresh flavor and are great in sauces. Black peppercorns are picked when the plant is not quite ripe. They are left to dry out and the outer shell shrivels and turns black, and thus the name. The black peppercorns have the strongest flavor of the three. Black Tellicherry peppercorns from India are considered the gold standard of peppercorns.

White peppercorns are left to ripen on the vine. The outer skin is removed and the interior is what becomes white peppercorns. These peppercorns have a smooth, tannish-white shell, are smaller than black peppercorns, and are milder in taste.

Always finish your steaks with a sprinkle of coarse, crunchy sea salt like fleur de sel or Maldon sea salt flakes.

Steak Myths

Bring meat to room temperature.

Salt in advance.

To test for doneness, cut into steak with a knife.

Steak Facts

Dry steak with paper towels.

Oil lightly all over to keep juices in.

Salt just before cooking.

Turn once halfway through the cooking time for the best crust.

Use an instant-read meat thermometer or the A-OK method (see the facing page).

Let the meat rest before slicing.

Brush with melted butter, olive oil, compound butter, a sprinkle of finishing or special salt, or fresh herbs before serving.

INDOORS ON THE STOVETOP AND IN THE OVEN

This is basically how most steak chefs cook steaks in a restaurant. You sear the steak on both sides on an indoor grill or in a grill pan and let it finish cooking in the oven.

INDOORS—IN A CAST-IRON PAN ON THE STOVETOP: This is my favorite smoky, high-heat, "drama-in-the-kitchen" method. You preheat a dry cast-iron or carbon steel skillet on the stovetop for 5 to 6 minutes. Salt the pan and sear a dry steak in the pan, one side at a time. Then, let the steak rest on a rack as you cook the next steak. I cook steak this way for no more than four people and buy large enough steaks so that each steak can feed two people. Otherwise, it is too difficult to cook for a crowd one steak at a time.

CROSSHATCH MARKS

Steaks look steakhouse-perfect with crosshatch marks, which are so much easier to achieve than they look. Just before turning the steaks, rotate them a quarter turn to the right and grill for about 2 minutes. If cooking by the combo method, sear for 2 minutes, rotate a quarter turn and sear for another 2 minutes, turn over, and repeat, then move to indirect heat to finish cooking. To make sure you don't have three sets of marks, carefully place your steaks in the same position or turn them a quarter turn when you move them to indirect heat and the marks will be seared in during the final cooking time.

IS IT DONE YET? OR TESTING FOR DONENESS 1

Besides lighting the grill, knowing when the food is "done" to perfection makes many of us otherwise-confident cooks quiver in our proverbial boots. Not to worry, arm yourself with two tools:

• A timer

• An instant-read thermometer

If you are like most people today, you'll use the timer on your phone. That's what I do. Set the timer for the number of minutes that you think the food will need before turning, or whatever the next step may be. Base this estimate on the recipe or your past experience. Then, use your instant-read thermometer to check the internal temperature to see if your timing is correct. Invest in a good meat thermometer. These days you can buy instant-read thermometers that connect to your smartphone and will alert you that the steak needs to be flipped or taken off the heat. This is a great help when you are cooking for a party—just remember to keep your phone in your pocket! OXO, ThermoWorks, and Maverick make several models that work very well and have all kinds of extra features, like the ability to download your recipe into the app.

Remember, cooking and grilling steaks is much more of an art than a science, and the cooking times will vary slightly based on many factors, including wind, thickness of the food, starting temperature of the food, preheating the grill, and the cooking temperature. Once you get the hang of it, you'll realize that the mystery is part of the game and what makes it so much fun!

To make it easy for you, I've compiled a steak cooking chart based on the temperatures that I use when I cook beef. I like the meat cooked to the lower temperatures rather than the USDA-recommended medium and higher temperatures. My recommendations are the same as what the Certified Angus Beef (CAB) brand recommends. The truth is that when I am cooking whole-muscle roasts such as beef tenderloin, strip roasts, and prime rib, I often remove the meat from the grill or the oven when the internal temperature of the thickest part of the meat is at 120°F so that any residual heat and carry-over cooking will bring it to 125°F. Use the simple chart that follows as your internal temperature/testing for doneness guideline.

TEMPERATURES FOR STEAK

RARE	125°F
MEDIUM-RARE	135°F
MEDIUM	145°F
MEDIUM-WELL	150°F
WELL	160 °F to 170°F

Notes: Remember that the temperature will rise as much as 5°F as the steak rests. The USDA recommends an internal temperature of 145°F for steak that is medium, but in my book, medium means overcooked.

The USDA recommends that all ground meat, including beef, veal, pork, poultry, and lamb, be cooked until it's no longer pink. If you still have questions, consult the USDA website: usda.gov.

TESTING FOR DONENESS 2: A-OK TRICK

If you read a lot of cookbooks or watch a lot of cooking shows, you've probably seen someone make a fist to show you how to test the doneness of meat with your finger. When I was first taught this trick, I understood

---

A Note on Reverse Sear

Reverse sear is all the rage these days. Instead of searing the meat, then cooking it through, you cook the meat through and then sear it. Before it had the moniker of "reverse sear," I called it "char" or "char-crusted." I employed this technique on any meat—mostly large steaks and whole beef tenderloins—that were cooked by the indirect method the day before I wanted to serve it.

For example, on day one, I would smoke or cook a steak sous vide. The meat would rest in the refrigerator overnight and just before serving, I'd brush it with olive oil, sprinkle it with coarse salt, and sear it over high direct heat. I found that searing cold cooked beef gave me a beautiful charred crust and warmed the already cooked meat just enough to serve but not overcook it.

If you like a nice caramelized crust and prominent grill marks, I don't see the reason for the reverse sear. The original sear and cook method that I discussed on page 196 is—in my book—the best method. If you want to try the sous-vide reverse sear method, try the Indoor/Outdoor Tomahawk Steak on page 22.

---

where it was going, but I thought it was too difficult to get other people to see the point. So I took the same principle and created my "A-OK" tip. Here it is:

1. Everyone knows the OK sign, where thumb and forefinger make a circle. Start there: Make an OK sign and hold it.

2. Feel the meaty part of the palm, just under the thumb, with your other forefinger. That feeling is **raw**. You really will be resting your other forefinger on your palm. There's no need to poke your palm.

3. Next, move your thumb to your middle finger and feel how the palm has gotten a little tighter; that is **rare**.

4. Next, move your thumb to your ring finger and feel how the palm tightens again; that is **medium**.

A few years ago, I was grilling beautiful beef tenderloins with my good friend and coauthor of *Pizza on the Grill*, Bob Blumer. We were cooking for a posh private party and had a $300 Prime beef tenderloin in our hands. Our "prime" (pun intended) objective, besides making sure all the wine glasses were filled, was to serve the beef charred on the outside with a beautiful ruby-red center.

I was in charge of the meat. I took my job very seriously, and using my trusty A-OK doneness test (see page 201), I knew I took the tenderloin off at the right time. We let the meat rest for about 7 minutes and then carved and plated it. Well, I was so disappointed: The meat was a pleasing pink but not the color I was looking for. There was nothing left to do but serve our guests, take our bows, and pretend that we had intended to serve rosy instead of ruby-red meat. After our guests had been served, we walked back to the kitchen to plate our next course, and what did we see but a gorgeous ruby-red piece of tenderloin staring straight at us! If we had just waited another 10 minutes, it would have been on their plates like that! I've learned through my experience that any piece of meat that weighs over 3 pounds needs between 15 and 20 minutes to rest.

5. Finally, move your thumb to your pinkie finger and feel the palm under the thumb again. It should be really tight by this time, and that is what **well-done** meat feels like when you poke it with your finger.

This test takes a while to master. While you are still getting the hang of it, make the OK sign that corresponds to the doneness you like your steaks. For example, I like mine rare so I'd put my middle finger on my thumb, then feel my palm and the steak. When the steak is rare, it will feel the same as my palm. Alternate between poking your palm and poking the meat until you memorize how the tension feels on the meat. But the proof is in the eating! Take your steak off the grill, let it rest, and cut into it—were you right?

RESTING MEAT

If you cook meat (or poultry), you are familiar with the instructions to let meat rest before slicing and serving. Besides seasoning with the Trilogy (see page 198) and cooking it properly, I find letting the cooked food rest is the single most important factor for serving juicy, perfectly cooked meat.

The resting process allows the juices to relax and redistribute themselves throughout the meat. When any protein is exposed to high heat, the juices are forced toward the exterior of the food. When you remove it from the heat, the food relaxes and the juices are redistributed evenly throughout the food. I prefer to let my meat "rest" or "sit" uncovered by aluminum foil, but some people cover their food to keep the heat in. I don't do that, in general, because the covering starts causing the food to steam, making my perfect crusts soggy.

Where Steak Comes From and Major Characteristics

When I sat down to write this book, I decided that it would be educational and fun to begin the process at the source. So I called my good friend Pat LaFrieda (third-generation butcher, author of *Meat*, and all-around great guy) and asked him how he would feel about cutting steaks, grilling them, and tasting them with me. I wanted to get the perspective of America's most beloved butcher—the butcher who made the famous Shake Shack blend and who supplies New York City with steaks. He was game, because Pat is always game! Weber sent us my favorite grill, the Summit 450, and we set it up at Pat LaFrieda Meat

Purveyors near the New Jersey Turnpike. If anyone had told me that I would be grilling Prime steak by the New Jersey Turnpike in the middle of the summer, I would have thought that they were crazy! But grill we did! We grilled and we tasted America's favorite steaks and a few that have yet to become popular. Following is A Steak Primer Grid, which showcases all the different steaks in order of where they come from on the cow, beginning at the shoulder and going toward the tail.

CUTS OF STEAK

There are four basic major (primal) cuts into which beef is separated: chuck, rib, loin, and round. The smaller muscle groups pertinent to steak include sirloin (part of the loin), flank, short plate, shank, and brisket.

I've included flavor in the grid, even though it proved to be very difficult to pin down. I decided to rate it on the intensity of the beef flavor using a range of 1 to 4, with 1 being the lightest in flavor (think filet mignon) and 4 being the strongest in flavor (think Prime ribeye, aged meat, and cuts like skirt and hanger).

Here is a key to the grid. Every steak is defined by its name and the muscle group it's cut from. These are followed by:

FLAVOR INTENSITY

1 = Lean: soft, clean, light, delicate

2 = Lean with some fat: clean, flavor chameleon (it will take on the flavor of a marinade)

3 = More marbling: juicy, big, beefy, rich

4 = Aged: very rich, nutty, deep, full-flavored

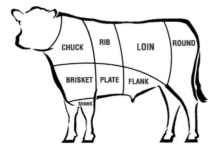

Several individual words like *gamy*, *fatty*, and *caramelized* are used to refer to what happens when the meat is cooked. For example, when a steak is prepared so that it has a prominently caramelized crisp crust, you get a roasty, toasty flavor.

TEXTURE

Fine (tender), **medium,** or **coarse** (chewy)

The finer the texture of the meat fibers, the more tender it will be; the coarser the texture, the tougher the cut will be.

DEFINING CHARACTERISTICS

More specific information about the cuts.

PREP NOTES

If there is an important tip for the cut's preparation, it's noted here.

PRICE

So many people ask me about price as it relates to steak that I wanted to find a way to give home cooks an idea about the costs associated with different steaks. "The market is a quagmire," said one meat expert to me. Meat prices fluctuate so much that it is difficult to give an exact price—or even a price range—for the steaks. For example, some cuts like skirt steak used to be inexpensive, but now that skirt steak is popular, it has become a much higher-priced cut of beef. But it is possible to categorize cuts of meat by price. I am grateful to Clint Walenciak, director of packing for Certified Angus Beef, aka "the CAB price man," who steered me in the right direction. Clint spent a lot of time helping me assign price levels to the various steaks. He also fact-checked the rest of the chart for me, making sure that the information was accurate.

$ = Lower price: value cuts

$$ = Medium price: sirloin and flank

$$$ = High price: loin and strip

$$$$ = Highest price: luxury cuts, bone-in steaks, anything dry-aged

A Steak Primer Grid

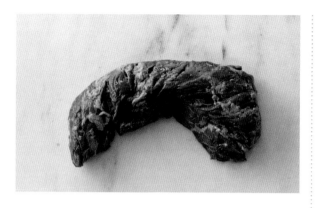

PETITE TENDER

AKA: Shoulder tender, mini filet mignon, teres major

Muscle group: Chuck

Flavor intensity: 2

Texture: Medium

Defining characteristics: Similar in shape to tenderloin, but only weighs 12 to 16 ounces, thus its name. Not nearly as buttery and tender as the true tenderloin.

Price: $$

FLATIRON

AKA: None

Muscle group: Chuck

Flavor intensity: 3

Texture: Fine/Medium

Defining characteristics: Second most tender cut of beef. Flatirons are cut from a top blade that has a tough piece of sinew running through the middle. Once removed, the blade can be divided into 4 steaks, weighing about 12 ounces each.

Price: $$

SIERRA

AKA: Minute steak, pepper steak

Muscle group: Chuck

Flavor intensity: 2

Texture: Coarse

Defining characteristics: Cut from the chuck roll or shoulder. An economy cut that looks similar to a flank steak. Well marbled but tough.

Prep notes: Benefits from being sliced into thin strips and stir-fried or from being pounded before cooking, like a pepper steak or a minute steak.

Price: $

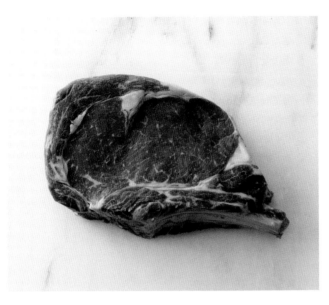

BONE-IN RIBEYE

AKA: Cowboy, cowboy with "frenched" bone, tomahawk (see below for distinctions)

Muscle group: Rib

Flavor intensity: 4

Texture: Medium

Defining characteristics: Well marbled and thought to be the most flavorful steak on the animal. The bone-in ribeye has a shorter bone than the frenched cowboy or the tomahawk.

   All three steaks are the same cut. The ribeye is a combination of the "eye" and the "cap." The "eye" is the center of the rib muscle. The "cap" is the accordion-like cap of meat on top of the ribeye. The "cap" is technically the *spinalis dorsi* and revered by serious meat lovers. This cap is sometimes removed and made into a "ribeye cap roast."

Price: $$$

TOMAHAWK

AKA: Bone-in ribeye

Muscle group: Rib

Flavor intensity: 4

Texture: Medium

Defining characteristics: A bone-in ribeye steak with the rib long bone intact is known as the tomahawk. The bone is typically 8 to 12 inches long. The steak is cut based on the thickness of the bone and is typically at least 2 inches thick.

Prep notes: This is a good choice of steak for cooking sous vide and searing over high heat before serving.

Price: $$$$

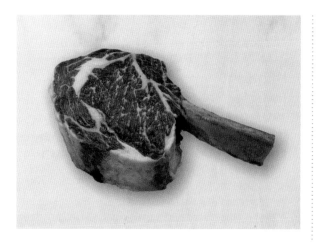

COWBOY WITH A "FRENCHED" BONE

AKA: Bone-in ribeye

Muscle group: Rib

Flavor intensity: 4

Texture: Medium

Defining characteristics: If the bone is "frenched," or cleaned for presentation purposes, it is then known as the cowboy. A regular bone-in ribeye is often referred to as a "cowboy steak," but the real cowboy steak has a cleaned 2-inch bone. It is incorrect to call it a "frenched cowboy."

Price: $$$$

BONELESS RIBEYE

AKA: Delmonico

Muscle group: Rib

Flavor intensity: 3

Texture: Medium

Defining characteristics: The ribeye steak with the bone removed. Sometimes called the Delmonico steak after the nineteenth-century New York City restaurant that popularized it.

Price: $$$

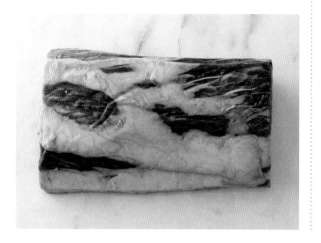

RIBEYE ROAST

AKA: Boneless prime rib

Muscle group: Rib

Flavor intensity: 3

Texture: Fine/Medium

Defining characteristics: The ribeye roast is a part of the whole rib muscle before it is cut into individual ribeye steaks. It is tender, rich, and beefy, with a fine grain and generous marbling.

Prep notes: A great "steak" for a crowd. It takes a little over an hour to cook a 6-pound roast to rare/medium-rare, and then it can be sliced for a crowd.

Price: $$$

RIBEYE CAP ROAST

AKA: Spinalis

Muscle group: Rib

Flavor intensity: 4+

Texture: Coarse

Defining characteristics: Technically it's the *spinalis dorsi* and sold as a ribeye cap roast. The late, great meat lover and food writer Josh Ozersky lived for the spinalis muscle, and Pat LaFrieda created the ultimate steak for Josh Capon's Bowery Meat Company by turning this ribeye cap into a BRT (bone, roll, and tie) roast that can be sliced into a steak. These days, you can buy a ribeye cap roast or a ribeye cap steak.

Prep notes: This is one steak—for me—that needs to be cooked to a full medium to bring it to full flavor.

Price: $$$$

T-BONE

AKA: None

Muscle group: Loin

Flavor intensity: 3

Texture: Fine/Medium

Defining characteristics: Cut from the short loin across the spine with the telltale "T-bone" separating the tenderloin and the strip steak. You get both the "tender" tenderloin and the meatier and more flavorful "strip" steak on both the T-bone and the porterhouse. Plus, either steak delivers the most iconic steakhouse presentation.

Price: $$$$

PORTERHOUSE

AKA: None

Muscle group: Loin

Flavor intensity: 3

Texture: Fine/Medium

Defining characteristics: The T-bone and the porterhouse are the same cut, but the porterhouse is cut from further back on the loin. Thus, the nugget of tenderloin is bigger on the porterhouse steak. You get both the "tender" tenderloin and the meatier and more flavorful "strip" steak on both the T-bone and the porterhouse. Plus, either steak delivers the most iconic steakhouse presentation.

Price: $$$$

BONE-IN STRIP LOIN STEAK

AKA: Shell steak

Muscle group: Loin

Flavor intensity: 3+

Texture: Medium

Defining characteristics: Tender, juicy, marbled, and meaty, the strip has great flavor, is easy to eat, and is a steak lover's favorite.

Price: $$$$

BONELESS STRIP LOIN STEAK

AKA: This quintessential steakhouse steak is known by many names, including New York strip, Kansas City strip, ambassador steak, and hotel-cut strip steak.

Muscle group: Loin

Flavor intensity: 3+

Texture: Medium

Defining characteristics: With the chine bone and the spine removed, the strip loin steak becomes a boneless strip loin steak. This is a very popular choice because there is no bone to cut around, the meat cooks more evenly, and you can eat the whole steak without having to cut around fat and bone.

Price: $$$

STRIP ROAST

AKA: None

Muscle group: Loin

Flavor intensity: 3+

Texture: Medium

Defining characteristics: The strip roast is a part of the whole strip loin muscle before it is cut into individual steaks. This is the same major muscle as the rib so it can be prepared similarly to ribeye steaks and roasts.

Prep notes: This is a great "steak" for a crowd. It takes about an hour to cook a 6-pound roast to rare/medium-rare, and then it can be sliced into steaks for a group.

Price: $$$

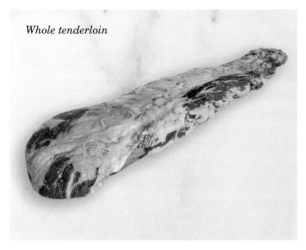

Whole tenderloin

TENDERLOIN

AKA: Filet mignon, chateaubriand

Muscle group: Loin

Flavor intensity: 1

Texture: Fine

Defining characteristics: The most tender and most expensive cut. It is made up of very small and fine meat fibers that make it tender when it is sliced and cooked. It is a long muscle that is inside the spine and runs from the body to the hind leg. It tapers off to a point as it moves closer to the head. The "chateaubriand" is cut from the thicker part of the tenderloin, near the hind leg.

Filet mignon is the name of the steak that is cut and portioned from the whole tenderloin. It should be cut 2 inches thick for grilling. Follow recipe directions for other methods such as pan-searing or baking.

Prep notes: Carpaccio (a thinly sliced and pounded raw beef dish) is made from the tenderloin or a piece of filet mignon.

Price: $$$$

Chateaubriand

Filet mignon

BONE-IN FILET

AKA: None

Muscle group: Loin

Flavor intensity: 2

Texture: Fine

Defining characteristics: It is sold with a part of the T-bone (transverse process). Perfect for a steakhouse WOW! presentation.

Prep notes: The bone in the filet will increase the cooking time by a few minutes.

Price: $$$$

TENDERLOIN TIPS

AKA: None

Muscle group: Loin

Flavor intensity: 1

Texture: Fine

Defining characteristics: If your butcher sells tenderloin tips, they are likely the trimmings from making perfect "center-cut" filets mignons.

Prep notes: These pieces of tenderloin make excellent kebabs (page 80), chili, beef stroganoff (page 120), and so on.

Price: $$$

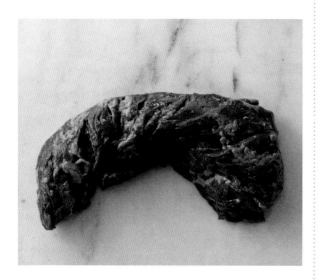

HANGER

AKA: Butcher's steak, hanging tender

Muscle group: Short loin, referred to as "thin meat" just like skirt steak

Flavor intensity: 4

Texture: Medium/Coarse

Defining characteristics: The meat hangs from the diaphragm; thus its name. It used to be taken home by the butcher, earning the nickname "butcher's steak." Strong in flavor; some think it has slight overtones of a "liver-like" taste.

Prep notes: It is sold as *onglet* in France and commonly served as a bistro steak or steak frites (page 155). It is excellent ground into hamburger meat and served rare.

Price: $$

FLANK

AKA: Sometimes sold as "London broil"

Muscle group: Flank

Flavor intensity: 2

Texture: Coarse

Defining characteristics: From the lower belly. It has long meat fibers and can be very chewy if not sliced against the grain.

Prep notes: A good steak for marinating. It must be sliced against the grain.

Price: $$

OUTSIDE SKIRT

AKA: Skirt steak

Muscle group: Plate

Flavor intensity: 4+

Texture: Medium/Coarse

Defining characteristics: From the diaphragm, near the lungs. Doesn't fall into one of the prime cuts groupings or "middle meat" steak groups. Referred to as "thin meat" just like hanger steak.

The outside skirt is smaller (about 3 inches) and narrower and has better texture than the larger inside skirt steak. The rich beefy flavor of the skirt steak is a favorite among butchers and chefs—myself included.

Prep notes: Cook to medium-rare for best results.

Price: $$

INSIDE SKIRT

AKA: Skirt steak

Muscle group: Plate

Flavor intensity: 4+

Texture: Very coarse and chewy

Defining characteristics: Cut from deeper inside the cow next to the lungs. Doesn't fall into one of the primals or "middle meat" steak groups. Referred to as "thin meat" just like hanger steak. Inside skirt steak is about twice the width (5 to 6 inches) of outside skirt steak.

Prep notes: Often used for fajitas and benefits from a marinade.

Price: $$

TRI-TIP

AKA: Triangle steak

Muscle group: Loin/sirloin

Flavor intensity: 2

Texture: Medium/Coarse

Defining characteristics: The tri-tip or "triangle" steak is cut from the sirloin/round at the back of the cow. Cut from the bottom sirloin, it usually weighs 3 to 4 pounds and is the signature cut from Santa Maria, California.

Prep notes: Rubbed with spices and sometimes marinated, it is grilled whole and served as "Santa Maria barbecue" (page 56).

Price: $$

BALL TIP

AKA: Ball tip steak, ball tip roast

Muscle group: Loin

Flavor intensity: 2

Texture: Coarse

Defining characteristics: These steaks come from the top butt. It is one of the largest loin cuts and is generally sliced into steaks for surf and turf at value restaurants or ground for chili, burgers, or meat loaf.

Prep notes: Benefits from marinating.

Price: $$

TOP SIRLOIN STEAK

AKA: None

Muscle group: Loin

Flavor intensity: 2

Texture: Medium/Coarse

Defining characteristics: One of the largest loin cuts. Sirloin is lean, has no intramuscular fat, and is not particularly tender or flavorful on its own.

Prep notes: Benefits from marinating. It is more tender when cut into cubes for kebabs.

Price: $$

Basic Steaks
STEAK 101

This is the easy 5-minutes-a-side way to cook a steak. It works well for a strip steak, a small ribeye, a flatiron, or a 2-inch-thick filet mignon.

Serves 4

> 1 to 4 boneless New York strip steaks or other favorite (steakhouse) variety such as ribeye or filet mignon (12 ounces each and at least 1 inch thick)
>
> Extra-virgin olive oil
>
> 1 teaspoon coarse kosher salt, or more as needed (optional)
>
> 1 teaspoon whole black peppercorns, coarsely ground (optional)
>
> Steak Butter (optional; recipe follows)

Outdoor Grilling Method: Direct/Medium-High Heat (about 400°F)

❶ Preheat the grill with all burners on high. Once preheated, adjust the temperature to medium-high heat for direct grilling.

❷ Wrap the meat in paper towels to rid it of excess moisture. Replace the paper towels as needed.

❸ Just before grilling, brush both sides of the steaks with oil and season with salt and pepper, if desired.

❹ Place the steaks directly over medium-high heat for about 5 minutes. Flip the steaks over and continue cooking for about 5 more minutes for medium-rare (135°F on an instant-read thermometer).

❺ Remove the steaks from the grill and set them on a platter. Top each one with ½ tablespoon of Steak Butter, if desired. Allow them to rest for at least 5 minutes, but no longer than 10 minutes, before serving.

Indoor Cooking Method: Stovetop and oven

❶ Wrap the meat in paper towels to rid it of excess moisture. Replace the paper towels as needed.

❷ Preheat an oven-safe grill pan on the stovetop to medium-high heat and the oven to 350°F.

❸ Just before cooking, brush both sides of the steaks with oil and season with salt and pepper, if desired.

❹ Place the steaks directly on the grill pan and cook until nicely grill-marked on one side, 1 to 2 minutes. Using tongs, flip the steaks over. Transfer the grill pan to the oven and cook for about 7 minutes for medium-rare (135°F on an instant-read thermometer).

❺ Remove the steaks from the oven and set them on a platter. Top each one with ½ tablespoon of Steak Butter, if desired. Allow them to rest for at least 5 minutes, but no longer than 10, before serving.

Indoor Cooking Method: Stovetop only

I love this red-hot cast-iron pan stovetop method and actually employ it on my grill as well as my stovetop. Cooking this way outdoors means no smoky kitchen. It does create a lot of smoke, but the crust is the best crust that you can get on a steak.

Serves 1 or 2

> 1 New York strip, filet mignon, or ribeye steak (about 16 ounces and at least 1 inch thick)
>
> Extra-virgin olive oil
>
> Coarse kosher salt
>
> Freshly ground black pepper (optional)

Special Equipment: Cast-iron or carbon steel skillet (I prefer the Lodge 10½-inch square pan)

❶ Wrap the meat in paper towels to rid it of excess moisture. Replace the paper towels as needed.

❷ Meanwhile, place a dry cast-iron skillet on the stove and preheat it over medium-high heat until a drop of water sprinkled on the surface "dances" and evaporates instantly.

❸ Just before cooking, brush the steak all over with olive oil and season lightly with kosher salt and pepper, if using. Place the steak in the preheated pan toward one side, and let cook for 3 to 5 minutes, pressing down gently to ensure even contact between the steak and the pan. Using tongs, flip the steak over to the other side of the pan, and continue cooking. You should wind up with a nice, even crust after another 3 to 5 minutes. Using tongs, hold the steak upright so you can brown the fat on the sides.

❹ At this point, the steak should look done, be a bit smaller in size and firmer, and have a deep-brown caramelized crust on each side. It is time to check for doneness. The meat should feel tight and

slightly springy, not raw and mushy, to the touch. If using an instant-read thermometer, insert it horizontally through the side into the center to read the temperature. Medium-rare is 135°F.

❺ Remove the steak to a rack set in a sheet pan and let rest for 5 to 10 minutes. You can tent it lightly with aluminum foil, but not so tightly that the steak will begin to steam. Slice and serve.

STEAK BUTTER

A compound butter gives your steak a steakhouse presentation and adds that little extra lushness to the meat. This is what changes the steak from backyard beef to a real backyard treat—you may never go out for steak again!

Makes 1 log; generous ½ cup

Once the skillet is hot, add the steak to one side.

8 tablespoons (1 stick) unsalted butter, at room temperature

4 teaspoons minced fresh parsley

2 teaspoons granulated garlic

2 teaspoons dried tarragon

❶ Combine the butter, parsley, garlic, and tarragon. Mix well.

❷ On a large piece of plastic wrap or parchment paper, drop the butter in spoonfuls in a row about 5 inches long. Roll the butter up in the wrap and smooth it out to form a round log about 5 inches long.

❸ Twist the ends to seal and refrigerate until the butter is hard and easy to cut into pieces, at least 2 hours. Well wrapped, the butter will keep refrigerated for 1 week and in the freezer for 1 month.

Once cooked on the first side, flip the steak over to the other side of the skillet.

Hold the steak up using tongs, and finish cooking by searing the sides.

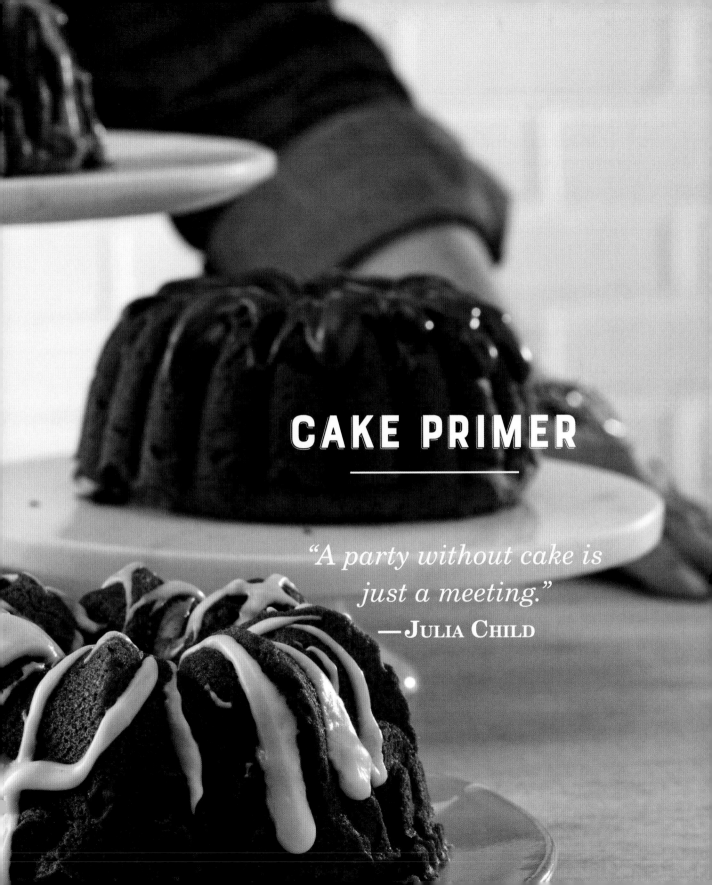

CAKE PRIMER

"A party without cake is
just a meeting."
—Julia Child

Cake 101

When I started to write this book, I quickly realized that I was going to have a huge amount of cake. Because cake is made to share, I decided to embark on a five-week trip to the homes of friends and family that I dubbed my "Steak and Cake Tour," or "cake tour" for short.

That way, I could bake, they could invite friends to come and taste the cakes, and I would have instant feedback. This trip also helped me edit my list of cakes. I had well over 100 cakes when I began and in creating the "cake list" for each stop, I assembled a list that I knew my hosts would love. For example, my sister Mary Pat loves blueberries, so I knew that I had to reserve my lemon-blueberry Bundt cake for her. I was right because it ended up being her favorite cake. In fact, after we all tasted a sliver of it, she squirreled it away and kept the rest for herself. I could always tell which cake was the real winner because that cake instantly went into the host's freezer instead of being offered to others to take home.

When I came back home and unpacked my notes, I looked at my cake list—it was a list of my favorites and my crowd-pleasers. There were a number of classic cakes that I had wanted to include that didn't make the cut. I wrestled with this fact but then realized, with the help of my editor, Suzanne Rafer, that it was okay to have an eclectic curated list of cakes that reflected my personal tastes. After all, she said, "this is a quirky book." So in the end, this is not an exhaustive compendium of cakes but instead a handpicked selection that matches up beautifully with my steak recipes and is reflective of a cross section of the country from North Carolina to New York to Chicago to Houston to California, where the cakes were eaten and loved.

If you have never baked a cake before, it can be intimidating. The cake section of my Steak and Cake class was the most rewarding because I saw people's self-esteem and confidence grow in three hours. Because the class was hands-on, everyone got to make steak and bake cakes. And each week, there

would be at least one person attending who had never baked a cake before and thought that they couldn't do it. I would make sure my beginner bakers made the Tex-Mex Chocolate Sheet Cake on page 127. It is impossible to mess up, and the end result is so delicious that it will have even those with a lifelong fear of baking doing the happy dance! It is easier than you think to bake a cake from scratch, and the results are generally so much better than you can buy at a bakery or a restaurant. I've found that all it takes is that initial success for someone to become a baker. It's like jumping off the high dive for the first time—scary at first, but ultimately exciting and satisfying, and you can't wait to do it again!

Basic Pans

When I first started baking and cooking, I would buy the pan I needed once I chose a recipe instead of buying lots of pans just because they looked interesting. I was lucky enough to live across the street from a Williams Sonoma store, and slowly, over the years, I have collected many pans and have tested different materials to discover what works best.

To illustrate: I love all kitchen equipment and love to troll antique stores and flea markets looking for gadgets and old pans—I am sure I got this from my mother! But ultimately, the best end result is the goal. Even though my mother was emotionally attached to her grandmother's hexagonal tin cake pans, I suggested that we try good-quality (platinum-process) silicone cake pans. I knew that it seemed like a sacrilege and a dishonor to family tradition, but I wanted a better cake. Eventually we did try the silicone and realized that they worked better than the antique family heirlooms. It was a sad day for tradition, but better for the cakes.

CAKE PAN CONSTRUCTION

METAL: If you buy metal baking pans, light-colored pans are preferable. Many companies sell dark-colored baking pans, and sadly, buying them is a mistake, because these pans tend to overbake cakes.

Cake pan manufacturers use many metals, including stainless steel. I like the heavy-gauge aluminized steel, as well as anodized aluminum, and some heavy-duty stainless-steel pans that All-Clad made years ago. Whatever you choose, choose a light-colored, heavy, sturdy pan that will bake evenly.

One of my favorites is the Fat Daddio's brand of anodized aluminum bakeware, which brings professional-quality equipment to the home cook. Their 9 x 13-inch pan bakes the perfect sheet cake. They have so many pans, and they are all good. Wilton also makes good-quality, classic, light-colored aluminum pans. While I was creating the recipes for this book and shooting the photographs, I most often used the Cuisinart Chef's Classic nonstick

six-piece bakeware set in the gold finish. It is made of heavy-gauge aluminized steel and bakes evenly and consistently. The set includes a 9-inch loaf pan, a 9-inch square pan, two 9-inch round cake pans for layer cakes, a 6-cup muffin tin, and a 17-inch sheet pan, all for a very reasonable price. It is a good choice if you need all the basic shapes.

SILICONE: I love silicone. When it was first introduced in the United States, I worked with Lékué to bring their baking pans from Spain. I found that silicone prevents the cake from overbaking—providing that you take the cake out of the oven in time—and keeps the crumb moist and tender. This is especially helpful if you are a new baker.

Lékué taught me that you must buy platinum-process silicone for health and for consistent and even heat transfer. The non-platinum process can leave impurities in the silicone that affect the baking. I still like Lékué a lot and am very partial to their brilliant porcelain and silicone springform pan. Because the silicone sleeve doesn't heat up like metal, you can bake cheesecake without a water bath, and the cheesecake will have a tender and creamy texture.

Silicone baking pans generally do not have any hard structure, which makes them easy to "squish" into a cabinet. This also means that you must place the traditional silicone pan on a sheet pan before you place it in the oven to bake. However, that has changed with the new line of Trudeau baking pans.

Trudeau makes some of my new favorite silicone baking pans. They are platinum-process and have all the properties of silicone—even heat, easy release, dishwasher-safe—but they also have a metal skeleton that eliminates the need to place the pans on a sheet pan before baking. This new structured silicone is big news for silicone cake pan lovers!

PORCELAIN: My favorite porcelain is made by the original French porcelain company, Revol. In the spirit of full disclosure, I partnered with Revol to create a line of bakeware and cookware called Elizabeth's Everyday Essentials, but that is a testament to how fantastic these pans are! The pans perform exceptionally well and are beautiful to boot. My favorite pans for cake are the Revol Les Naturels loaf pan, the Les Naturals rectangular baking dish, and the Elizabeth's Everyday Essentials Super Square Baker.

GLASS AND CERAMIC: The traditional 9 x 13-inch Pyrex glass pan is now sold as a 3-quart Pyrex. This is a pan that just about everyone has in their kitchen. However, the new Lodge ceramic "stoneware" pans bake better and are sized in the traditional 9 x 13-inch and 8 x 8-inch sizes. They can be used for a sheet cake or for making the Margarita Tres Leches Cake (page 150) and Anthony's Grandmother's "Earthquake Cake" (page 153), among others. In my experience, the light-colored metal, stoneware, ceramic, and porcelain pans bake more evenly than the glass pans, but you can adjust your cooking times. Just make sure that a toothpick inserted in the center of the cake comes out clean, and you will be set.

CAKE PAN SHAPES

BUNDT OR TUBE PANS: Both pans—the distinctive Bundt and its plainer cousin—are known for their graceful round shapes with a center hole. The most well-known Bundt pans come from Nordic Ware. However, many other companies make a version. If you love cast iron, Lodge's Legacy series recently brought back the fluted cake pan that was a mainstay in their line for forty years. I used this pan for the Old Virginia's Best Pound Cake (page 118), and it baked beautifully!

ROUND LAYER PANS: Back in the day, round cake pans were typically 8 inches in diameter. Today, most of the round cake pans on the market are 9 inches. You can find both 8-inch and 9-inch round cake pans made by many companies; they are typically 2 inches deep, and that is what you want. All of the layer cakes in this book will work for both 8- and 9-inch round cake pans. Just make sure you divide the batter evenly between the pans. If you are making a three-layer cake, the 8-inch pans work better.

SQUARE CAKE PANS: Square cake pans come in many materials: metal, silicone, glass, ceramic, and porcelain. The most common sizes are 8 x 8 or 9 x 9 inches. If you use an 8-inch-square pan for these recipes, the cake will be a little thicker than if you use a 9-inch square—just make sure that the pan sides are at least 2 inches high. Both sizes and all the materials work well. My preference is for a square pan with sharp, not rounded, corners.

LOAF PANS: These pans come in a variety of sizes, with the average pan measuring 9 x 5 inches or 8½ x 4½ inches. Since loaf pans are not standardized, my rule of thumb is to fill them only two-thirds full, and if there's batter left over, I make a mini loaf or muffins with the extra batter.

SHEET CAKE PANS: Note: These pans are not to be confused with half sheet pans (see below). Sheet cakes are easy to make. They're great for parties and large groups because they can be cut into many pieces. You can leave them in the pan and frost only the top, or you can remove them from the pan, place them on a cake board (Wilton makes a simple white cardboard board that is 10 x 14 inches and fits a 9 x 13-inch sheet cake perfectly), and frost the top and the sides. Traditionally, sheet cakes were baked in pans that were at least 9 x 13 inches and 2 to 3 inches deep. Today, you can find deep sheet cake pans in just about every size. Wilton, Nordic Ware, and Fat Daddio's all make great sheet cake pans.

If you are traveling with your cake (think potlucks), look for the pans that come with domed plastic lids. Most layer cake batters can be baked in a deep 9 x 13-inch pan if you're looking to make a party-size sheet cake.

HALF SHEET PANS/JELLY ROLL PANS: This hardworking restaurant pan is having a moment due mostly to the popularity of "sheet pan suppers." This is the pan that I use to support my silicone bakeware and make it easier to remove a Bundt pan from the oven. It is a must in your kitchen and is the pan to use for

the Tex-Mex Chocolate Sheet Cake (page 127) and my German Chocolate Sheet Cake (page 128). Many companies make sheet pans; I like Nordic Ware, Cuisinart, and Fat Daddio's. If you are traveling with the Tex-Mex Chocolate Sheet Cake, the domed lid sold with the half sheet pan by Nordic Ware is very handy. Make sure to buy a cooling rack that will fit into the sheet pan. USA Pan makes a nice set of a half sheet pan and cooling rack that are sold together.

MEASURING CUPS AND SPOONS

Baking and cooking are all about measuring. You can measure in two ways: by weight or by volume. This book lists all measurements for both the steak recipes and the cake recipes by volume, using the American measuring cup system.

If you do not have the proper measuring cups and spoons, you will need to invest in three separate sets—dry measuring cups, liquid measuring cups, and measuring spoons. You can't interchange the dry-measure and the liquid-measure cups. However, you can use the same measuring spoons for salt, sugar, spices, and liquid flavorings.

Measuring cups for dry ingredients are usually colored plastic or metal. I prefer the metal measuring cups because they clean up easier, but I have used both. They commonly come in sets of four or five pieces: ¼ cup, ⅓ cup, ½ cup, 1 cup, and sometimes ⅛ cup.

Measuring cups for liquid ingedients are usually clear plastic or glass. I prefer glass measuring cups and use them for both sweet and savory cooking. They usually come in three configurations: 1 cup, 2 cups, and 4 cups. OXO makes a ¼ cup size as well.

Measuring spoons are usually colored plastic or metal. As with the dry measuring cups, I prefer the metal variety. They commonly come in sets of four or five pieces: ¼ teaspoon, ½ teaspoon, 1 teaspoon, 1 tablespoon, and sometimes ⅛ teaspoon. (It has been decided that a "pinch" of salt is just under ⅛ teaspoon, so newer sets sometimes include the ⅛ teaspoon.) Sometimes ¼ tablespoon and 2 tablespoons are also included in a set.

Basic Ingredients for Making Cake Batter

Most cakes are a combination of flour, sugar, butter or oil, and an ingredient to make the cake rise. The rising ingredients include baking soda, baking powder, egg whites, or a combination of these.

FLOURS

To get a light and airy cake structure, you need a flour with a lower protein content. All-purpose flour has a medium protein level, and cake flour has the lowest protein content. Bread flour has the most; you would never want to make a cake with bread flour. All flours are bleached to some extent, but "unbleached" all-purpose flour means that there are no chemical bleaching agents used in the processing of the flour. My favorite is King Arthur Unbleached All-Purpose Flour. My favorite cake flour is Swans Down. All cake flours have been chemically bleached to bring the protein level down. The lower protein level is what makes the crumb on the cake so soft and tender.

ALL-PURPOSE: All-purpose flour comes in two basic forms—bleached and unbleached—and can be used interchangeably. All-purpose flour is a blend of high-gluten hard wheat and low-gluten soft wheat. It's a fine-textured flour milled from the inner part of the wheat kernel and contains neither the germ nor the bran. U.S. law requires that all flours not containing wheat germ must have niacin, riboflavin, thiamine, and iron added; some mills also add vitamins A and D, and these flours are labeled "enriched." Most flour on the market today is presifted, requiring only that it be whisked, then spooned into a measuring cup and leveled off.

CAKE FLOUR: Many family cake recipes that have been handed down from generation to generation call for cake flour. Made from soft wheat and chlorinated or bleached, Swans Down cake flour is famous for being sifted twenty-seven times. Swans Down has been sold since 1894.

ALTERNATIVE FLOURS: These days there are so many alternative flours that I can't begin to name them all. Besides all-purpose and cake flour, I generally only use nut flours to bake a cake. Almond is my favorite, followed by hazelnut and coconut. It is important to note that nut flours absorb a lot more liquid, so you can't substitute them for wheat flour cup for cup. The best gluten-free flour that I have used is called Cup4Cup, but admittedly, I have only used it to make pizza dough. I have never made a cake with it. I will leave the gluten-free experiments to the gluten-free experts.

MEASURING FLOUR

The first thing that you need to know when you're following a cake recipe is how to measure flour. Too much flour and your cake will be heavy and chalky; too little flour and your cake will be dense and spongy. I grew up measuring and sifting and measuring again, but sifting is really no longer necessary because flour is sifted before it is packaged. In addition, my observations from teaching my many steak and cake classes is that measuring and sifting flour twice is a deterrent to baking a cake. I have eliminated the sifting steps, and I have not found that any of my cakes have suffered at all. It *is* necessary to aerate the flour, but you can do that at the same time that you mix in the salt and any spices and leavening agents (such as baking powder or baking soda) by whisking the flour and dry ingredients together.

Use the correct measuring cup. Dry measuring cups come in graduated sizes and are usually plastic or metal. (Liquid measuring cups are usually glass or plastic and look like pitchers with cup notations on the side.)

Using a scoop or a spoon, lightly fill the measuring cup and shake gently to level it off or sweep across the top with a table knife. You don't want to pack the flour in.

Pour the measured flour into a bowl and whisk to incorporate air into the flour. This is the perfect time to whisk in any other dry ingredients. Most recipes

Fresh vs. Sweetened Dried Coconut

I like pretty much anything with coconut in it. And for baking you have two main choices—sweetened dried coconut and freshly grated coconut. Today you can also buy unsweetened dried coconut, but I usually use that only when I'm making homemade granola. Some cakes, like German Chocolate Sheet Cake (page 128), call for the sweetened dried variety—a grocery-store staple. My Mother's Freshly Grated Coconut Cake (page 68) calls for fresh coconut because the cooked icing is already sweet and the light white cake is best paired with the delicate fresh coconut flavor.

If you don't want to crack and peel your own coconut, you'll find frozen grated fresh coconut in Asian grocery stores or frozen Just Coconut Chunks from Trader Joe's.

in this cookbook call for all-purpose flour, but some of them call for cake flour. If you want to substitute cake flour for all-purpose flour, you must add an additional 2 tablespoons of cake flour to every cup of all-purpose. For example, 1 cup of all-purpose flour equals 1 cup plus 2 tablespoons of cake flour.

Occasionally, there are directions in this book that are not standard but that I have found create a superior result. For example, some of the sugar will be whisked into the flour. This is a little unusual, but if the recipe calls for it, do it. I also have found that whisking citrus zest into the flour ensures that the zest is well distributed throughout the cake, and I call for that step throughout the book. Likewise for cocoa powder.

THE SUPPORTING CAST—BUTTER, MILK, SUGAR, SALT, NUTS, AND FLAVORINGS

As we all learned from the story of the Three Little Pigs, if you don't have good-quality materials, your entire house may collapse. This is the case for cakes as well. Butter, sugar, salt, and nuts help build the foundation of your cake, and you want to use the best ingredients to make the best cakes.

UNSALTED BUTTER: This is also sometimes referred to as sweet butter. It is always best to use unsalted butter when baking; salted butter can make the cake too salty. It is better to be able to control how much salt you use in a recipe, whether it is sweet or savory. Soften butter by bringing it to room temperature on the counter, not in the microwave. I call for butter measures by the tablespoon, stick, or cup. Remember this rule of thumb: 1 pound of butter is usually divided into 4 sticks. Each stick is the equivalent of 8 tablespoons or ½ cup. If you buy a ½ pound of butter, that is equivalent to 2 sticks or 1 cup.

MILK: If a recipe calls for milk, you want to use whole milk unless the recipe specifically calls for a different kind. My sister Mary Pat likes to say that using milk with a lower fat percentage (1 percent, 2 percent, and skim) is "akin to building a house with sticks instead of bricks." Use a liquid measuring cup to measure milk.

These are generally made from glass or transparent plastic.

SUGAR: Granulated white sugar is best for cake batters because of the size of the grain. Never use confectioners' sugar in a cake batter unless the recipe specifically calls for it. It is too fine and has cornstarch added to it. If a recipe calls for brown sugar or demerara sugar, then use it. Otherwise, stick to granulated white sugar. Use a dry measuring cup to measure sugar. White sugar is filled to the top of the dry measuring cup, which is usually solid plastic or metal. Dark brown and light brown sugars are packed into the measuring cup.

Confectioners' sugar is dipped and measured like flour and then sifted to remove any lumps. It is the sugar most often used in frostings, icings, and glazes.

SALT: I call for fine sea salt, like La Baleine, sold in a blue canister and available in most supermarkets. This fine-grain salt—as opposed to kosher salt—is incorporated into the batter quickly and evenly. While Morton's iodized salt works, I think it has a chemical metallic aftertaste. Salt is generally measured using measuring spoons or a pinch between your thumb and forefinger. A pinch should never be more than ⅛ teaspoon.

NUTS: Adding flavor and texture, nuts are important in so many cakes. I like to say that as a Southerner, I use pecans like other chefs use salt and pepper. I think they enhance everything, especially when toasted (see box, page 85).

FLAVORINGS: I tend to use liqueurs to flavor cakes and frostings because they taste less artificial. For example, I use 99 Bananas liqueur instead of banana extract in my Banana Pudding Ice Cream Cake (page 162) because it enhances the natural banana flavor instead of giving it an artificial banana flavor.

Extracts are very popular flavorings, especially vanilla. If a cake calls for vanilla extract, you can substitute an extract of your choosing. Most besides vanilla are very concentrated, but some of them are a lovely addition. My favorite extracts include lemon, orange, almond, coconut, and peppermint. It is best when possible to choose real extract over imitation, but some of the extracts, such as coconut, are not available in any form except imitation.

You can also use citrus zest, citrus juice, and fruit purees to add flavor. Start with a small amount the first time you bake a cake. Next time you bake the cake, build the flavor if you think it's needed.

Spirited Flavorings

Any of your favorite liquors and liqueurs can make an excellent flavoring for frosting, icing, glazes, and syrups.

> Amaretto
> 99 Bananas
> Bourbon
> Baileys Original Irish Cream
> Chambord
> Cognac and other brandy
> Cointreau
> Crème de menthe
> Domaine de Canton (ginger)
> Frangelico
> Grand Marnier
> Kahlúa
> Kirsch
> Limoncello
> Luxardo (Maraschino cherry)
> Peach schnapps
> Peppermint schnapps
> Rum
> Sambuca
> Triple sec

Baking Cakes

PREPARING THE PANS

FAT AND FLOUR (F&F) METHOD: If you learned to bake from your mother or grandmother, as I did, preparing cake pans was a big part of baking a cake. We would start by drawing an outline of the cake pan on waxed paper or parchment paper, cutting it out, and making sure it fit in the bottom of the pan. Often, I would have to retrim it to fit because the outside dimension of the pan is actually about ¼ inch larger than the inside. Next, you would have to grease the pan with butter or Crisco, sprinkle with flour, tip the pan, and tap it to evenly distribute the flour all around the bottom and the sides—shaking out the excess until you had a coating of "fat and flour," or F&F for short. Then the paper would be inserted on the bottom to ensure that the cake didn't stick.

BAKING SPRAY: You can still go through all of these F&F steps or do what professional pastry chefs and seasoned bakers—including myself—do and use a baking spray. The spray is formulated with both fat and flour. My favorite brand is Baker's Joy, but Pam also makes a baking spray. They work the same, but I don't like the artificial vanilla scent that has been added to the Pam version. When using a baking spray, I prepare my pans just before I pour batter in them. However, for ease, I note in my recipes to prepare the pans when you preheat the oven. Either way is okay. I hold my pan over the sink to catch any spray that goes into the atmosphere, methodically spray in a circle around the edges, and then fill in the bottom. I use a liberal amount of the spray and never have any sticking issues.

TESTING FOR DONENESS

You can tell a cake is done when a toothpick inserted in the center comes out clean. At this point, the cake will start to pull away from the sides of the pan. If the cake has shrunk from the sides and there is a ⅛- to ¼-inch space between the sides and the cake, it is most likely overbaked.

HOW TO REMOVE CAKES FROM THE PANS

Remove the cake from the oven and let the pan cool for the number of minutes stated in the recipe. Then, run a butter knife around the edge of the pan to make sure that none of the cake is stuck to the sides. Invert the cake onto a wire cooling rack and tap the bottom of the

cake pan in all the corners and the middle. With one hand on either side of the pan, carefully and slowly lift it off the cake. If you aren't frosting the cake and want to preserve the top crust for presentation, invert the cake again onto another cooling rack and let it cool top side up.

STICKAGE: Cakes that stick to the pan and rip when you try to remove them to cool break a baker's heart! My editor, Suzanne Rafer, has had this happen on more than one occasion. As she says, "I've pasted together more than several Bundts," so I gave her the advice that I give everyone: Spray the pan with Baker's Joy and go ahead and use more than you probably need. This is especially important if you are using the intricate Bundt pans that have so many nooks and crannies that cake can adhere to. On page 132, you can see the only cake that was baked for our photo shoot not using Baker's Joy—and a tiny patch of cake stuck to that pan. We photographed it just like that, without pasting it back onto the cake, because I know

that that happens to home cooks all the time, and I wanted to show that the cake was still beautiful with no effect on the flavor at all. But for best results, use Baker's Joy.

A NOTE ON CAKE COOLING RACKS

I think that the manufacturers of cooling racks must have had cookies on their minds when they designed them, because the shape is mostly rectangular. This is convenient, because they fit into sheet pans nicely and are integral for great roasting. But most cakes are round or 8 or 9 inches square, and the extra sides of the cooling racks can be awkward. So imagine my delight when I discovered that Nordic Ware makes round cooling racks. They are heavy-duty, store easily, and are just the right size for round layer cakes, square cakes, loaf cakes, Bundt cakes, and so on. The only cakes that they won't work for are the cakes that you make in a 9 x 13-inch pan—and for those, you can use a standard rectangular cooling rack.

BASIC CAKES

Sometimes the perfect cake is a simple yellow cake with a chocolate frosting or a fluffy white cake with an American buttercream. That's why I included a basic cake section. If you're making cupcakes for a party or your son's or daughter's classroom, this is the section that you can refer to for a simple yellow, white, or chocolate cake. These are my three favorite versions for traditional layer cakes, party sheet cakes, and cupcakes.

YELLOW BUTTER CAKE

This all-American beauty was my mother's go-to cake. When we were kids, she served it most often with a chocolate fudge icing or an American buttercream. It is a solid, multipurpose yellow cake recipe that is also great for large-occasion sheet cakes and cupcakes.

Baking spray, for preparing the pans

12 tablespoons (1½ sticks) unsalted butter, at room temperature

1½ cups granulated white sugar

3 large eggs

2¼ cups all-purpose flour

2½ teaspoons baking powder

1 teaspoon fine sea salt

1 cup whole milk

2 teaspoons pure vanilla extract

Pans: Two 9-inch round cake pans or cupcake tins, or one 9 x 13-inch pan

① Position a rack in the center of the oven and preheat the oven to 350°F. Spray the cake pans with baking spray.

② Cream the butter and sugar together with an electric mixer on medium-high speed until light and fluffy, 3 to 5 minutes. Add the eggs one at a time, beating well after each addition, until thoroughly mixed.

③ Place the flour in a medium-size bowl. Add the baking powder and salt and whisk well to combine. Pour the milk into a glass measuring cup and stir in the vanilla.

④ Add a little of the flour mixture to the butter mixture and mix well on medium-low speed. Add a little of the milk mixture and mix. Alternate the flour and milk in small batches until it is all incorporated into the batter. Stop the machine and scrape down the side of the bowl as necessary.

⑤ Pour the batter into the prepared cake pans. If using 2 pans, make sure to divide the batter evenly. Lightly tap each pan down on the counter to make sure the batter is evenly distributed and to remove excess air bubbles.

⑥ If baking layers, bake until they pull away from the sides of the pans and a toothpick inserted in the center comes out clean, 30 to 35 minutes. A 9 x 13-inch pan will take longer to bake—40 to 45 minutes. Cupcakes will take 15 to 20 minutes. Begin testing the layers at 25 minutes, the sheet cake at 30 minutes, and the cupcakes at 15 minutes. Test again in 5-minute increments because every oven bakes differently. Depending on your oven, it may take a little less time or a little longer to bake. Use the visual clues and the toothpick test as your definitive test.

⑦ Cool cupcakes or layers in the pans for 10 minutes, then remove them from the pans and let cool completely on wire cooling racks before icing or assembling. A cake baked in a 9 x 13-inch pan, commonly referred to as a sheet cake, can be left in the pan and iced only on the top, or it can be removed from the pan and iced and decorated on the top and the sides. It is easier to transport a sheet cake while it is still in the pan.

WHITE CAKE

S implicity is the keynote of all true elegance," according to Coco Chanel. And when you are looking for elegant simplicity, a delicate white cake is just that. I use a modified version of this white cake in both the Homemade Confetti Birthday Cake (page 48) and My Mother's Freshly Grated Coconut Cake (page 68). In any incarnation, it's delicious—pure and simple.

> Baking spray, for preparing the pans
>
> 12 tablespoons (1½ sticks) unsalted butter, at room temperature
>
> 1¾ cups granulated white sugar
>
> 2⅔ cups all-purpose flour
>
> 3½ teaspoons baking powder
>
> ¾ teaspoon fine sea salt
>
> 1⅓ cups skim milk
>
> 2 teaspoons pure vanilla extract or other extract of your choosing
>
> 4 large egg whites (about ½ cup)

Pans: Two 9-inch round cake pans or cupcake tins, or one 9 x 13-inch pan

① Position a rack in the center of the oven and preheat the oven to 350°F. Spray the cake pans with baking spray.

② Cream the butter and sugar together with an electric mixer on medium-high speed until light and fluffy, 3 to 5 minutes.

③ Place the flour in a medium-size bowl. Add the baking powder and salt and whisk well to combine. Pour the milk into a glass measuring cup and stir in the vanilla.

④ Add a little of the flour mixture to the butter mixture and mix well on medium-low speed. Add a little of the milk mixture and mix. Alternate the flour and milk in small batches until it is all incorporated into the batter. Stop the machine and scrape down the side of the bowl as necessary.

⑤ Beat the egg whites in a clean mixer bowl with the whisk attachment until stiff peaks form. Gently fold the whites by hand into the cake batter.

6 Pour the batter into the prepared cake pans. If using 2 pans, make sure to divide the batter evenly. Lightly tap each pan down on the counter to make sure the batter is evenly distributed and to remove excess air bubbles.

7 If baking layers, bake until they pull away from the sides of the pans and a toothpick inserted in the center comes out clean, 30 to 35 minutes. A 9 x 13-inch pan will take longer to bake—40 to 45 minutes. Cupcakes will take 15 to 20 minutes. Begin testing the layers at 25 minutes, the sheet cake at 30 minutes, and the cupcakes at 15 minutes. Test again in 5-minute increments because every oven bakes differently. Depending on your oven, it may take a little less time or a little longer to bake. Use the visual clues and the toothpick test as your definitive test.

8 Cool cupcakes or layers in the pans for 10 minutes, then remove them from the pans and let cool completely on wire cooling racks before icing or assembling. A cake baked in a 9 x 13-inch pan, commonly referred to as a sheet cake, can be left in the pan and iced only on the top, or it can be removed from the pan and iced and decorated on the top and the sides. It is easier to transport a sheet cake while it is still in the pan.

CHOCOLATE CAKE

This tender and very dark chocolate cake is made with cocoa powder instead of melted unsweetened chocolate. I like the beautiful deep color that you get from using cocoa powder, and it eliminates the step of melting the chocolate. This basic recipe can also be used in many ways: a layer cake, a sheet cake, or cupcakes. Try it with a buttercream made with cocoa powder and Frangelico (page 38).

Baking spray, for preparing the pans

12 tablespoons (1½ sticks) unsalted butter, at room temperature

1⅔ cups granulated white sugar

3 large eggs

2 cups all-purpose flour

⅔ cup unsweetened cocoa powder

¼ teaspoon baking powder

1¼ teaspoons baking soda

½ teaspoon fine sea salt

1⅓ cups cold buttermilk

1 teaspoon pure vanilla extract

Pans: Two 9-inch round cake pans or cupcake tins, or one 9 x 13-inch pan

1 Position a rack in the center of the oven and preheat the oven to 350°F. Spray the cake pans with baking spray.

2 Cream the butter and sugar together with an electric mixer on medium-high speed until very fluffy, 3 to 5 minutes. Add the eggs one at a time, beating well after each addition, until thoroughly mixed.

❸ Place the flour in a medium-size bowl. Add the cocoa powder, baking powder, baking soda, and salt and whisk well to combine. Pour the buttermilk into a glass measuring cup and stir in the vanilla.

❹ Add a little of the flour mixture to the butter mixture and mix well on medium-low speed. Add a little of the buttermilk mixture and mix. Alternate the flour and buttermilk in small batches until it is all incorporated into the batter. Stop the machine and scrape down the side of the bowl as necessary.

❺ Pour the batter into the prepared cake pans. If using 2 pans, make sure to divide the batter evenly. Lightly tap each pan down on the counter to make sure the batter is evenly distributed and to remove excess air bubbles.

❻ If baking layers, bake until they pull away from the sides of the pans and a toothpick inserted in the center comes out clean, 30 to 35 minutes. A 9 x 13-inch pan will take longer to bake—40 to 45 minutes. Cupcakes will take 15 to 20 minutes. Begin testing the layers at 25 minutes, the sheet cake at 30 minutes, and

the cupcakes at 15 minutes. Test again in 5-minute increments because every oven bakes differently. Depending on your oven, it may take a little less time or a little longer to bake. Use the visual clues and the toothpick test as your definitive test.

⑦ Cool cupcakes or layers in the pans for 10 minutes, then remove them from the pans and let cool completely on wire cooling racks before frosting or assembling. A cake baked in a 9 x 13-inch pan, commonly referred to as a sheet cake, can be left in the pan and iced only on the top, or it can be removed from the pan and iced and decorated on the top and the sides. It is easier to transport a sheet cake while it is still in the pan.

AMERICAN BUTTERCREAM

This sweet and creamy frosting originates from the back of the box of Domino confectioners' sugar. It is now referred to as "American buttercream" in baking circles, which romanticizes a simple frosting. I am assuming that it earned that moniker because of its ubiquitous popularity on cupcakes and birthday cakes. It is also a snap to make, and that makes it a good choice for both the novice baker and any sweet frosting lover. It is easily colored and flavored, which makes it customizable. You can also substitute a favorite liqueur for some of the cream—think Grand Marnier, Frangelico, or Kahlúa.

Important note: This basic recipe hasn't changed since my mother was making birthday cakes for my sisters and me. Back then, round cake pans were 8 inches in diameter and about 1½ inches deep. Today, however, standard round cake pans are 9 x 2 inches. This recipe will make enough frosting for a small two-layer cake or a 9 x 13-inch sheet cake (especially if it only has the frosting on the top and is served in the pan). If you make two 9-inch round cake layers, you will need almost twice the buttercream to achieve a good cake-to-frosting ratio, meaning that you will need to double this recipe. However, if you are not a mile-high frosting person, the single recipe will be enough for you.

Another note: While it is okay to use a whisk when combining flour with dry ingredients, confectioners' sugar needs to be sifted to avoid lumps of sugar in your icing.

VANILLA AMERICAN BUTTERCREAM

Makes enough for a lightly frosted cake. Double the recipe for a heavy frosting-centric cake.

> 1 box (1 pound) confectioners' sugar, or more if needed
>
> Pinch of fine sea salt, or more if needed
>
> 8 tablespoons (1 stick) unsalted butter, at room temperature
>
> 1 teaspoon pure vanilla extract or other flavoring, or more if needed
>
> 3 to 4 tablespoons heavy (whipping) cream, or more if needed

① Sift the confectioners' sugar and salt together in a medium-size bowl.

② Cream the butter until light and fluffy with an electric mixer on medium speed, about 2 minutes.

③ With the mixer still on medium speed, slowly add the sugar to the butter. You want to make sure that you don't have sugar flying all over the kitchen.

④ When the sugar is incorporated, add the vanilla and the cream, 1 tablespoon at a time, until your desired spreading consistency is reached. (Other flavorings, such as liqueurs like Grand Marnier, Frangelico, Kahlúa, and limoncello, can be substituted for some of the cream, if desired.) If the frosting is too stiff, add a little more cream. If it's too loose, add a little more sugar. Taste for balance and add a touch more salt and vanilla, if needed.

CHOCOLATE AMERICAN BUTTERCREAM

Makes enough for a lightly frosted cake. Double the recipe for a heavy frosting-centric cake.

> 3 to 4 ounces unsweetened chocolate, depending on how chocolaty you want your buttercream (see Note)
>
> 1 box (1 pound) confectioners' sugar, or more if needed
>
> Pinch of fine sea salt, or more if needed
>
> 8 tablespoons (1 stick) unsalted butter, at room temperature
>
> 1 to 2 tablespoons heavy (whipping) cream, or more if needed
>
> 1 teaspoon pure vanilla extract or other flavoring, or more if needed

❶ Melt the chocolate in the top of a double boiler over simmering water or in a microwave-safe bowl in the microwave. Take care not to overheat the chocolate. Set aside to cool.

❷ Sift the confectioners' sugar and salt together in a medium-size bowl.

❸ Cream the butter until light and fluffy with an electric mixer on medium speed, about 2 minutes.

❹ Slowly add the sugar to the butter. When the sugar is incorporated, add the vanilla and cooled melted chocolate. Add the cream, 1 tablespoon at a time, until your desired spreading consistency is reached. (Other flavorings, such as liqueurs like Grand Marnier, Frangelico, Kahlúa, and limoncello, can be substituted for some of the cream, if desired.) If the frosting is too stiff, add a little more cream. If it's too loose, add a little more sugar. Taste for balance and add a touch more salt and vanilla or other flavorings if desired.

Note: If you don't have unsweetened chocolate squares, whisk 2 generous tablespoons of unsweetened cocoa powder into the confectioners' sugar before adding the sugar to the butter.

BASIC GLAZE

This glaze is best for loaf and Bundt cakes. In my experience, most people love a little sugary icing on the top of simple cakes, with the exception of a banana loaf. A glaze can be as simple as water and confectioners' sugar, but I like to use milk or cream to make the glaze because I think a little bit of dairy softens the sugary flavor. You can add extracts, citrus zest, juice, spirits, and liqueurs to the glaze to boost the flavor.

Makes 2 cups, enough for 1 to 2 loaves or 1 Bundt cake

> 2 cups confectioners' sugar, sifted
>
> Pinch of fine sea salt
>
> Pinch of spice, such as ground cinnamon, freshly grated or ground nutmeg, and ground mace (optional)
>
> 3 tablespoons heavy (whipping) cream or milk, or a combination of vanilla, liqueur, flavorings, or extracts that equals about 3 tablespoons

Mix the sugar, salt, spices (if using), and cream together in a medium-size bowl with a fork until shiny and smooth and all of the lumps are worked out.

VARIATIONS

To make a chocolate glaze: Melt 2 ounces of unsweetened chocolate in the top of a double boiler over simmering water. If you are used to melting chocolate in a microwave, you can do so, but it scorches easily in the microwave and a double boiler is failsafe. Add it to the sugar a little at a time. Don't add the cream, as the melted chocolate will take its place. If it's too thick once the chocolate is added, add cream a little at a time until you have the right consistency.

To make a chocolate glaze with cocoa powder: Whisk 3 tablespoons of unsweetened cocoa powder in with the confectioners' sugar. Add the cream to the dry ingredients. Taste, and if it needs more chocolate, add up to 1 tablespoon more of cocoa powder.

BAKER'S SYRUP

This syrup is designed for layer cakes and Bundts. It is brushed on a cake as it cools and will keep the cake moist and/or add another layer of flavor, as in the Whiskey Buttermilk Bundt Cake on page 6.

Makes ½ cup

¼ cup filtered water (see Note)

¼ cup granulated white sugar

1 teaspoon pure vanilla extract or 2 tablespoons bourbon or liqueur, such as Grand Marnier or Frangelico

Pour the water into a heat-resistant glass measuring cup and add the sugar. Microwave on high for 1 minute. Remove and stir to combine—all of the sugar should be melted and mixed into the water. If not, microwave for 30 seconds more. Add the vanilla or other flavorings and stir well. This will keep for up to 1 month in the refrigerator; store in a closed container, like a Mason jar.

Note: Use filtered water, if possible, for a cleaner taste.

FLUFFY WHITE COOKED FROSTING

AKA ITALIAN MERINGUE, WHITE MOUNTAIN, OR SEVEN-MINUTE FROSTING

All three of the cooked frostings named in the subhead above are similar in the sense that they are made by slowly pouring very hot syrup in a thin stream into stiffly beaten egg whites and result in snowy-white, marshmallow-like, creamy frostings. Some versions use cream of tartar to stabilize the frosting, and this one uses light corn syrup to keep it together. It is a fantastic recipe, but once you start, you can't take your eyes off it until it is done.

Makes enough for a 2-layer cake with a thin layer of frosting

> ⅔ cup granulated white sugar
>
> Pinch of fine sea salt
>
> 3 tablespoons filtered water
>
> ⅓ cup light corn syrup, such as Karo
>
> 2 large egg whites (⅓ cup)
>
> 1½ teaspoons pure vanilla extract

❶ Place the sugar, salt, water, and corn syrup in a heavy-bottomed saucepan. Bring to a boil slowly over medium-high heat without stirring until the syrup spins a 6- to 8-inch-long thread when poured from a spoon and registers 242°F on a candy thermometer. Cover the saucepan.

❷ Reduce the heat to low and simmer the syrup. Keep the saucepan covered only during the first 3 minutes to keep the sugar from forming crystals on the side of the pan.

❸ While the sugar syrup is cooking, beat the egg whites in a medium-size bowl until they hold stiff peaks.

❹ When the syrup is ready, pour it very slowly in a thin stream into the beaten egg whites, beating constantly. Add the vanilla and beat until the frosting holds its shape, about 5 minutes. Spread immediately on the cake's cooled layers.

STABILIZED WHIPPED CREAM

Whipped cream that's not been stabilized is delicious dolloped as a garnish on just about any dessert, but if you're using it to frost a cake, it needs to be stabilized. I used to stabilize whipped cream with gelatin until I picked up this tip from my mother, who learned it from Rose Levy Beranbaum. Since almost everyone has a box of cornstarch in their pantry, I am a convert to this new way of making whipped cream frosting. This is a nice light option for pound cake, strawberry shortcake, or any time you are looking for a cake topping that is less sweet or whipped cream that will keep its shape.

VANILLA WHIPPED CREAM

This recipe makes about 2 cups, which is perfect for adding as a garnish, but if you want to frost a two-layer cake you will need to double the recipe. I like to use vanilla bean puree so that you can see flecks of the vanilla bean through the soft white clouds.

> 2 tablespoons confectioners' sugar
>
> 1 level teaspoon cornstarch
>
> 1¼ cups heavy (whipping) cream
>
> ½ teaspoon pure vanilla bean puree or pure vanilla extract

❶ Place a mixing bowl and (preferably whisk) beater in the freezer for at least 15 minutes, but preferably 30 minutes.

❷ Off the heat, combine the sugar and cornstarch in a small saucepan and gradually stir in ¼ cup of the cream (keep the remaining cream in the fridge).

Mix well. Slowly heat the cream mixture over medium heat until you see a little steam coming off the liquid and the sugar is melted. Be careful not to bring the mixture to a boil or the cream will turn into a jelly-like substance. You want it to be a pourable liquid.

❸ Once steaming, pour the mixture into a clean bowl and cool completely to room temperature. Stir in the vanilla.

❹ Beat the remaining 1 cup of cold cream in the chilled bowl just until traces of beater marks begin to show distinctly. Add the cooled cornstarch mixture in a steady stream, beating constantly. Beat just until stiff peaks form when the beater is raised. You can store the stabilized whipped cream in a lidded container for up to 3 days in the refrigerator.

CHOCOLATE WHIPPED CREAM

This recipe makes about 2 cups, which is perfect for adding as a garnish, but if you want to frost a two-layer cake you will need to double the recipe.

    2 tablespoons confectioners' sugar

    1 level teaspoon cornstarch

    1¼ cups heavy (whipping) cream

½ teaspoon pure vanilla bean puree or extract

1 tablespoon unsweetened cocoa powder

❶ Place a mixing bowl and (preferably whisk) beater in the freezer for at least 15 minutes, but preferably 30 minutes.

❷ Off the heat, combine the sugar and cornstarch in a small saucepan and gradually stir in ¼ cup of the cream (keep the remaining cream in the fridge). Mix well. Slowly heat the cream mixture over medium heat until you see a little steam coming off the liquid and the sugar is melted. Be careful not to bring the mixture to a boil or the cream will turn into a jelly-like substance. You want it to be a pourable liquid.

❸ Once steaming, pour the mixture into a clean bowl and cool completely to room temperature. Stir in the vanilla and the cocoa powder.

❹ Beat the remaining 1 cup of cold cream in the chilled bowl, just until traces of beater marks begin to show distinctly. Add the cocoa mixture in a steady stream, beating constantly. Beat just until stiff peaks form when the beater is raised. You can store the stabilized whipped cream in a lidded container for up to 3 days in the refrigerator.

SWISS MERINGUE

My friend and pastry chef Paola Marocchi introduced me to Swiss meringue. It is similar in texture and flavor to the other cooked icings, but because you cook the egg whites with the sugar, it is more stable and can be made in advance. This is an especially good choice for My Mother's Freshly Grated Coconut cake on page 68.

Makes enough for a generous layer of frosting on a two-layer cake.

5 large egg whites ($^2/_3$ cup)

1$^1/_3$ cups granulated white sugar

Pinch of fine sea salt

1 teaspoon vanilla bean puree

$^1/_2$ teaspoon cream of tartar

❶ Whisk together the egg whites, sugar, and salt in the top of a double boiler. Pour water to a depth of 1 inch in the bottom of the double boiler and simmer the egg white mixture over the water until the temperature reaches 140°F on a candy thermometer, 8 to 10 minutes. The mixture will be thick and foamy.

❷ Using a mixer fitted with the whisk attachment, beat the egg white mixture on high while adding the vanilla bean puree and the cream of tartar. Continue beating on high until the mixture becomes glossy and medium-stiff peaks form, 4 to 5 minutes. Transfer to a nonreactive container or pastry bag and refrigerate until ready to use.

MILK CHOCOLATE CREAM CHEESE FROSTING

I added cream cheese to my aunt's traditional chocolate frosting to balance the sweetness of the cake.

Makes enough for a sheet cake or two-layer cake with a thin layer of frosting

8 tablespoons (1 stick) unsalted butter, at room temperature

1 package (8 ounces) full-fat cream cheese, at room temperature

1$^1/_2$ teaspoons pure vanilla extract

3 cups confectioners' sugar, sifted

3 heaping tablespoons Dutch-process cocoa powder

Pinch of fine sea salt

1 tablespoon whole milk or half-and-half

❶ Cream the butter and cream cheese together in a large bowl with an electric mixer until very smooth, 3 to 5 minutes. Add the vanilla and beat for 30 seconds more.

❷ Whisk the sugar, cocoa, and salt together in a small bowl. With the mixer on low, slowly add the sugar mixture to the butter mixture. About halfway through, add the milk. Make sure to incorporate fully between additions.

❸ Once all is incorporated, increase the mixer speed to medium and beat for 1 to 2 minutes, stopping the mixer to scrape down the side of the bowl as necessary. Cover until ready to frost the cake.

A LITTLE SOMETHING EXTRA

RASPBERRY ROLL-UP WITH LIMONCELLO WHIPPED CREAM

Here is my take on a Swiss roll or jelly roll. It is pretty as a picture, exposing a roll of raspberry jam and fresh raspberries when sliced. This butter- and oil-free cake is best eaten the day it is made. I like balancing its lightness with a lemony whipped cream, but if you are a chocolate person, a raspberry-spiked chocolate ganache will tickle your jelly roll in all the right places.

Makes 8 slices

FOR THE CAKE

Baking spray, for preparing the pan

3 large eggs

¾ granulated white sugar

½ cup self-rising flour

1 tablespoon ground almonds or almond flour, such as Bob's Red Mill

Confectioners' sugar

4 tablespoons raspberry jam, no sugar added

½ pint fresh raspberries, plus more for serving

FOR THE LIMONCELLO WHIPPED CREAM

1 cup heavy (whipping) cream, chilled

2 tablespoons confectioners' sugar

1 tablespoon limoncello

Zest of ½ lemon

FOR THE RASPBERRY CHOCOLATE GANACHE

½ cup plus 1 tablespoon whipping cream

4 ounces semi-sweet chocolate, chopped into small pieces

2 tablespoons raspberry jam

Pinch of salt

Pan: Lékué Jelly Roll Kit or other jelly roll pan (about 12 x 17 inches), or sheet pan

❶ Position a rack in the center of the oven and preheat the oven to 425°F. Spray the jelly roll pan with baking spray and, if necessary, line the bottom with parchment paper (see Note).

❷ Whisk the eggs and granulated sugar with an electric mixer fitted with the whisk attachment on medium speed until the mixture is thick and pale, 10 minutes. It gets very thick and fluffy and silky looking.

❸ Whisk the flour and ground almonds together. Sift it over the egg mixture and fold in.

❹ Pour the batter into the prepared pan and lightly tap the pan down on the counter to make sure the batter is evenly distributed and to remove excess air bubbles. Bake until the cake is golden and pulls away from the sides of the pan, 13 to 15 minutes. Remove from the oven and continue with Step 5 before the cake cools.

⑤ Lay a piece of waxed paper slightly longer than the cake on your work surface and dust thickly with confectioners' sugar.

⑥ Turn the cake onto the sugar-dusted paper. Spread jam all over the the warm cake, sprinkle with the fresh raspberries, and roll tightly using the waxed paper to guide the roll. Let stand seam-side down for 5 minutes, then transfer to a wire rack to cool completely.

⑦ While the cake is cooling, make the Limoncello Whipped Cream: Whip the cream and sugar just until soft peaks are formed, 3 to 4 minutes. Add the Limoncello and zest, and continue beating until stiff peaks form.

Or, if you'd prefer, make the Raspberry Chocolate Ganache: Heat the cream in a microwave to just under boiling, about 1 minute, or in a small saucepan on the stovetop over medium-low heat. Add the chocolate to the cream and stir vigorously with a fork until all the chocolate is melted. Add the raspberry jam and salt and stir until well combined.

⑧ Serve the cake with more raspberries, and either the whipped cream or chocolate ganache, as desired.

Note: Lékué Silicone has a Jelly Roll Kit that includes a flexible silicone jelly roll pan that eliminates the need to line the pan with parchment paper; you roll up the filled cake using the silicone pan as a guide. You do, however, need to place the silicone jelly roll pan on a metal sheet pan during baking. Sprinkle on the confectioners' sugar after the cake is rolled.

THE MATCHUPS

TRI-TIP SANTA MARIA WITH LOW-AND-SLOW CABBAGE AND OLD-FASHIONED GARLIC BREAD,
page 56

TUSCAN STEAK WITH WHITE ANCHOVY AND TRUFFLE BUTTER AND GRILLED LEMONS,
page 61

SURF AND TURF LOBSTER WITH HOMEMADE PASTIS CREAM AND STEAK,
page 97

WILD PERSIMMON CHRISTMAS FRUIT AND NUT CAKE

This recipe is the wonderful and delicious brainchild of my mother, Marylin Odom Karmel. My mother took her family's traditional recipe for wild persimmon cookies and merged it with her mother's fruitcake to create this superlative version of wild persimmon fruitcake, aka Christmas fruitcake. It is a confection that we all looked forward to every year. Because it is a big job for one person, I would go home to North Carolina two weeks before Thanksgiving each year to bake the cakes with my mother. But the preparations began a month earlier; since wild persimmons are truly wild, my mother would forage around Greensboro and in her front yard for a month to get the fruit puree for these cakes. But, in 2007, the drought rendered the trees in Greensboro bare. Luckily, I remembered that my friend and fellow persimmon lover Bill Smith knew someone in Chapel Hill who foraged them for his restaurant, Crook's Corner. It was a happy trade of persimmon puree for fruitcake, and a new tradition was born! We usually double this recipe, and my mother would always say, "Put in all of the fruit and nuts, it [the cake] will hold."

Makes 3 or 4 minis for giving and 2 large fruitcakes for the family, depending on your loaf pans

FOR THE CAKE

Baking spray, for preparing the pans

1 cup (2 sticks) unsalted butter, at room temperature

⅔ cup (packed) light brown sugar

⅔ cup white granulated sugar

4 large eggs

2 cups persimmon pulp (see Note), cleaned and sieved

2 cups cake flour

1 teaspoon baking soda

1 teaspoon baking powder

1½ teaspoons ground cinnamon

1 teaspoon ground mace

½ teaspoon ground cloves

½ teaspoon ground allspice

¼ teaspoon fine sea salt

¼ cup apricot brandy, such as Jacquin's, plus more for curing

9 cups dried fruit (see below)

¼ cup all-purpose flour

3½ pounds pecan halves (save ½ pound for decorating the tops), lightly toasted (see page 85)

FOR THE FRUIT

Mix the following dried fruits in any combination to equal roughly 9 cups

Mission figs, stemmed and cut into quarters

Calimyrna figs, stemmed and cut into quarters

Dried cherries

Dried cranberries

Whole dried Turkish apricots, each cut into 4 long strips

Golden raisins

Currants

Date pieces

Pans: 3 or 4 minis (6 x 3½ x 2) and 2 large (9 x 5 x 3) loaf pans; 2 sheet pans

You'll also need: 3 feet of cheesecloth per cake, for wrapping

① Position a rack in the center of the oven and one directly under it. Preheat the oven to 275°F. Spray the cake pans with baking spray.

② Cream the butter and sugars together with an electric mixer on medium speed until light and fluffy, about 4 minutes. Add the eggs one at a time, beating well after each addition. Then, continue beating to make sure the ingredients are well combined, about 2 minutes more. Slowly mix in the persimmon puree and continue beating until very smooth and golden in color.

③ Whisk together the cake flour, baking soda, baking powder, spices, and salt. Add the flour mixture and the brandy to the butter mixture alternately in batches, mixing on low speed until incorporated. Stop the mixer and scrape down the side of the bowl as necessary. Once everything is incorporated, increase the speed and mix until silky.

④ Mix the dried fruit with the all-purpose flour in a large bowl (you do this so the fruit won't all sink to the bottom). Add the pecans and toss to mix the fruit and nuts together.

⑤ Add the fruit mixture to the batter slowly, stirring after each addition. Stir in all the fruit and nuts that the batter can handle—when you think you can't incorporate anymore, add another cup. Mix with a wooden paddle or whatever is easiest to move the batter around. This will take elbow grease.

⑥ Once the batter is made, spoon it into the prepared pans, filling each three-quarters full (the cakes won't rise very much). Pack the batter down with a spatula or large spoon. This step is very important or the cake will not be dense and full. Add more batter if necessary.

⑦ Place the loaf pans on sheet pans with sides to make it easier to pull them out of the hot oven. Bake until the cakes are brown and slightly raised and a

THE MATCHUPS

PORTERHOUSE FOR TWO
WITH STEAKHOUSE SPINACH AND
WILD MUSHROOM SAUTÉ,
page 67

MARY PAT'S INDIVIDUAL BEEF WELLINGTONS,
page 86

MY MOTHER'S BEEF STEAK STROGANOFF,
page 120

toothpick inserted into the center comes out clean, 2 hours for small pans (3 or 4 pans on 2 racks) or 2 hours and 10 minutes for large pans (2 large pans). Cool the cakes in the pans set on a cooling rack for 2 hours, then remove them from the pans to the wire cooling racks to cool completely.

⑧ Once the cakes are cool, begin wrapping them. You will need a 3-foot length of cheesecloth per large cake and half of that if you make mini fruitcakes. Unfold the cheesecloth and soak it in the apricot brandy. Wrap each cake completely and tightly in the cheesecloth. You'll wind up with several layers of cheesecloth around each cake. Place each cake in a resealable plastic bag and place them in the refrigerator. Every few days, open the bags and sprinkle the cheesecloth with a little more brandy until the cakes are "cured." We do this for 5 to 6 weeks before Christmas Eve, and the fruitcake only gets better. When you are ready to give the fruitcake to a friend or family member, give the cheesecloth a final sprinkling of brandy and wrap the cake in aluminum foil. Place the foil-wrapped cake in a heavy-duty resealable plastic bag and keep it in the refrigerator.

⑨ To serve, slice the cake when cold into the thinnest possible pieces, so that it resembles a stained-glass window. Rewrap any remaining cake in the cheesecloth, foil, and plastic bag. You can continue curing—and sprinkling it with apricot brandy—for a couple of months and it will keep, shrouded in brandy-soaked cheesecloth, indefinitely in the refrigerator.

Note: Wild persimmons grow in North Carolina and southern Indiana. Enterprising growers sell the pulp online. Google "persimmon pulp" to find the current purveyors.

ROSE WHITE'S FAMOUS CARAMEL CAKE

Caramel cakes are a staple of the Southern pantry, and they show prominently at church picnics, family reunions, funerals, tailgates, and anywhere else you have more than two people. But long before this recipe was shared with the world—it was featured in *Saveur* magazine under the headline "World's Best Caramel Cake"—I had the pleasure of eating it, because the famous Rose is Rose Deshazer White, who has worked with me for almost as long as I have been working. Soon after we met, Rose brought me a piece of her caramel cake, and it made me melt! It's no wonder—although she has lived in Chicago for many years, Rose learned how to make it at the apron strings of her Mississippi-born mother. In fact, she still makes the caramel icing with the same saucepan and spoon that her mother gave her. Though I am certain that those heirlooms bring a little something special to the mix, I am confident that your cake will be equally famous made with your own pan and spoon.

Makes 16 slices

FOR THE CAKE

Baking spray, for preparing the pans

3 cups cake flour

2 teaspoons baking powder

½ teaspoon fine sea salt

1 cup whole milk

1½ teaspoons pure vanilla extract

1 cup (2 sticks) unsalted butter, at room temperature

2½ cups granulated white sugar

4 extra-large eggs

FOR THE CARAMEL ICING

1 cup (2 sticks) salted butter

4¼ cups granulated white sugar

2 cans (12 ounces each) evaporated milk

Pans: Three 8-inch round or two 9-inch round cake pans

❶ Position a rack in the center of the oven and preheat the oven to 325°F. Spray the cake pans with baking spray.

❷ Stir the flour, baking powder, and salt together in a medium-size bowl. Mix the milk and vanilla together in a small bowl.

❸ Cream the butter and sugar together with an electric mixer on medium speed until light and very fluffy, 3 to 5 minutes. Add the eggs one at a time, beating well after each addition. Add the flour mixture and the milk mixture to the butter mixture alternately in small batches. Beat well after each addition. Stop the machine and scrape down the side of the bowl as necessary.

❹ Divide the batter evenly among the prepared cake pans. Lightly tap each pan down on the counter to make sure the batter is evenly distributed and to remove excess air bubbles.

❺ Bake until the layers pull away from the sides of the pans and a toothpick inserted in the center comes out clean, about 35 minutes. Cool the cakes in the pans for 10 minutes before removing them to wire cooling racks to cool completely.

❻ Make the caramel icing: Melt the butter in a medium-size saucepan over medium-low heat. Add the sugar and let cook until golden brown, stirring constantly, 8 to 10 minutes. Add the evaporated milk and reduce the heat to low. Stir and let cook—do not let it form bubbles or boil over—until the icing gets noticeably thicker, another 8 to 10 minutes. Continue cooking until the icing forms a soft ball or registers 240°F on a candy thermometer, 10 to 15 minutes more. Remove the pan from the heat and beat the icing with a hand mixer until glossy, cooler, and spreadable. This will take another 5 minutes.

❼ Assemble the cake: You will need to work quickly because when the caramel icing cools, it has the texture of fudge, making it difficult to spread. Carefully trim a thin slice off the rounded tops of the 2 layers to even them out. Place 1 layer bottom side up on a serving plate and spread the top generously with frosting. Top it with the second cake layer and frost it, then place on the third layer, if there is one. Frost the sides of the cake and finish off by frosting the top layer. Chill the cake in the refrigerator to set the icing for at least 1 hour.

❽ Serve or let sit, covered, at room temperature to serve the next day. If there are leftovers, you can cut the remainder into slices, wrap each individually in plastic wrap, and freeze for up to 1 month.

THE MATCHUPS

KNIFE & FORK COUNTRY CLUB STEAK SANDWICH
WITH BLOODY MARY SALAD
WITH HORSERADISH VINAIGRETTE,
page 15

NEW YORK STRIP WITH RED WINE BUTTER AND
SPINACH ARTICHOKE CASSEROLE,
page 47

MY MOTHER'S BEEF STEAK STROGANOFF,
page 120

If you want to
see friends or
relatives smile,
bake them a cake!
cake = love

CONVERSION TABLES

Please note that all conversions are approximate but close enough to be useful when converting from one system to another.

OVEN TEMPERATURES

FAHRENHEIT	GAS MARK	CELSIUS
250	½	120
275	1	140
300	2	150
325	3	160
350	4	180
375	5	190
400	6	200
425	7	220
450	8	230
475	9	240
500	10	260

Note: Reduce the temperature by 20°C (68°F) for fan-assisted ovens.

APPROXIMATE EQUIVALENTS

1 stick butter = 8 tbs = 4 oz = ½ cup = 115 g

1 cup all-purpose presifted flour = 4.7 oz

1 cup granulated sugar = 8 oz = 220 g

1 cup (firmly packed) brown sugar = 6 oz = 220 to 230 g

1 cup confectioners' sugar = 4½ oz = 115 g

1 cup honey or syrup = 12 oz

1 cup grated cheese = 4 oz

1 cup dried beans = 6 oz

1 large egg = about 2 oz or about 3 tbs

1 egg yolk = about 1 tbs

1 egg white = about 2 tbs

LIQUID CONVERSIONS

U.S.	IMPERIAL	METRIC
2 tbs	1 fl oz	30 ml
3 tbs	1½ fl oz	45 ml
¼ cup	2 fl oz	60 ml
⅓ cup	2½ fl oz	75 ml
⅓ cup + 1 tbs	3 fl oz	90 ml
⅓ cup + 2 tbs	3½ fl oz	100 ml
½ cup	4 fl oz	125 ml
⅔ cup	5 fl oz	150 ml
¾ cup	6 fl oz	175 ml
¾ cup + 2 tbs	7 fl oz	200 ml
1 cup	8 fl oz	250 ml
1 cup + 2 tbs	9 fl oz	275 ml
1¼ cups	10 fl oz	300 ml
1⅓ cups	11 fl oz	325 ml
1½ cups	12 fl oz	350 ml
1⅔ cups	13 fl oz	375 ml
1¾ cups	14 fl oz	400 ml
1¾ cups + 2 tbs	15 fl oz	450 ml
2 cups (1 pint)	16 fl oz	500 ml
2½ cups	20 fl oz (1 pint)	600 ml
3¾ cups	1½ pints	900 ml
4 cups	1¾ pints	1 liter

WEIGHT CONVERSIONS

U.S./U.K.	METRIC	U.S./U.K.	METRIC
½ oz	15 g	7 oz	200 g
1 oz	30 g	8 oz	250 g
1½ oz	45 g	9 oz	275 g
2 oz	60 g	10 oz	300 g
2½ oz	75 g	11 oz	325 g
3 oz	90 g	12 oz	350 g
3½ oz	100 g	13 oz	375 g
4 oz	125 g	14 oz	400 g
5 oz	150 g	15 oz	450 g
6 oz	175 g	1 lb	500 g

ACKNOWLEDGMENTS

This book was a long time in the making! The contract was signed in 2014 and I went out on my Steak and Cake Tour in 2015. I completed the book in 2016, but between my schedule and my editor's schedule, it took another 3 years to get the book photographed and published. Luckily steak and cake never go out of style!

You may notice when you read the book that there are three people mentioned often. Those three people are my baking musketeers and were my three hosts of "cake week" during my tour—my mother Marylin, my sister Mary Pat, and my kindred culinary spirit Bob Blumer.

This book was inspired by the Steak and Cake class that I taught at the Institute of Culinary Education (ICE) for many years. So my biggest thanks has to go to Rick Smilow and the staff at ICE for making it so easy for me to teach my class and for continuing to support me in all that I do. Almost the full menu from that class made the cut for this book.

Second, I have to thank my friend and editor, Suzanne Rafer, for loving this book as much as I do and for "skipping" retirement to see this book to the finish line. I am also indebted to the rest of the Workman team, including the book's fabulous designer, Janet Vicaro and head of publicity Rebecca Carlisle. Plus Suzie Bolotin, Jenny Mandel, Lathea Williams, Cindy Lee, Kate Karol, Hillary Leary, Barbara Peragine, Orlando Adiao, and Anne Kerman, who are all great partners and have made me a part of the Workman family from day one.

This is the first time that I have employed readers during the writing process. Thanks go to my mother, and Mary Pat, Bob Blumer, and my former editor from *Fine Cooking* magazine, Rebecca Freedman, for all of their excellent feedback. I am indebted to each and every one of them for being honest and generous with their opinions.

Besides my readers, I was lucky enough to have the support of so many people. My biggest cheerleader was my father Louis, who asked me daily (until his untimely death) if I had finished the book! My mother is so much a part of this book that words can't express my gratitude. Even though she was sick from chemo, she helped me through the editing process and pairing the steaks and cakes right up until she lost her battle with ovarian cancer. I owe my love of baking and cooking to her. She was my mentor and collaborator, and I will miss working with her in the kitchen for the rest of my life.

On the home front, my longtime friend and colleague Kirsten Teissier has lived through this book on an almost daily basis. I have to thank her for her support, help, friendship, and always having my back no matter what. More thanks to her husband and my bourbon buddy, Nat, for letting us monopolize all the conversations and turning many of them into grilling and food discussions.

Big hugs to my childhood friend and barbecue partner, David Lineweaver, and our four-legged family of cockapoos, Baxter, Madison, and Gracie. They have been there during the whole long process of writing this book. It was difficult to cook steak, night after night, and not give in to the begging eyes of these three, but nary a bone went to the dogs! My sisters and their families have been a great audience and great critics. Likewise my "adopted" brother Bob and his wife Kate. We have enjoyed many steaks and many cakes together as I refined recipes or cooked and baked just to share my favorites with them! Thanks MP, Karl, August, Alexander, Max, Hazel, Cat, Cyril, Olivia, Nat, Luc, Axel, and Rocky! And thanks to Jenny for all the kitchen help.

The photography in this book is stunning! I have never published a book with so many gorgeous, mouthwatering photos. A huge depth of gratitude goes to my photographer and friend, Steve Hamilton. He took this project on as a labor of love and I so appreciate the way his photos bring my recipes to life. He and his team worked so hard and it shows. Much thanks to the whole Stephen Hamilton team including, photo assistants Ben Weston and Jack Wheeler; producer Deirdre O'Shea; manager Patti Schumann; stylist Melanie Francis; chef Justin Brunson; and pastry chefs Paola Marocchi and Kathy Skutecki. As you can see in the photo portraits, we cooked hard but never lost our sense of humor! Steve powered through on a daily breakfast of waffles and the rest of us relied on our favorite tools to get us through the day.

Most of the portraits feature our individual "can't live without" tools—no surprise that mine are my blending forks!

Support for this book extended far and wide and I have many more people to thank. Dee Buxton picked up where my parents left off—as the best neighbor my sisters and I could possibly have. A lifetime of thanks goes to Sharon Franke for sharing her intel and always supporting me. And to Sarah Abell, my Thundercloud sister—always speaking the truth and cheering me on.

My friends at Weber have supported me through my whole career. Big thanks go especially to Mike Kempster and Brooke Jones. Mike Kempster was the person who literally ignited my passion for grilling when Weber was my client more than 20 years ago. I love grilling today even more than I did back then.

More thanks go to Mary Rogers from Cuisinart for supplying so much equipment for testing, and also to Cuisinart's longtime PR team and my friends Rachel Litner and Dan Kulp, who always have a solution to my houseware needs.

Mark Kelly sent so much Lodge (cast iron) to the photo shoot that I could have opened a store—but he was spot-on, as I used almost every bit of it. Thank you, Mark, for your kindness, for your generosity, and for urging me to try the carbon steel skillet, which is my new favorite steak skillet!

My friends at Revol have also been very generous with their gorgeous French porcelain. Merci beaucoup to Tenaya Santos Da Silva, Olivier Passot, Amélie Keromnes, and everyone else in the USA and France.

I am lucky enough to call Pat LaFrieda a friend. I have known Pat since I opened Hill Country Barbecue Market in 2007. Besides being America's most charismatic butcher, Pat is truly the sweetest and most eternally generous person in the New York food business. When I asked him if I could come to Pat LaFrieda Meat Purveyor headquarters in New Jersey to grill and taste steak with him for my Steak Primer Grid tasting notes, he didn't blink an eye! It was a wacky idea, and even wackier grilling on the New Jersey Turnpike, but the experience and Pat's insight made the Steak Primer Grid come to life!

Soon after I began working on this book, I met Mary McMillen from Certified Angus Beef. Mary is one of this book's biggest supporters and rallied the CAB troops to help me with anything I needed. Special thanks go to Mary, Clint Walenciak, Michael Ollier, Diana Clark, and Beth Barner. As I say in the book, I thought CAB was a marketing entity and found out that it is really all about quality. I have to thank everyone at CAB for their ongoing support, including hundreds of pounds of CAB steaks that I tested, tasted, and photographed. Helping CAB provide these steaks to me in both New York and Chicago were my friends from Master Purveyors, DeBragga, and Purely Meats. A special nod (respectively) to Steve Gold and Mark Solasz; Marc Sarrazin and Lydia Liebchenand; and Matt Ronan and the team of butchers at Purely, who hand-cut untold numbers of steaks for photography.

Susan Jardina represents some of my favorite brands and thanks go to her for sending my favorite Lékué platinum silicone baking pans, Shun knives (including my favorite cake knife—the 6-inch classic serrated utility), and the beautiful wood products from J.K. Adams.

During the final testing and photography of the book, I discovered a new line of pots and pans from France. I first fell in love with the fact that the Cristel line has detachable handles—that come in a rainbow of colors—and then when I started cooking with it, I fell in love with the performance. Thanks to Tenaya for introducing me to the brand, and thanks to Alex Campbell and Pierre Sur for your interest and support of my book.

I love all kinds of knives and have a large collection of them. But it took a lunch at a steakhouse in Chicago for me to realize that the elegant, slightly S-shaped non-serrated knives from France work so much better than the classic American serrated steak knives. Thanks to Alex Delecroix from Opinel, who brought those knives for our lunch, and to their PR person Katie Flagg for the Opinel steak knives pictured in the book.

More thanks go to these companies for sending products that I used in testing and/or photography: Guittard Chocolate Company, Breville, Fat Daddios, Wilton, KitchenAid, Staub, Trudeau, Nordic Ware, Memphis Wood Fire Grill, Joule, Maverick, Thermopen, Joseph Joseph, and Vista Alegre.

Thank you one and all!!

INDEX

(Page references in *italics* refer to illustrations.)